The Masks of Odin

A SUNRISE LIBRARY BOOK

Elsa-Brita Titchenell

The Masks of Odin

Wisdom of the Ancient Norse

THEOSOPHICAL UNIVERSITY PRESS
PASADENA, CALIFORNIA

THEOSOPHICAL UNIVERSITY PRESS
POST OFFICE BOX C
PASADENA, CALIFORNIA 91109-7107

The paper in this book is FSC Certified Mixed Sources,
chlorine-free, 30% Post Consumer Recycled fiber.

Library of Congress Information

Author:	Titchenell, Elsa-Brita, 1915-2002
Title:	The masks of odin: wisdom of the ancient norse
Edition:	1st ed.
Published:	Pasadena, Calif. : Theosophical University Press, 1985.
Description:	xv, 294 p., [5] p. of plates : facsims. ; 22 cm.
ISBN:	978-0-911500-72-1 cloth (alk. paper)
	978-0-911500-73-8 softcover (alk. paper)
Subjects:	Mythology, Norse. Eddas. Theosophy.
Other Title:	Edda Saemundar. English. Selections. 1985.
Notes:	Includes translation of lays from the Poetic or Elder Edda, glossary, bibliography, index.
Call No.:	BL860.T54 1985
Contol No.:	85-40652

Printed in the United States of America

Contents

ᚠoreword

A GOOD MANY PEOPLE hearing of the Edda or of the Norse myths think mainly of Balder, the sun-god, who was slain by a twig of mistletoe; or they may conjure up mighty Thor, hurler of thunderbolts and lightning, whose footsteps make the earth quake. Or perhaps they remember Loki, trickster, mischief-maker without malice, who seems constantly to stir up trouble, yet as often by imaginative wit and intelligence resolves the difficulties he has caused.

The Masks of Odin is a provocative study of "the wisdom of the ancient Norse." While it portrays the various aspects and forms that Odin assumes in order to gain knowledge of the nine worlds inhabited by gods and giants, humans, elves, and dwarfs, Elsa-Brita Titchenell has a larger purpose in view. As a serious student of both Edda and Theosophy, her loom is cosmic in reach, its warp representing the *theosophia perennis* or enduring god-wisdom and its woof the Edda, whose many-colored threads she weaves into colorful and often inspiring patterns of interpretation.

The world's oldest traditions hold that long ago all peoples, however widely separated, were the common inheritors of a body of sacred truths initially imparted to the earliest humanities by divine beings from higher regions; and, further, that myth-makers of every land were in greater or less degree transmitters of this archaic wisdom/science. Against this backdrop the author undertakes to interpret some of the more important sagas of the Norse Edda, retranslating them from the Swedish text and comparing it with the original Icelandic. Her aim is not to hammer out just another version of the Edda when already several in

English are available both in prose and verse, but rather "to penetrate to the core of inspired meaning" hidden within the world's mythic lore. To attempt this would have been out of the question, she believes, but for two radical changes in the general thought life: first, the disclosure about a century ago of a significant portion of the universal theosophic philosophy by H. P. Blavatsky and its emancipating effect on the human spirit, and second, the new developments in Western science.

In Part I Elsa Titchenell outlines the broad features of the principal characters involved in the drama of cosmic and terrestrial creation as recorded in the Edda, including the gifts to early mankind of spirit, mind, and vitality by three Aesir (gods) so that we humans in time might become "godmakers." Relating theosophic teachings and current findings of astrophysics and physics to traditional mythic symbols she depicts the ancient mythographers as philosophers and scientists of stature. To the Norse bards or *skalds*, the interplay between gods and giants represented the continuous interaction of spirit and matter on a series of "shelves" or planes as "rivers of lives" moved, each after its own manner, through mansion after mansion of planetary and solar spheres within Allfather-Odin's domain.

In Part II, the author's *Notes* preceding the translated lays provide the reader with an invaluable guide through the often bewildering maze of metaphor and symbolic allusion. The opening saga is the well-known *Völuspá* or Sibyl's Prophecy, that tells of the formation of worlds, of Odin's search for wisdom in the spheres of matter, and of the "toppling of the world tree" when the gods withdraw and earth is no more — until the Vala (Sibyl) sees another earth rising from the sea as old ills are resolved and the Aesir return. In the High One's Song, we read of Odin's consummate experience when for nine whole nights he "hung in the windtorn tree," the Tree of Life, so that he might "raise the runes" and drink the mead of omniscience.

There is much to delight and instruct in the retelling of lay after lay, each with its own story and truth to impart. Admittedly only a portion of the available material is treated, and this is drawn chiefly from the Poetic or Elder Edda of Saemund the Wise. Cognizant, moreover, of the challenge posed by the mystery-language of symbolism in use by the poet-philosophers of old, the author is hopeful that others will find in this "fragment of runic wisdom" the stimulus to pursue further and more complete studies of the ancient Norse records.

Whether writing as Eddist or theosophist, amateur scientist, mythographer, or translator, Elsa-Brita Titchenell by lucid and perceptive scholarship has earned for *The Masks of Odin* an honored place among Edda literature.

GRACE F. KNOCHE

Preface

IT WAS IN THE EARLY 1950s when the writer picked up a book at random in the Theosophical University Library in Altadena — a beautifully bound volume of the *Edda* in Swedish. Though familiar since childhood with at least some portions of the Norse "god-stories" this was the first time I had read the poetic lays of the Elder Edda. Browsing through the verses and delighting in their picturesque "kennings," I was enjoying the quaint turns of phrase when suddenly, as by a lightning bolt, I was struck by a dazzling flash of meaning, a hint of basic truth. Skeptical at first, I began to read with greater attention and soon became convinced that the Edda ranks among the world's sacred traditions as a genuine scripture, a goldmine of natural history and spiritual treasure. This is connoted also by its Swedish name: *gudasaga* — a divine story or *god-spell* — the archaic form of the word "gospel."

Many years later, after much scrutiny and comparison with other myths, enough evidence of the Edda's scriptural content had accumulated to warrant collating at least a few fragments that seem to have secreted in them a discernible esoteric meaning. Among the great wealth of material in the Norse myths it has been necessary to be selective, partly because there are several versions of many of the tales, partly because the purpose of this book is to bring out and suggest interpretations of those myths which are of particular relevance in our time.

Most of the lays and stories herein are translated from the *Codex Regius* — the "royal codex" — which was written down by Saemund the Wise a thousand years ago, though their content has doubtless been known much longer than that. Today they are luminous with meaning due to two seemingly independent circumstances: first, the disclosure of a generous portion of the universal theosophic philosophy in the late nineteenth century and the broadening influence this has exerted; and second, following closely thereafter, the development of a more enlightened science in the West.

The story of *Codex Regius* is itself a fascinating one. King Frederik III of Denmark sent Thormod Torfaeus to Iceland with an open letter dated 27 May 1662 which empowered him to purchase ancient manuscripts and other material containing information on Icelandic history. He delivered it to Bishop Brynjolv Sveinsson, an ardent collector of memorabilia since his accession to the bishopric of Skalholt in 1639. Soon afterward the bishop sent the king a gift of several manuscripts; Torfaeus made a catalogue of these which Gudbrand Vigfusson lists in his Prolegomena to the *Sturlunga Saga.* In this collection the manuscript cited as No. 6 is titled "Edda Saemundi; quarto." It was a treasure of the Royal Library at Copenhagen until a few years ago when it was returned to Iceland, where it is now housed in the Arna Magnussonar collection. No one knows how Bishop Brynjolv came in possession of it, but he must have acquired it some twenty years before Torfaeus' arrival as he had inscribed the first page with his own name in Latin, Lupus Loricatus (contracted to ⅃⅃),* with the date 1643; he also had a copy made on white parchment.

Several versions of the Edda are extant in part. One collection of handwritten texts is that of Arne Magnusson, believed to emanate from the same source as Saemund's; another is the *Codex Wormianus* (from which are taken the Songs of Rig and Waywont), and *Flatöboken.* The Spells of Groa, Verywise's Exchange, and

---

*Cf. plate 1 of the photographic reproduction of Völuspá from the Codex Regius manuscript, following p. 83.

the Lay of Odin's Corpse are from Swedish translations of paper copies; these do not occur in *Codex Regius*. The Song of the Mill is from Snorri's *Edda*.

The lays rendered here were first translated into English from the two Swedish versions of Gödecke and Sander, with frequent reference to the commentaries of the Swedish scholar Viktor Rydberg; thereafter the result was compared with the Wimmer and Jónsson *Saemundar Eddu*, a photographic facsimile of the old Icelandic *Codex Regius* manuscript with a printed transliteration facing each page. It is a continuous text with no divisions and only an inserted title to mark the beginning of each lay. Most translations break it into verses of six or eight lines as indicated by the rhythm, but we have chosen in many cases to write the verses as quatrains. There is no rhyming, but an alliterative pattern which with the distinctive tetrameter used in many very early epics gives the lays a peculiar charm.

The Edda consists of two main divisions, as do most scriptures that deal with the creation of cosmos and the evolution of mankind. The first applies to the surrounding world, the second to the "heroes": races of humanity and their development through stages of immaturity into the thinking, self-conscious men and women we have become. The latter tales sometimes make use of geographic features and of actual historic events to illustrate the much larger picture they disguise. This work concentrates mainly on the earlier portion, which deals with grand principles and universal events, searching out the basic philosophy of divine nature which is valid throughout the vicissitudes of the human venture.

In translating, both alliteration and meter have unfortunately very often had to be sacrificed, as our purpose is to convey the philosophic and scientific import rather than merely reproduce the poetic style. There already exist several English renditions in verse and prose, many of them accompanied by detailed analyses of the verse forms used in the original. In brief, our aim is not to produce merely another translation but to attempt to penetrate to the core of inspired meaning often concealed within myths. Interpreting and clarifying that inner sense in the Edda is made possible by resorting to the foremost elucidating work of our time, *The Secret Doctrine*, whose author, H. P. Blavatsky, juxtaposed a prodigious array of myths relating to cosmogony as well as human history and the destiny of living beings. In that work are keys showing that the same majestic pattern underlies the varied expressions of different mythic scriptures; we are given an overview of the universe, its periodicity of function and repose, and we discern how divine consciousness reflects itself periodically as a kosmos in space and time.

To find the information the Edda contains we must examine the etymology of names and their connotations, which in some cases are numerous. For this Cleasby's *Icelandic Dictionary*, completed by Gudbrand Vigfusson in 1869, has proved of inestimable value for it contains copious quotations from the original manuscripts and sometimes presents a strikingly intuitive perception. *Undersökningar i Germansk Mitologi (Teutonic Mythology)* by Viktor Rydberg also contains scrupulous examination of terms and much information.

One great problem with a book such as this is to arrange the material in a practical manner without necessitating undue repetition. The lays are reproduced in English with the flavor as nearly unchanged as may be and each one is preceded by explanatory notes. In addition certain themes are given special attention; inevitably some of these will occur more than once though each approach is somewhat different. In the notes, verse numbers are given to indicate whence an interpretation has been derived. Needless to say, many meanings are often contained in a single passage, and frequently they are mere hints requiring some personal insight on the part of the reader, for it is not always possible to elucidate each symbol adequately, nor is it necessary. The spelling of names is intentionally inconsistent, some being given in Icelandic (e.g., Aesir), others in Swedish (e.g., Äger), both to make them easier to distinguish visually by the English-speaking reader and because in many cases the root of a name has a suggestive meaning in one language but does not occur, or has a slightly different connotation, in the other. There are also many instances where the Icelandic grammatical variants, or a Swedish plural or definite form, would make an otherwise familiar word all but unrecognizable, necessitating inevitable compromises in an English rendition. Also, where Swedish uses å we have favored using the Icelandic á. When possible, names have been translated into English to enable a reader to find his own interpretation. A glossary and index have been provided.

Acknowledgments

Many thanks are due to a number of people who have helped bring this book into being: first to the late James A. Long who, during his leadership of the Theosophical Society, encouraged my study of the Edda and included eight articles on its theosophic content in Volume IV of the magazine *Sunrise* during 1954–5, with some half dozen more appearing later over a period of years; also to Kirby Van Mater, without whose prodding this book would never have been begun; thereafter to Sarah Belle Dougherty, who read the manuscript and proposed shuffling the material into better order; to Gertrude (Trudy) Hockinson who typed and retyped large portions of the manuscript; to Rod Casper of Millikan Library at the California Institute of Technology, who helped me procure research materials; A. Studley Hart, who performed some editorial magic; my dear friend Ingrid (Binnie) Van Mater, who not only read the work with a clear and critical eye but also checked the entries of the index and glossary and assisted with all the ticklish unavoidable tasks that must precede completion of a book. Thereafter she, Manuel Oderberg, Eloise and Studley Hart proofread it. In addition I must thank the production staff of Theosophical University Press, notably Will Thackara, Raymond Rugland, Mark Davidson, and John Van Mater, Jr., who took endless pains with the craftsmanship of the work. Above all, my grateful thanks are due to Grace F. Knoche, without whose constant support none of the above would have come about.

ELSA-BRITA TITCHENELL

May 31, 1985
Altadena, California

Part 1

COMMENTARY

Myths — A Time Capsule

AMONG THE MOST INTRIGUING THINGS about myths is the air they have of being more permanent than life. Anonymous and timeless, they seem to exist uncreated in some universal limbo, waiting to be discovered. Their message is as eternal as boundless space, as pervasive as the energies that swirl cosmic dust into spirals and spin atomic worlds into the organized formations that are larger worlds.

There can exist but one truth, one all-embracing reality, which is the common property of all mankind. It has always existed and it exists today. Out of the white light of that primordial truth radiate the mythologies and scriptures of the world and, though the light still remains, it is diffracted through innumerable human minds into the prismatic colors of partial knowledge and diverse beliefs. Nevertheless, by comparing the different mythologies we may still discern in them the truth which gave them rise.

Among the many expressions of ancient lore in various parts of the globe we find that the Norse Eddas contain science and philosophy of a high order, a rounded knowledge which also constituted religion to some long forgotten people who must have preceded the Viking age by no one knows how long. Judging by the thoughts they incorporated in their tales they included in their world picture an awareness of many of the forces and potencies we know by different names and which have been rediscovered by science during the past century or so. Considering that the Norse tradition, though dating back in essentials to an unknown prehistory, has had to pass through the rough-and-tumble world of the Viking warriors and has no doubt had to draw on a more vivid palette in depicting the adventures of gods and giants than originally used, it is remarkable how much profound philosophy is recognizable to us today.

Many generations which told and retold the tales probably lacked understanding of their import; for them the tales served merely to while away the long dark nights and people the skies and earth with gods and heroes. If they incidentally preserved the ancient lore for later, more receptive generations, who is to say this was not an objective of the mythographers? It truly is a miracle that these songs and stories continue to exist at all, when you consider how few of our bestselling books survive even the year of their publication. If myths recorded merely commonplace events, real or imaginary, they would have been forgotten long ago. Their longevity must be due to a built-in permanence which rests on a substratum of reality, quite independent of climatic and regional traits which lend their coloration to the stories. Most people are familiar with a wealth of classic tales, epics, and the mythologies of several groups of people; we learn them as children and, as parents, pass them on without questioning whence they have come, simply because they are interesting and we enjoy them. And yet in our languages the very word "myth" has come to mean something spurious without any basis in fact. Transmitted for ages by word of mouth, sung by rememberers who had to learn by rote incredible quantities of verse, it is a moot question whether those bards were less exact than the written word. We all know how vehemently children object to any change in the wording of the classic fairy tales. Perhaps they instinctively recognize that these stories are sacred and must be protected from adulteration.

Not all myths are of course equally meaningful. Some are merely entertaining; others strongly suggest factual science, albeit worded in an unfamiliar dialect, while subjects which we regard as discrete and separate — astronomy, biology, anthropology, psychology, physics — are treated as an integrated whole. Allusions to long forgotten history are meaningless to us; however, myths dealing with themes having timeless and universal application — the creation of worlds, astronomical events, natural history — preserve for ages science, philosophy, and religion, and emerge from obscurity whenever a generation is receptive to their message.

As every mythology descended from the oldest traditions echoes the same grand cosmogony and imparts similar instructions for ethical living in its own distinctive code, we can partly decipher that code by comparing various systems. Without such decoding many a fairy tale, archaeological find, legend, opera, and myth, remains empty of significance, a cover without a book, a frame surrounding a blank canvas. But if we look for the inner message in the myths we may indeed find them a valuable time capsule — not full of *things*, but compact of wisdom which in the guise of stories keeps intact our heritage of all that has lasting value.

THE LANGUAGE OF MYTHS

Mythology is not just a collection of stories; it is a language. Like other languages it uses symbols to convey ideas according to standard associations: symbols such as "up," "high," "lofty" denote things that are noble and elevating, and "down," "low," "base" things that are ignoble and undesirable.

A kind of symbol often found in the Eddas is the "kenning." It used to be believed that to give your real name to a stranger was to give him power over you, and so a descriptive epithet, a kenning, was preferred. To understand the Eddas we must therefore examine the etymology of names, for more often than not this will supply a key to the part played by a character in a particular situation. We have tried to translate the kennings as they occur, so as to give the reader an opportunity to discern their meanings for himself. Often a kenning is used also to draw attention to the particular aspect of a person or object which is relevant at the time.

For example, as the sorrowing Idun lies weeping, fallen from the Tree of Life, the lay recounts how "tears fell from her brain's shields." To translate this "from her eyes" would of course be permissible but would rob the poem of its distinctive flavor. Similarly, the Tree of Life, Yggdrasil, is seldom designated twice in the same way. It may be called the "life supporter," "the shade giver," "the soil mulcher," "the noble ash tree," "Odin's horse," or "Odin's gallows" (whereon he is crucified).

The Norse myths also make use of puns, which can be a most effective and intricate method of teaching. One outstanding example is the tale of Cinderella, whose very title holds a wealth of wisdom. She is the French Cendrillon, and the English Little Polly Flinders (who sat among the cinders). It is a tale too well known to need repeating, and the symbology is quite clear. Briefly, the orphaned child is enslaved by the wicked stepmother and her brood of evils: the human soul that has lost touch with its father in heaven comes under the sway of the lower side of nature with which it is not truly kin. Note that it is a stepmother, not a true parent, who plays the villain. Alienated from its proper place, the soul labors to regain its rightful condition. By purity and virtue it earns the help of its fairy godmother, the spiritual soul. Many tales use this theme of a mysterious godmother and giver of gifts, which latter represent a soul's finer qualities unfolded through merit. This elven power uniting the human soul with its divine source is the channel (elf) which confers on its child all earned spiritual endowments.

The Norse Cinderella is named *Askungen* — (*ask* ash + *unge* child), "the ash child." She is a scion of the "noble ash tree," Yggdrasil, the Tree of Life, which bears the worlds with all their life forms on its branches. All living beings are children of the cosmic Ash Tree from the minutest particle to the largest. What is more, each of us is not only a member of the cosmic tree, but a tree of life in his own right.

The ash child is also cyclically reborn from the ashes of its former self, like the phoenix. There is also a connection with Gullveig, "the thirst for gold," which urges the conscious mind to seek the "gold" of the mystical alchemists — wisdom. Gullveig is said to be "thrice burned and thrice reborn, yet still she lives" (Völuspá 22).

If Askungen is written *ás-kunnigr*, there are revealed further meanings of this versatile term: first, "god-kin" — i.e., of divine lineage; and again, "god-knowing" — having knowledge of divinity; and "knowing as a god" — possessing divine wisdom; and yet again "known to the gods." Any one of these could describe the rare soul who has attained human perfection. A further meaning emerges if we divide the word *ás-kungen*: this means "the king of aesir," implying that the ruler of the gods is inherent in the story's orphaned waif. Thus an ingenious play on words makes the title of this fairy tale convey a rich philosophy.

Many interpreters have emphasized the part played by racial migrations in the mythic histories, and doubtless the Odin whose exploits and leadership live on in story form did represent an early people, possibly from one of the deeper strata of Troy, as has been suggested by more than one mythologist. Nevertheless, this in no way disallows other applications of the sagas — astronomical, psychological, and spiritual. The same applies to others of the divine cast of characters. The entire pantheon represents properties existing in nature — and in ourselves — and they evidently have a vital importance not only for us terrestrial kingdoms, but they also affect the quality of life throughout the solar realm.

The effective imparting of ideas demands three factors: first, the message to be imparted; second, the means of expression used to convey the message; third, an understanding mind prepared to receive it. It follows that mythic scriptures must draw on perennial common knowledge and recurring events to illustrate their truths. Therefore things that figure in the public mind are in evidence throughout the myths: war and battles are prominently featured, because these have all too frequently been a familiar part of the human scene; moreover they vividly portray the conflict that takes place in the soul of an individual who has embarked on the pursuit of inner goals and high ideals. This furtherance of human progress toward a nobler stature is in large part what the epics aim to encourage.

THE HERO TALES

The hero tales of the Eddas have a markedly dual character. They are both quasi-historical and legendary, and they deal with a profusion of events which interlink large numbers of characters in a web of plots and counterplots, feuds and subterfuge. Many of the incidents related are so involved and their protagonists so numerous that tracing the thread of the stories poses a challenge to the most dedicated genealogist. However, with some background of mythic methodology we may discern a glimmer of light pointing to a pattern that fits the progression of the earliest human races, their characteristics, and their methods of living and means of propagation.

The theosophic philosophy places man among the creators of our world from the very beginning, when he and the globe itself were still not of physical substance as we now know it, but condensing very slowly from a primordial nebula. The names of the earliest heroes give us interesting confirmation of this, if they indeed represent distinct groups of humanity during that stage of formation. If their exploits are a way of symbolizing the progress of these early races, we can trace our ancestry from amorphous wisps of cloud to gelatinous and finally fleshy beings;

from sexless to androgynous to bisexual organisms; and from unthinking, dreamy, non-conscious movers into gradually awakening intelligences. By the more experienced kingdom of the lowest gods the protohumans were guided and taught to plan, to cultivate and to harvest, to fashion objects, temper tools, and in the course of time to become self-sufficient and independent. In the hero tales we may see, by the manner in which the characters interact, how life forms altered over immense lengths of time and thereby also changed the composition of the globe. Successive phyla, human and nonhuman, followed one another, competing for habitat and viability, with antagonists and relatives conquering and superseding one another and with multiple marriages bringing radically different offspring into the picture. Some were neither human nor bestial but curiously malleable creatures, performing unexpected and uncritically accepted acts.

To relate the epics to humanity's prehistory would demand the untangling of the many intertwined threads of narrative — a monumental undertaking with no surety of correct interpretation or sequence. The lengthy saga of *Sigurd Fáfnesbane* (bane of Fáfnir) is suggestive of those remote aeons. The Germanic version is well known as part of the *Nibelungen* cycle.

The name Nibelungen, or *Niflungar* in the Norse, means "children of the mist" (*nifl* nebula). Strongly reminiscent of the "Sons of the Fire Mist" in *The Secret Doctrine*, these too appear to be forces which were instrumental in bringing into being the primordial world. The Niflungar were followed by the *Völsungar*, which means "children of *völsi* (phallus)," a much later humanity which by then had begun to propagate by sexual means — a development which theosophy places in the third and subsequent humanities.

Interspersed with the saga are numerous feuds which evidently have reference to a succession of races, branch races, and lesser tribes, as well as to various types of rudimentary consciousness characteristic of peoples in the early stages of our planet's life. The story contains a welter of deception and revenge, blood feuds carried on through generations, all told in the dispassionate, unjudging narrative style which is one of the hallmarks of genuine mythology. Appraisals are the province of fiction and reflect the passing mores of an age; mythic accounts record events without praise or blame.

Hidden within the symbolism of these tales with their many digressions we may detect, by the very abundance of anecdotes, the ages-long sweep of the early development of our planet, when its matter was still condensing and all the kingdoms of nature were in process of formation. Increasing substantiality and variety of form afforded the means for physical evolution, while it also set in motion the momentum which would tend to retard the development of spirituality. Before the turning point this was mercifully counteracted by the event recorded as the coming of Rig, when a ray of the god Heimdal, "the whitest Áse," entered humanity in three successive stages.* Our lineage is therefore thrice divine. Also, like Sigurd (Fáfnesbane), we are god-taught and, like him, deluded by the wiles of matter, we must repair and reconstitute the sword we have inherited: the will by which to overcome illusion and awaken the sleeping Valkyrie in the soul.

SCIENCE IN THE EDDA

In order to recognize references to facts and artifacts in legends and mythic tradition we ourselves must be familiar with the things they refer to. It takes a technologist of the same kind to recognize a description of another's technological invention, and it takes knowledge of a natural phenomenon to recognize a description of it in myth. References in the myths to electricity, magnetism, or conductivity passed unnoticed by scholars of

---

*The Lay of Rig, ch. 18.

earlier centuries who knew little or nothing of such things; that the Edda's "winged wagons" and "featherblades" — like the Sanskrit "celestial cars" of the Hindu *Mahābhārata* and *Rāmāyana*[1] — may have described instruments of flight, escaped recognition before we had recourse to aviation. Now that we use airplanes routinely, we can, if we will, find strong indications that not only air travel, but also the Van Allen belts, the earth's magnetic field, black holes, and QSOs[2] were known to the makers of the myths. We have yet to learn what prodigious forces were used by some builders of cyclopean monuments and pyramids, and how they moved boulders weighing tons and shaped them with jewel-like precision in places as widely separated as Egypt, Peru, Britain, and Cambodia.

Archaeoastronomers are fairly sure that many if not all of the henges of Britain — Stonehenge being one among hundreds and certainly the best known — were built and used to study the movements of celestial bodies; alignments of dolmens were apparently used to calculate eclipses among other things, something which requires refined long-term observation and precise calculation. Some of these structures are thought to have harbored universities for other studies as well. Both the old and new worlds contain remains of a variety of devices: mounds, stone circles, medicine wheels, petroglyphs, and buildings, which served to align stars and planets. Scandinavia and Britain abound in mysterious stone circles, miniatures of the better known henges, formed of stelae placed in round or oval formation. My friends and I used to play in such a "stone ship" on a hillock on an island in the Baltic. We found after weeks of digging that the stones, which stood only about two feet high, were buried so deep that we never succeeded in rocking any of them. For the sod to have accumulated nearly to their tops they

---

1. Swedish: *vingvagn, fjäderblad;* Sanskrit: *vimāna.*
2. Quasi-stellar objects, popularly called quasars.

must have been of considerable age. (Other stone ships are probably later Viking burial sites; it was the practice to lay a dead chieftain aboard his vessel, set it alight and send it burning out to sea, a custom superseded by burial with goods, ship and all.) Older stone circles are so placed that they may well have provided sighting markers for solstices, equinoxes, sun dogs (those mysterious reflections on both sides of a rising or setting sun), and possibly more sophisticated observations as well, such as the heliacal rising of certain stars.

Many things which seem absurd or inconsistent in myths are explainable once we reverse our point of view: instead of looking down on their authors as ignoramuses and up at the universe from the material level, we can regard the cosmos as an expression of life and lives, as a vital, composite organism containing unimaginable reaches of consciousnesses and infinite grades of substances. Today increasing numbers of scientists are entering the realm of philosophy and conceding that the human race is an intrinsic part of a universal system of life. A recent textbook on astronomy contains the following:

> Astronomy teaches that we are creatures of the universe, children of the stars, offspring of the interstellar clouds. We are products of cosmic evolution. We are also part of the process of cosmic evolution. Perhaps we are the universe's way of becoming aware of itself. You and I and the other living creatures in the cosmos — when we look into space, we see the source of ourselves. And to those wide-open spaces we add hope, fear, imagination, and love.[3]

The Norse myths regard sun, moon, and planets as the dwellings which "beneficent powers" have formed for their habitation. Some of these mansions, disposed on a series of "shelves" — different grades of substances — are given such names as Bredablick

---

3. Michael Zeilik, *Astronomy: The Evolving Universe*, 1979 ed., p. 501.

(Broadview), Himmelsberg (Mountains of Heaven), Lidskjälf (Shelf of Compassion),[4] Sökvabäck (Deep River), and other suggestive epithets. Obviously it is not possible to describe in human terms the supernal spheres of the gods, but we may assume that the stellar and planetary spheres we see in the sky are the visible bodies of their deities, that is, of conscious energies each one with its distinct individuality. The myths that deal with these "gods" and "goddesses" and with their shelves and the halls they have built for themselves thereon give the impression of a family: a group of related individuals having pronounced characters and dispositions. They act on one another, react to one another, and generally behave as one might expect members of a family to conduct themselves.

Although the mythographers revered these "beneficent powers" as the mighty movers of the spheres, there is no hint in the earliest traditions of worship in the modern sense of the word; there is a recognition of their "worthship" as universal powers who have graduated from former "giant" worlds and who precede us on the evolutionary path, blazing the trail of human destiny for future aeons. Nor are the deities confined to the visible solar and planetary worlds which represent them. Their scope is far vaster, something we know today on physical grounds: space probes have shown that a planet is surrounded by an envelope of magnetic plasma so immense that the visible globe has been compared to a baseball in the nose of a blimp. The mighty solar wind also pours forth torrents of plasma, which mingles with the planetary magnetospheres, flattening them on the daylight side (facing the sun) and propelling them far into space on the nightside.

Despite differences in expression, modern science and an-

---

4. *Lida* suffer or *blid* side, rank, or alignment. By implication this "shelf" may suggest the gods' being aligned by our side or, more likely, "suffering" or "feeling with" — as in the Latin *compassion* and the Greek *sympathy* from *pathein*, to suffer, endure and, by extension of meaning, to bear the burden of.

cient myths describe the solar system in very similar ways: myths as a hierarchic being wherein streams of vital energies — the Edda's rivers of lives — flow from mansion to mansion, linking the divine energies (consciousnesses) in a webwork of life and motion; physical science as a huge organization wherein gravitational effects produce tides and in unexplained ways affect growth cycles on earth. On a much larger scale galaxies in clusters and superclusters of galaxies are found to interact, being gravitationally bound. Myths seem to be true to nature in describing the solar system as a vast composite wherein seen and unseen worlds correspond to every permutation of god-giant — energy-matter — interactions, paralleling interactions of psychological and other intangible influences, such as we are familiar with in the human sphere.

In line with this view, astrophysical science has for some time been debating the relative probability of a "closed" versus an "open" universe. The answer depends on how much matter exists in space, unseen and apparently undetectable by presently available means. Whatever the outcome of this debate, for our purposes it is enough that invisible, inaudible, intangible, by physical means seemingly undetectable, matter has been accorded scientific respectability. This approaches mythic science which has always implied the existence of nonphysical substances. Not that myths need either confirmation or denial; their message can stand on its own merits.

If the vast preponderance of matter is unseen, it becomes simple logic to regard the globes in the sky as parts of larger systems of worlds that we do not see but that may be analogous to and perhaps interact with corresponding unseen parts of our own nature. In theosophic tradition the visible spheres of our solar system are considered the grossest components of their respective planetary beings. They are their bodies; we may surmise or sense, but cannot see, their souls. To carry the idea one step further, they interact with one another much as human beings interact without physical contact. Certainly we share our thoughts and feelings, at times inspire and become inspired by one another; so too may the invisible components of the solar system help to build and influence other invisible, and visible, components. This would agree well with the idea that rivers of lives, comprising all kinds of characteristics (and matching substances), flow through the immense solar body along magnetic paths of attraction, each life an entity in its own right as well as a minute portion of the whole. Some of these lives imbody in mineral forms — those possessing the ponderous, earthy character we find it hard to imagine as "life"; others have progressed to the vegetable stage with its great variety of possibilities; others to animal status and still greater diversity; and we represent the human stage. All through the system interconnectedness is demonstrable as we take our places in the biological food chain, where we transform and transmute the matter of the globe; more importantly, we process properties of consciousness of vastly different kinds. All the beings that traverse the stages of existence up to the limit we have reached, inhabit their appropriate spheres of life within the greater being we all help compose. It is then not so strange to suppose that we, one of the rivers of lives, have a home for every aspect of our nature in some domain of the solar universe. This seems to be what the myths imply in their cryptic way.

The intriguing descriptions given in Grimnismál of the twelve mansions of the gods, each on its "shelf" (plane), are extremely suggestive of the pattern given in *The Secret Doctrine* and later elaborated by G. de Purucker in *Fountain-Source of Occultism*. There it is plainly intended to connect each deity and its corresponding planet with an invisible portion of our own planet's inner being, showing a relationship of each to each linking all the parts of every individual component of the solar system. Intricate correspondences connect every character of the celestial scenario with every one of the others, and these explain the complex interrelationships of the Norse deities as nothing else could; the same applies to the Greek and other pantheons. When myths give assurance of a continuum wherein worlds exist outside our perception, both "above" and "below" the familiar range of frequencies which characterizes matter, and still form part of our universe; when they indicate that our familiar proportions continue indefinitely above and beneath our "line of sight" and that apparently empty space is a fullness of lives unperceived by us; we have no means of either proving or disproving this information until we become able to apprehend and experience the "shelves" and "mansions" of which they speak. Interpretation is therefore largely an individual matter. A myth that refers to Freya does not always specify whether the visible planet Venus is intended, or the unseen characteristic power which sponsors and has particular concern for our humanity; or, it may be the Venus-inspired portion of our planet that is intended. In any case, we cannot set limits on the versatility of nature; the limitations are in us.

One interesting possibility that presents itself as we contemplate the astrophysical universe concerns the extraordinary prevalence in space of binary stars and galaxies. They far outnumber the single ones and in many cases are paired in such a way that while one component is building its physical sphere the other is etherealizing — radiating away its substance. In certain instances the former is "cannibalizing" the latter. If we consider the theosophic pattern of solar and planetary deities imbodying, accreting substance to themselves, and forming their habitations, while other gods of the same system are in process of dying, it appears that where spheres are progressing toward more substantial imbodiment and others of the same system are relinquishing theirs, such a pair of twin globes when traversing the "shelf" of our perception may quite possibly be seen as a binary system.

Unless we claim to possess complete knowledge — which

no intelligent person would presume to do — we must concede that there may well be conditions of life unknown to us. Myths imply, though they cannot describe, a universe filled with evolving consciousnesses using life forms, most of which are unknown to our senses. To the mythmakers all nature was one living whole, wherein greater and lesser systems lived and interacted, each unit being primarily a consciousness which activated and animated a suitable body. It was apparently taken for granted that worlds of other kinds of matter interpenetrated and sometimes interacted with our own though most often beyond our awareness. Their way of describing such familiar phenomena as electromagnetism gives us a clue to the manner in which myths may contain factual information. It would be interesting to speculate on how we would explain our own knowledge to survivors of a major catastrophe and how much recognizable science would remain after a few tellings. Imagine, for instance, explaining the way electricity works — something most easily illustrated by an electric storm — and how this information would be transmogrified after a few generations: inevitably it would give rise to a new Indra, Jove, or Thor hurling thunderbolts across the sky, and soon a new Olympus or Ásgárd of mighty and capricious deities would once more occupy the heavens.

SKALDS AND TEACHERS

In that distant dawn when humankind first became aware of itself as thinking, knowing, selective, the oldest traditions agree that this awakening occurred because higher intelligences, more experienced souls of mankinds of the past, mingled their essence with the early humans. This act of their compassion gave us the undying vision of reality which is our link with the divine ground of life.

The myths, if they hold any meaning for us at all, are a

guide to that inner light, kindled when our kind was still ignorant of good and evil, when choice did not yet exist — a light which remains unquenched within our deepest consciousness. They tell us of worlds and humans undergoing the experience of life in order to consummate our perfectibility, and of the holy purpose for which we exist. Their tales are sometimes obscure, often moving, sometimes funny. They hold our attention even when we do not understand them, hinting, beckoning our dormant insight, urging us to rouse our intuitive intelligence and find the kernel of truth they conceal.

The bards who chanted the mythic sagas were past masters at suggesting majestic avenues of thought without specifically stating any doctrine that could be coagulated into set and brittle opinions. The beauty of their tales lies in the flights of wondering they prod the mind to take and in the ever-broadening vistas that are glimpsed beyond each larger understanding. Perhaps no mythology so fully turns the keys to nature's arcana as do these relics of the Norsemen's forebears. Some of the purest versions of the universal wisdom may well be those contained in the Eddas for, being somewhat less known than the Greek and Roman myths, they have been less adulterated. The myths of the Mediterranean area have been so garbled and lampooned since the closing of the Mystery schools that the public mind of later centuries has seen in their gods little more than reflections of human foibles. Exoteric and unexplained to begin with, their meanings have through Europe's Dark Ages been further misunderstood and misinterpreted. As a result people have come to regard all myths as childish fancies of those who worship whatever they fail to understand. If we had greater insight into the noble truths these tales were originally intended to convey we might enrich our own spiritual climate. The mythic heritage of the remote northern lands seems to have given a safer refuge than most to the wisdom of the ages.

Nobody knows how long the Norse stories were passed on

by word of mouth before they were recorded. It may be a very long time indeed since the last civilization flourished which possessed knowledge of the spirit of man, the universe's origin and destiny, and the course of evolution. The mythmakers were doubtless the wisest among humankind; the Norse bards, like those of ancient India and other lands, couched their knowledge in rhythmic verse that could be easily memorized and so kept current through millennia, even if only as a diversion. One who learned and chanted the Norse songs was a *skald*, a word still used in Sweden to mean "poet." However, the connotation given it in the Eddas is that of one possessing wisdom, spiritual knowing, and it is closely bound to the idea of the mead, the sustenance of the gods. The *skaldemjöd* (poetic mead) denotes the Mysteries, the wisdom sought by Odin, chief of the creative gods, in his quest through spheres of matter — the "giant world."

Secreted in mythology are spiritual truth, logical philosophy, and also scientific facts. Indeed, the latest discoveries in science often prove to be indispensable to an understanding of the science in the myths. We may never know how the unknown peoples of distant antiquity came by this knowledge unless we recognize that truth is innate in the intelligence-level of life represented on earth by the human race. The ancient legends relate that the gods created humans out of their own substance, "in their own image" as the Bible has it, and that for ages divine teachers walked the earth with us, training the newborn intelligences to understand and work with nature's ways. In the course of time, as the human race pursued knowledge and gained experience of good and evil, through the exercise of free will, the innocence of those days was lost. In the headlong progress toward more material interests, humanity drifted away from its divine preceptors. Thereafter, our race must *earn* its liberation: our human consciousness must learn to know truth from error and deliberately free itself from the lures of matter in order to assume its rightful place among the gods.

It is from that very early time, when gods and humans mingled, that many of the mythic tales take their rise. If they are often obscure to us it is not surprising, for they have doubtless passed through many phases of human, fallible remembrance; and our understanding, like our skepticism, follows from our inward attitude. With our present knowledge and the open-mindedness which is gradually prevailing over the dogmatic opinions of the past, once we recognize in any myth a reflection of a truth which has been independently discovered by science or the new scientific philosophies and religious nonsectarian thought, it becomes easier to see the same natural truth in other systems.

Edda means "great-grandmother" and, by extension of meaning, "matrix," suggesting "world mother." The word is apparently derived from *veda*, the Hindu scriptures or sacred *vidyā* (knowledge, from *vid*, to know, to perceive) from which stem the German *wissen*, the Swedish *veta*, and the old English *wit* — all words which mean "to know." The *skalds* held an honored position for they possessed knowledge and, even in Viking times, the *drott* (druid) was still revered as one who possessed the godly wisdom. (Later the word became used to designate a brave and noble chieftain, a warrior-king, more suited to the warlike race the Vikings had by then become.) This wisdom, or Edda, was imparted by the skalds who traveled from community to community of the farmers who dwelt along the many bays and inlets of the Scandinavian lands. Such a bay is called a *vik* and a dweller on their shores became known as a *viking*.

In all justice it should be mentioned that the Vikings who are popularly reputed to have terrorized Europe and some of whom evidently visited America long before Columbus made his famous journey, though a rough and simple people, had strong notions of honor and morality. Many of them are held to have lived by a disciplinary code few moderns would care to maintain. Among the marauding pirates on the high seas, merchantmen ran a risky gauntlet with their goods and it was the Vikings whom they enlisted for protection. These Norsemen with their reputation for strength and valor provided armed escort and became the insurance agents of the continent. (The bodyguards of all the emperors of Byzantium from the ninth to the twelfth century were Vikings.) No doubt there were some among them who succumbed to the temptation of running their own "protection racket," but this should not be held against all the Norsemen who on the whole were a civilizing influence for centuries. They instituted law and order — the famed Danelagh — wherever they settled, and Iceland was, a thousand years ago, the original home of democratic parliamentary rule and had the earliest known judicial system of trial by a jury of equals. But this is by the way.

As time went on it is doubtful whether the wisdom concealed in the songs and sagas was completely understood even by the skalds; they may also have overlaid the substance with some embellishments to suit their audience, or omitted less popular tales from their repertoire. Human fallibility in the oral transmission must also be allowed for, as we have no way of knowing how far back in the misty past these relics of wisdom were first formulated. We do know that Saemund the Wise (1057–1133 A.D.), after having studied in France, opened a school at Oddi in Iceland, where he is believed to have written down the Elder or Poetic Edda. The Younger Edda is attributed to Snorri Sturlusson (1178–1241), who attended the school at Oddi as a pupil of Saemund's grandson during which time he must have become acquainted with the lays. Most of them, including several that are no longer extant in the poetic form, he recast into prose. Many scholars find his retelling easier to understand than the rather obscure poems of the Elder Edda.

In their introduction to the *Corpus Poeticum Boreale, the Poetry of the Old Northern Tongue* (1883), G. Vigfusson and F. York Powell point out that much of the material mentioned in the prose commentaries on early poetic myths is either not found in the verses that have survived or is very sketchy and incomplete. They conclude from this that the prose versions, whether by Snorri Sturlusson or some commentator, must have been taken from more explicit but no longer extant originals. Indeed the two scholars refer to parts of the Völuspá cited in one prose version as "a confused, pell-mell jumble of broken, distorted verses, as if the lines of the poem had been shaken up together in a bottle" (p. xcviii); and they make the probably valid assumption that after the first formulation of wisdom into myth by any great seer or seers, the "Era of Production is closed, the Age of Commentators, Copiers, Glossators begins, and we are happy if we can get the book as it then stands before the Age of Neglect and Decay has come on and the work has partly perished" (p. xcvii).

About 1890, the Swedish scholar Fredrik Sander published his *Rigveda-Edda*, wherein he traces the Germanic tradition to the ancient Aryan. His study convinced him that Norse mythology came from India and preserves Hindu myths more faithfully than do the classic Greek and Roman, which are much disfigured. Max Müller considered the Edda tradition to be older than the Vedas; others, including Sven Grundtvig, regard the Eddas as originating in the early Iron Age; still others postulate an early Christian origin. Whatever their age may be, the *content* of the myths agrees with the oldest records in many parts of the world, which forces the conclusion either that they all stem from a single source, a prehistoric formulation of science, philosophy, and mysticism once common to all mankind or, alternatively, that each one arose independently and coincidentally — a notion too preposterous to be seriously entertained. In any case, the evidence points to a single body of lore having inspired the traditions whose relics are to be found everywhere on the face of our globe.

The present study is limited almost entirely to a portion of the Saemundar Edda for two reasons: first, because of the overwhelming vastness of the subject matter covered even in the relatively few lays included here coupled with the conviction that, reduced and incomplete though they may be, what has been selected is at least unadulterated. While these verses probably contain less than the once known truth we may feel reasonably sure that they have not been elaborated to contain more, i.e., very little if any spurious matter added by later authors. The other reason for our selection is the recognition in this material of truths that are currently found more fully explored in modern theosophical literature. Many of these truths, moreover, after having been overlooked for centuries in the popular religions, are now being discovered almost daily by the new scientific research, which agrees with the theosophic teachings in many and surprising ways.

Ours is a far more liberal age than any in history. When Christianity spread over Europe, the zealots of the new religion systematically destroyed the temples and shrines of earlier gods and massacred those who persisted in the pagan rituals. The heathens of the northern lands, whose custom of unlimited hospitality and absolute tolerance in religious matters left them wide open to exploitation, found themselves converted or were destroyed before they could take steps to prevent such unexpected and high-handed annexation. They fell under the control of Roman popes who instituted the use of the Latin language and orthodox gospels in the place of native tongues and scriptures. The Norse religion soon became a hybrid of partially understood Christianity grafted on a, by then, degenerate pagan root. Only distant Iceland, whose population and priesthood were relatively inaccessible and impossible for the church to supervise, escaped the methodical destruction of its shrines and traditions. Even the Christian priests there ignored the new rules — of celibacy for instance — and continued in the ways of their forebears, using the tongue of their fathers and passing on the ancient lore to their children. It was there that Saemund the Wise lived and wrote down the poetic Elder Edda, preserving the phrasing whose rhythmic meter evokes intuition in the hearer. Snorri later elaborated on the laconic verses and related the tales that deal more particularly with human races and their development. The myths have given rise to numberless folk-tales and fairy tales which have been adapted to various media for expression, from nursery rhymes to grand opera, by such diverse transmitters as Mother Goose and Wagner, and they include collections made by students of folklore such as the brothers Grimm in the nineteenth century.

Of the numerous promulgations of the universal wisdom in gospels, stories, teachings, and evangels, each new light that is kindled continues to burn only so long as truth remains of paramount importance to its adherents. Sooner or later attrition sets in: human institutions, founded to preserve the message, take precedence over it and obscure it; thereafter attention is focused on the mask — method and ritual — while reality is overlooked. Misinterpretations, misunderstandings, and super-stitions rapidly prevail as inspiration is lost and the sacred knowl-edge once more forgotten. The mythic deities, from having been majestic laws of universal nature, become personified as gods and heroes whose actions appear unpredictable for lack of the wisdom once contained in the now empty rites — all that remains of a once companionable association of humans with the divine powers governing the universe.

Yet myths live on. This is the eternal mystery: the indestruc-tible core of truth, garbed in a hundred guises, which has inspired mankind through all ages. In every land have lived some few who, by courageously venturing into the spheres where spirit dwells inviolate, have brought back with them a draught from the imperishable fount of truth. These descendants of the early mythmakers are the *skalds*, the poets and seers who keep un-broken the lines of communication between humanity and the gods. They bring the eternal wisdom down through the centuries while the rest of us continue to delight in the "god-spells" that rouse within the depths of us a vague remembrance of a sacred trust. The voices of the bards can never die, for they sing the pattern of eternity. Their appeal is to the undying part of us, even while the mortal self may scoff as Loki does when, uninvited and unprepared, he enters the banquet hall of the gods.[5]

---

5. Cf. Loki's Flyting, p. 214.

2

The Tree of Life — Yggdrasil

EVERY MYTHOLOGY FEATURES a Tree of Life. In the biblical account the "jealous" deities (*elohim*) — usually translated "the Lord God" — when the humans had eaten of the fruit of the tree of knowledge of good and evil, feared "lest he put forth his hand, and take also of the tree of life, and eat, and live for ever." They therefore set "a flaming sword which turned every way, to keep the way of the tree of life."[1] In the Bantu myths a rather awesome Tree of Life pursues the goddess of fertility and with her begets all the kingdoms of nature;[2] in India, the Aśvattha[3] tree is rooted in the highest heaven and descends through the spaces bearing all existing worlds on its branches. The concept of a tree branching into worlds is a universal one. Interestingly enough we still continue a tradition of adorning a tree with multicolored globes representing the many varieties of worlds pendent from the branches of the world tree although the meaning has long been lost.

In the Edda, the Tree of Life is named Yggdrasil, apparently for several reasons. This is another of the ingenious puns the bards of the Norsemen used to convey their message. *Ygg* has been variously translated in conjunction with other words as "eternal," "awesome" or "terrible," and also "old" or rather, "ageless." Odin[4] is called Yggjung — "old-young," equivalent to the biblical "Ancient of Days" — a concept the mind can

---

1. Genesis 3:22, 24.
2. *Indaba, My Children*, pp. 3–13.
3. *Bhagavad-Gītā*, ch. xv.
4. Also called Woden or Wotan.

grasp only in the wake of intuition. Yggdrasil is Odin's steed or, with equal logic, his gallows, the implication being of a divine sacrifice, a crucifixion of the silent guardian whose body is a world. In this thinking any Tree of Life, large or small, constitutes a cross whereon its ruling deity remains transfixed for the duration of its material presence. While Yggdrasil may refer to a whole universe with all its worlds, each human being is an Yggdrasil in its own measure, a miniature of the cosmic ash tree. Each is rooted in the divine ground of All-being and bears its Odin — omnipresent spirit which is the root and reason of all living things.

Any Tree of Life — human or cosmic — draws its nourishment from three roots that reach into three regions: one rises in Ásgárd, home of the Aesir, where it is watered by the spring of Urd, commonly translated as the past. However, the real meaning of the name is Origin, primal cause, the connotation being that of antecedent causes from which flow all subsequent effects. Urd is one of the three "maidens who know much" — the Norns, or Fates, whose farseeing gaze scans past, present, and future, as they spin the threads of destiny for worlds and men. "One was named Origin, the second Becoming; these two fashioned the third, named Debt. Fortune's lots, life and death, the fates of heroes, all comes from them."[5] *Urd*, the past, personifies all that has gone before and is the cause of both present and future. *Verdande* is the present, but it is not a static condition; on the contrary, it means Becoming — the dynamic, ever-changing, mathematical point between past and future; a point of vital importance for it is the eternal moment of choice for man, when conscious willing decision is made, directed by desire, either for progress or retrogression on the evolutionary path. It is noteworthy that these two Norns *create* the third, *Skuld*, meaning Debt: something owed, out of balance, to be

---

5. Völuspá, 20.

brought into equilibrium in the future — the inevitable result of all the past and of the present.

While the Norns are the Norse equivalent of the Greek Moirai or Fates who spin the thread of destiny, we recognize in them also what in the Stanzas of Dzyan[6] are called *Lipikas* — a Sanskrit term meaning "scribes" or "recorders." Like the Norns these are impersonal, implacable processes that automatically retain every event and set the stage for the balancing action of karma, the natural "law of consequences" or of cause and effect, which operates infallibly in all fields of action and determines the conditions met by every entity as a result of its past choices. In the unself-conscious kingdoms this is a purely automatic adjustment; in the human kingdom, every motive, noble or base, brings appropriate opportunities and obstacles that modify the future. Moreover, as the human awareness is capable of self-determined choice, it is also increasingly conscious of its responsibility for events to come. Each being is the result of all that it has made itself to be, and each will become what is in preparation through its present thoughts and deeds. The record of the everchanging complex of forces remains in its inmost identity the higher self in man, the individual's own Norn which the Edda calls his *hamingja*. In the Christian tradition it is our guardian angel.

Yggdrasil's second root springs from Mimer's well. This, the well of absolute matter, belongs to the "wise giant Mimer," source of all experience. It is said that Odin drinks each day from the waters of this well, but to do so he had to forfeit one of his eyes, which is hidden at the bottom of the well. In many popular tales where Odin is disguised as an old man in a blue fur coat, he wears a slouch hat to conceal the fact that he is lacking one eye. However, this is not the same as saying that

---

6. These stanzas form part of the ancient records on which *The Secret Doctrine* is a commentary.

he *has* only one eye. Can we be so sure that he had only two to begin with? The sacred writings of many peoples refer to a distant past when humanity possessed a "third eye" — organ of the intuition — which, according to theosophy, retreated inside the skull millions of years ago where it remains in vestigial form as the pineal gland, awaiting a time when it will once again be more functional than it is today. Such an interpretation gives us information not only on the meaning of the tale but on the picture language used in these myths. As immersion in the world of matter provides the experience which brings wisdom, consciousness (Odin) sacrifices part of its vision to obtain daily a draught from Mimer's well, while Mimer (matter) obtains a partial share of divine insight. Mimer is the progenitor of all giants, the timeless root of Ymer-Örgälmer, the frost giant from which worlds are formed.

Long ago, it is said, Mimer was killed by Njörd (time) and his body was thrown into a swamp (the "waters" of space). Odin retrieved his severed head and "confers with it daily." This suggests that the god, consciousness, uses the "head" or superior portion of its matter-associate, the vehicle or body, to obtain the distillate of experience. At the same time the giant achieves a measure of consciousness by association with the energic, divine side of nature. Duality appears to be universal: no world is so low, no consciousness so elevated as to be beyond this perpetual interchange, as the divine impulsion daily organizes and dwells in worlds of action, "raising runes of wisdom" by experience. Consciousness and matter are thus relative to each other on all levels, so that what is consciousness on one stratum of cosmic life is matter to the stage above it. The two sides of existence are inseparable. Both comprise every level of life as giants grow into gods and gods are graduates of former giant worlds, evolving toward still greater godhood.

Mimer's tree is Mimameid, the Tree of Knowledge, which is not to be confused with the Tree of Life, though the two are in certain ways interchangeable, for knowledge and wisdom are the fruits of life and living; conversely the application of wisdom to living brings immortality in ever loftier ranges of the Tree of Life.

Yggdrasil's third root reaches into Niflheim (cloudhome), where the clouds — nebulae — are born. This, like the other two realms, refers not to a place but to a condition. The name is highly suggestive as nebulae are stages in the development of cosmic bodies. The root is watered by Hvergälmer, source of all the "rivers of lives" — classes of beings.[7] These are what we call the kingdoms of nature which in their great variety of forms make up every globe. Niflheim, where lies the source of all these life types, contains the seething caldron of matter — primordial, undifferentiated substance out of which the matters of all ranges of substantiality and materiality are derived. It is the *mūlaprakṛti* (root-nature) of Hindu cosmogony, whose divine complement is *parabrahman* (beyond-brahman).

The intricate life system of Yggdrasil contains both facts of natural history and cosmological information which may be gleaned from the texts. For instance, the first root, springing from Ásgárd, the realm of the Aesir, watered by the well of the past, maps the "fates of heroes" from cause to effect for all hierarchies of existence, and the gods are no more exempt from this inexorable law than any other form of life. Yet every moment changes the course of destiny as each being acts freely within the limits of its own self-created condition.

The second root, watered by Mimer's well, draws its nourishment from the experience in matter earned by the divine eye of spirit, as Odin daily confers with Mimer's head.

The third root is watered by the many rivers of lives: all the different expressions needed to fill the requirements of all kinds of consciousnesses.

---

7. Grimnismál, 26.

During the first half of its life, Yggdrasil, the mighty Ash Tree, is named Mjötvidr (measure increasing); while in its process of growth the tree's energies are flowing from its spiritual roots into the worlds that are becoming. Its substances flourish on all levels, enriched by the nurturing wells that feed its three roots of spirit, matter, and form. After reaching full maturity, the tree becomes Mjötudr (measure exhausting); its juices then flow back into the root system, the life forces leave the matter realms, as the autumn of its life brings the fruit and seeds for succeeding lives to come. At length dormancy prevails during the ensuing frost giant — or rest cycle.

This metaphor of a tree, used in so many myths and scriptures to depict a cosmos, is remarkably exact. We know how on the earth with every spring the flow of forces infuses their growing power into each limb and leaf, giving beauty and perfection to blossoms, which in the course of time ripen into fruit which bears the seeds of future trees; and how, when the year draws to its close, the sap returns into the root system, nourishes it and provides firmer foundation for the next year's growth. We see an analogy to this in every human life as well: a baby's flesh is soft and delicate but increases in bulk and weight until middle life; thereafter the process reverses itself, culminating in the transparent fragility of the very old. So in the imbodiment of worlds do divine powers imbue latent, unformed matter with character, structure, and shape, increasing substance and solidity. The layered cosmos expands from within, branching through all grades of matter until the limit is reached for that phase of its evolution, whereupon the life forces retreat back into the spiritual realms as the divine root receives into itself the essence or aroma of the experience. So it is that consciousnesses imbody through multilevel worlds, earning the gods' mead of experience.

Yggdrasil nourishes all beings with a life-giving honeydew. The worlds pendent from its branches on all its shelves of existence receive from the divine roots what is needful for growth: predisposition from the well of Urd, material substance from the well of Mimer, and appropriate means of expression from Hvergälmer's rivers of lives. At death, when spirit withdraws as does the nutrient sap into the roots, the seeds of future imbodiments remain as an imperishable record while the empty shell of matter is recycled for future use, much as the leaves falling from a tree in winter become mulch to enrich the soil.

Yggdrasil is not immortal. Its lifetime is coeval with the hierarchy the tree is used to represent. Destructive forces are always at work and lead to its eventual decline and death: its leaves are eaten by four stags, its bark is nibbled by two goats, its roots are undermined by the serpent Nidhögg (gnawer from beneath). When it has lived its span, the mighty Ash is overthrown. Thus is taught the temporal nature of existence and the impermanence of matter.

Throughout the Ash Tree's life a squirrel makes its home in the tree and runs up and down the trunk maintaining communication between the eagle, or sacred cock, high in its crown, and the serpent at its base. The little rodent suggests life or consciousness, which spans the height and depth of existence. It is also pictured as a drill which can bore through the densest matter. In Hávamál, which relates how Odin sought the bardic mead concealed in the depths of a mountain, he enlisted the aid of the squirrel (or drill) to penetrate the rock and, in the guise of a serpent, entered through the bore hole. Once inside, he persuaded the daughter of the giant Suttung, who had the mead hidden in his underground domain, to give him drink of it, and thus he gained wisdom. This is an oft-recurring theme: the divine seeking the mead in matter, gaining and learning from it before returning to supernal worlds.

3

Gods and Giants

As we study mythologies in the light of the theosophic ideas we recognize that their gods are personified natural forces which are not static or perfect but represent evolving intelligences of many grades. Some are so far ahead of our condition that they surpass our loftiest imaginings, having in the past undergone the phase of rudimentary self-consciousness wherein we find ourselves at present and gained a spiritual stature we have yet to reach. Others may even be less evolved than the human kingdom. These would be on the way "down" toward matter, having not yet attained our stage of material development.

The Eddas' gods and giants are the two sides of existence, the duality from which worlds are formed. Gods are conscious energies, intelligences of many grades. They imbody in stars, planets, humans — in every form of life. This would include seemingly lifeless organizations of matter — rocks, storm clouds, ocean waves — that we do not generally think of as living but which, being organizations of atoms, possess the dynamism of the atoms that compose them, as well as their own unique characteristic structure and motion. The energies that supply this dynamism in the universe are the individually evolving consciousnesses the myths call gods.

The giants, their counterparts, are inertia: cold, unmoving, unformed. They become matter only when vitalized and set in motion by the gods and they cease to exist when the gods depart. The time periods during which the organizations, organisms, are endowed with life are the giants named in the Eddas; this is to say they are the life terms of the gods as well as their bodies.

In many stories we find one or more gods traveling to the giant world, visiting some giant "to see how his hall is furnished." There is often a confrontation between a god and a giant who compete in the classic guessing game wherein the protagonists take turns posing riddles which the other must solve. The loser forfeits his life. The meaning of this contest is transparently an exchange of information for the benefit of the hearer or reader and symbolizes in a masterly manner the way in which a divine energy informs the substantial side of its nature wherein it imbodies; in return it receives experience of existence and broadening understanding. The ensuing "death" of the giant (which always loses the encounter) represents a change of state, growth, as the rudimentary, material nature dies from its earlier condition by entering a more advanced stage of evolution.

Existence is apparently unending; entities are advanced or immature only in relation to other entities, never in any absolute sense either in time or in kind. Like the *aions* (aeons) of the Gnostics, the Norse giants are both worlds and time periods, as said; ages during which gods are imbodied in and interact with appropriate forms. Often a giant is called the "parent" of an individual, showing the properties of his age, as one might say a person is "a child of the renaissance" or "a product of his time." A shorter cycle within a greater may be referred to as a daughter of the giant, and several daughters would represent a series of cycles within a longer one.

When the gods form worlds and imbody in them they are said to be preparing the tables for their feast, for it is at the stellar, planetary, and other material "tables" that divine intelligences partake of the "mead" of experience whereby they are nourished.

In contrast to the giants, which act as vehicles or carriers of divine energies during the lifetimes of the gods, are the aions of non-life during which the gods are absent from existence, restored to their supernal spheres, leaving matter in a state of entropy. Such ages are the frost giants. They represent periods of inertia when no energies are present. During this total lack of motion there is no life or existence in the space so vacated; no atoms move, no forms are organized because no divine energy is present to give life to any beings. In Eastern philosophies such utter stillness is called *pralaya* (dissolution), when consciousnesses are in their appropriate nirvanas and matter is wholly dissolved. The only possible description of such a condition would be what science refers to as absolute zero (0° K, zero degrees Kelvin): total stillness, complete immobility, the absence of any kind of existence. To us it is of course a purely hypothetical state, unthinkable to living beings, but modern science approaches the idea of the frost giant very closely in recognizing that matter is the product of energies in motion — that without motion there would be no matter.

The Edda's Örgälmer (primeval sound),[1] like Brahmā, the "expander" of Hindu cosmogony, is the first breakthrough of vibrant motion which initiates the formation of a cosmos; the final giant Bärgälmer (sound of fruition), which is "ground on the mill" and "saved" for reuse, parallels Śiva, the destroyer/regenerator. It would be difficult to devise a more effective description of the big bang and black holes of astrophysical science than these mythic names. They suggest the systole and diastole of some great cosmic heart, the former pouring forth into manifestation the energies that organize a cosmos out of chaos, the latter reabsorbing the life essences into the unknown heart of Being, leaving bodily spheres to dissolve, ground on the mills of the gods into the frozen homogeneity of the frost giant.

In any kind of existence, whether it be the life of a galaxy,

---

1. *Ör* (Icel.) or *ur* (Sw.) is a prepositional prefix for which there exists no adequate English equivalent. It means "out of" and connotes an emanation from some primeval root or beginningless beginning.

a human being, or an atom, there is constant interplay between energy and inertia, consciousness and substance, spirit and matter, gods and giants. The pairs of opposites are forever linked, mutually indispensable. There could be no giant without its corresponding god, for it takes energy to organize the structure of atoms; on the other hand, gods need vehicles in order to acquire the experience whereby consciousness is nourished. Without material worlds of some sort, consciousness has no way of growing or of expressing itself. Hence gods and giants are forever mutually dependent on and relative to each other. So the mead of the gods is brewed in the giant Äger's brewhall (space) and served at the tables of solar and planetary systems. This is the Norse version of the Hindu thought that the universe exists for the soul's experience and emancipation.

In the course of ages the gods of the myths came to be regarded as humanoid personages; the Greek deities seem to have suffered most from this indignity, though the Eddas' too have been degraded with cheap ridicule in popular stories and commentaries. Their overlapping dynamic force fields and the gravitational effects they cause were depicted in popular stories as marital, extramarital, and incestuous relationships which have been judged as the misconduct of highly improbable deities by generations of laymen and scholars alike. The Edda itself gives an amusingly exaggerated example of this attitude in "Loki's Flyting."

ODIN

Chief among the Aesir is of course Odin. As Allfather he is the divine root of every being in all the worlds, the essence of divinity present in all life forms, in the smallest particle as well as in the cosmos itself. When Odin visits the giant worlds, he rides an eight-legged steed named Sleipnir (glider), fathered by Loki, and he uses numerous names and epithets signifying in each case his specific mission. He possesses a magic ring which dispenses eight more like itself every ninth night. This evidently refers to proliferating cycles wherein each curl, comprising a number of smaller curls, represents recurrent motion in both time and space: the wheels within wheels of biblical symbology. This spiral design can be found among plants and animals throughout nature, from the atomic worlds to the great sweeping movements of stars and galaxies in space.

The primary and most comprehensive lay of the Elder Edda, Völuspá, is addressed to Odin, the divine pilgrim, who traverses the worlds, searching the depths of matter for experience, runes of truth. For Odin is individual as well as universal. On the planetary level he is the guiding spirit of the planet Mercury; he is at once the inner god of every being on earth and the divine messenger, Hermod, who is also his son and corresponds to the Greek Hermes.

Odin's consort is Frigga, the wise mother of the gods, a model of benevolence and custodian of the secret wisdom. In Norse myths she corresponds to the Egyptian Isis and also in other systems to the universal immaculate mother from whom all the energic causes of life (gods) emerge, or descend. Frigga is referred to as the one who "knows every being's fate, though she herself says naught" (Lokasenna, p. 217). Her power is equivalent to that of Odin and, though her influence is all-pervasive, it is never forcibly intrusive. We observe too that Frigga is not recorded as occupying a mansion (cf. Grimnismál) though, as Saga, she shares one of Odin's. We may therefore infer that while Frigga is the unmanifest, passive aspect of Odin, the wisdom of her eternal past in the form of Saga (cf. p. 87n), represents her on the stage of life.

As Odin occurs on many levels — as a creative power in all the worlds, the Logos of classic Greek philosophy, and also as the informer of human spirit — he is omnipresent and is to be found at all stages of existence, sometimes disguised, often under different names, but always recognizable. This reinforces the idea that the divine essence is present in all forms of life as well as being the only self-existent ideal in nonlife when the cosmos is dissolved into nothingness. It is therefore not surprising to find Odin referred to as Allfather and to discover him under one mask or another in every tale and poem. The most prominent example is in Völuspá where Odin is addressed as "all ye holy kindred" — referring to all life forms in a universe. In Hávamál he is "The High One," in Vaftrudnismál he is Gagnrád (gainful counsel), in Grimnismál he is Grimner (hooded or disguised), in Vägtamskvädet he is Vägtam (way-wont: accustomed to roads). In Valhalla he greets his heroes as Ropt (maligned, misunderstood) and Nikar (ladler of misfortune) for reasons which will be explained (p. 79).

THOR

Another universally recognized deity is Thor, who corresponds to Jove or Jupiter of the Romans and in certain respects to the Greek Zeus. The source of all vitality and power, he too has many names suggestive of the different phenomena to which electromagnetic force applies. Thor is not only the Thunderer controlling the weather (paralleled by Jupiter the jovial and Jupiter Pluvius), he is also the regent of the planet Jupiter. When Thor goes by the name Vior he represents vitality, the life force that animates every being. As Lorride he is the electricity we know on earth and he visits us from the surrounding sky in lightning and thunder.

In the vastness of space Thor is Trudgälmer (sound of Thor), the sustaining energy (Fohat of Oriental philosophy) that organizes cosmos out of chaos and sets the galactic pinwheels churning. Trud or Thor is the impelling force which keeps atoms in motion and, like the Hindu Vishnu, maintains all things in action during their lifetimes. The hammer of Thor is Mjölnir (miller), the pulverizing force that destroys as well as creates. It is the electric circuit which always returns to the hand that sent it forth. Symbolized by the svastika, either three- or four-armed, it represents whirling motion, the ever moving power which never ceases while anything lives in time and space.

Trudgälmer has two sons: *Mode* (force) and *Magne* (strength), which suggest the two poles of electricity or magnetism on the cosmic level. Everything connected with Thor repeats the duality of bipolar power. His sons, centrifugal and centripetal action, manifest as radiation and gravitation in all forms of life. In the human arena we know these forces as hate and love, repulsion and attraction. Thor's iron belt forms the circuit for electrical current; his two steel gloves imply the duality of positive and negative polarity. His chariot wheels send sparks of lightning through the skies; for this reason, when traveling abroad he is unable to use the rainbow bridge of the gods, Bifrost,[2] as his lightnings would set the bridge on fire; he must therefore ford the waters (of space) that separate the worlds from one another. This apparently poses no problem to the god, so it is perplexing to find one lay devoted entirely to a rather monotonous exchange of braggadocio between Thor and the ferryman Hárbard whom Thor is trying to persuade to convey him across a river. It is evidently a ploy to demonstrate the need of a conductor to convey electric power. (The lay is not included here.) On the planet earth Thor's action is served by his two adopted children, Tjalfe (speed) and Röskva (work), familiar servants of our power-hungry civilization.

Thor's beautiful wife is named Sif. She has long golden hair which is the pride of all the gods. It represents the vitality of growth as well as the harvest which results from it and, analogically, the evolutionary power and urge to progress that maintains the course of existence for all beings.

---

2. Also called Bäfrast, Bilrast.

SOLAR AND OTHER DEITIES

The solar deity of our world is Balder. He dies and is reborn daily, yearly, and represents the lifetime of the sun. This is a way of describing the ever new aspects presented with each cycle, major or minor, as the sun-god "dies" and is "reborn" with every rotation and revolution of the planet earth. The soul of the sun is named Alfrödul, the "radiant elf-wheel," while the visible orb is nicknamed "Dvalin's toy." As the physical sun supports our life on earth, so its vital essence sustains our spiritual life.

When the sun-god is killed by his blind brother Höder (ignorance and darkness) — a moving tale related in Vägtamskvädet — Balder's devoted wife Nanna dies of a broken heart. She is succeeded by her half sister Idun who inherits her task of keeping the gods supplied with the apples of immortality. From the context it may be gathered that Idun represents our earth, while Nanna stands for the body of the moon which died a long time ago. In the theosophic pattern also the moon is the predecessor of our present living planet.

The planet Mars is represented in the Edda by the god Tyr — a word which means "animal," that is, an animate being, an energy, hence a god. Tyr is a heroic figure among his brother deities for having sacrificed his right hand to help bind Fenris, the wolf who, when set free, is destined to devour the sun.

The god of our planet earth, Frey, is the brother of Freya, the Norse Venus-Aphrodite. They are the children of Njörd who is represented by the planet Saturn and who also (like the Greek Chronos) stands for Time. Freya is the patron and protectress of the human race which she wears on her breast in the form of a gem — the Brisingamen: the spiritual intelligence in humankind (*brising* fire, specifically the fire of enlightened mind; *men* jewel). Frey's wife is Gerd, daughter of the giant Gymer.

LOKI

Among the gods a unique place is held by Loki. Having attained godhood, though of giant stock, he represents a most mysterious and sacred quality in human nature. On one hand he is the divine intelligence aroused in early humanity (the gem of Freya with which he is associated), and also the free will whereby mankind may choose its course for good or ill; on the other, he is the trickster, the renegade, who brings misfortune to the gods and is constantly being taken to task for his mischievous behavior, whereupon he is also the agent who remedies the situation he has caused. All in all, he typifies the human mind, clever, foolish, immature. When regarded in its most redeeming character, Loki is named Lopt (lofty) and applies to the elevating, aspiring traits in human intelligence.

There are many more gods in the pantheon, two of which require special mention: Forsete, justice, whose function in the Norse universe corresponds closely to that of karma in Oriental philosophies. Another is Brage, the personification of poetic inspiration, the wisdom of the skalds and divine illumination in the soul — of the universe and of man.

It is evident from the tales that Vaner are gods superior to the Aesir in a universe of many layers of perception, appercep-tion, insight, and comprehension, where the greater inspires the less which are contained within it, in unending successions of hierarchic lives. The two classes of gods, Vaner and Aesir,[3] apparently correspond to the Hindu *asuras* and *suras* (not-gods and gods, the former having a double meaning: either beyond gods or beneath gods). The Vaner are almost always referred to as "the wise Vaner," and seem to play no direct part in the

---

3. Singular: *van* and *áss* (Sw. *ås*); *r* preceded by a vowel is a plural ending (*vaner, åsar* or *aesir*). *Ås* also means the highest roofbeam of a house. May be anglicized as Vans and Ases.

spheres of life. The Aesir, on the other hand, inspire living celestial bodies, the planets in space. Dwellers in Ásgárd (court of the Aesir), they visit the giant worlds, usually in disguise, or send emissaries to represent them. A clear example of this is the avatāra Skirner — a "ray" of the god Frey — who is sent to woo the giant maiden Gerd on the god's behalf. Pure divinity can have no direct contact with matter but must be "disguised" or, to use a common electrical term, "stepped down" through a transformer or what the Norse myths term an *alf* (elf), meaning a "channel," a soul. The "disguises" of the gods are souls in every case appropriate to and characteristic of the mission in which they are engaged at the time.

In any mythology some of the most mysterious and difficult passages to understand are those dealing with the war of the gods. In the biblical *Revelation* it is Michael and the angels who battle the celestial dragon with his cohorts; in the *Rig-Veda* the battle is between *suras* and *asuras*, and in the Edda the same cosmic forces struggle in opposition as the Vaner and Aesir. Because Western thought has been long accustomed to viewing deity as a single divine personage, the only level of life above man in the cosmos, the Aesir are popularly believed to represent a more ancient and the Vaner a more recent class of deities respectively. There are, however, strong indications that these two types of powers belong to different levels of existence, one superior to the other; they may also parallel the Hindu *kumāras* (Skt. virgins) and *agniṣvāttas* (those who have tasted of fire), respectively gods who remain unmanifest and those who have imbodied in material worlds. This is supported by the verse (25) in Völuspá which tells of the Aesir being ousted from their celestial stronghold, leaving the Vaner "victorious" in the divine realms. The fray, which triggers the cosmic force of Thor and a new creation, appears to be the result of the burning of Gullveig (thirst for gold) which, like the enigmatic Phoenix, arises more beautiful after each cleansing by fire, "hoisted on the spears" of the gods. Like the alchemists' transmutation of base metal into gold, this mythic theme finds ready response in the human soul. We recognize its application to the hunger for enlightenment in man, which in the gods results in the creation of a universe; it is the urge that impels them to manifest. Paradoxically, the thirst for gold has also the opposite applicability in our human sphere where it may become greed for possessions.

At the council of the gods Odin put an end to the deliberations: should all the gods atone or solely the Aesir? The Aesir, "defeated," leave the field to the Vana-gods who remain in their heavens while the Aesir, ousted, undertake to enliven and enlighten worlds. This seems to identify the Aesir with the agni-ṣvāttas because they energize worlds in the cosmos. It is their presence in living beings that arouses the nostalgia of the soul for its spiritual home. For the gods it is a sublime sacrifice instigated by Odin, Allfather, the divine presence in the heart urging to growth of wisdom.

Once again the gods take counsel: Who had mingled the air with evil and given Od's maid to the giant race? This may be paraphrased: "Who had given to a race of humanity the power of free will to choose good or evil, and the intelligence (the Freya principle, Odin's daughter and manhood's bride — the higher human soul) with which to learn and grow through these decisions?"

Who indeed? No answer is explicitly given but, bearing in mind the divine "renegade," it is evident that an aspect of Gullveig is Loki — the lower nature evolved to self-awareness and thence to divine stature from a former material condition. His impish tricks are characteristic of human nature, undisciplined and imperfect, yet potentially godlike. Loki nearly always accompanies the Aesir on their travels through giant worlds and functions as intermediary there. He represents the bridge between god and dwarf (the spiritual soul and the animal nature) in man and evinces a marked duality, torn between noble and base impulses. When Loki stole Freya's Brisinga-jewel, human intelligence was diverted from its proper goal and misused for base purposes.

A pact made between the Vaner and Aesir resulted in an exchange of hostages.[4] The titans Mimer and Höner were sent by the Aesir to the Vaner, who in return sent the gods Njörd and his son Frey down to the Aesir. The Vaner soon found that Höner (intelligence on the cosmic scale) was useless unless Mimer (the protean basis of matter) was at hand to advise him (mind with no material field of action), so they cut off Mimer's head and sent it to Odin, who consults it daily and learns from it the secrets of existence.

To us the multilevel universe of mythic tales is an unaccustomed way of looking at things but it is implicit in most of the world's ancient cosmologies. Mimer alone has nine names on nine levels of life with nine skies and worlds. Other systems may use seven or twelve. Our western culture has limited the universe to three stories, with God upstairs, man in the middle, and the devil in the basement. This allows of no purpose for any form of life other than the human. All creation is beneath our own exalted state and evolving toward it and there everything apparently comes to a dead end. As for evolving consciousness and understanding, there is no provision for improvement or growth beyond the human stage, which gives us very little to look forward to and makes the concepts *infinity* and *eternity* irrelevant. In contrast, traditional lore postulates endless vistas of time and space, with life forms ranging through countless combinations of spirituality and materiality, where our world is a slim cross section on its own level. In such a universe one cannot automatically equate good with spirit and evil with matter; there is always a sliding scale of relativity where "good" is rightness, harmony in its own context, "evil" disharmony. The

---

4. From the Ynglingasaga of the Younger Edda.

perplexing biblical reference to "spiritual wickedness in high places" can be explained as denoting imperfection in a spiritual condition or as evil relative to a superior state. Throughout the myths gods and giants, energy and inertia, consciousness and substance, are inextricably linked, always relative, and not to be judged by our limited standards of good and ill. Yet they are constantly changing, growing from the less to the greater as the restricted expands its limitations, the self-centered becomes increasingly universal.

In Brahmanical literature gods and giants are also found under the guise of *lokas* and *talas*, among others. These represent the many worlds of manifestation, including the material world we inhabit. A loka is the upward-tending consciousness on any plane, the tala its corresponding downward-tending matter — the terms "up" and "down" being of course symbolic. This interrelatedness of gods and giants in eternal opposition is well depicted in the Grimnismál which attempts to describe the "shelves" of substance that build the "halls" or "mansions" of their respective dwellers, the gods.

The explanation of the war in heaven must be left to each one's intuition. One discerns a progression of divine intelligences inspiriting material worlds, veritable hells to these benign influences, so that lesser beings may receive some measure of their enlightenment. This undercurrent of the participation of the gods in inferior realms for the sake of their denizens is strongly felt in all the god stories of the Norsemen (or their predecessors in time) and may well be the real reason these tales appeal to us and continue to be honored and retold.

4

Cosmic Creation

BEFORE THE APPEARANCE OF any system of worlds, naught exists but darkness and silence — Ginnungagap (yawning void). The gods are withdrawn in their supernal spheres; space and time are mere abstractions, for matter is nonexistent in the absence of any organizing vitality. It is the *chaos* of Greek cosmogony before order, *kosmos*, comes into being. In the Stanzas of Dzyan[1] it is said: "Time was not, for it lay asleep in the infinite bosom of duration." The Edda calls this the Fimbulvetr (mighty winter) — the long cold night of Nonbeing.

As the hour approaches for the birth of a cosmos, the heat from Muspellsheim (home of fire) melts the ice massed in Niflheim (cloud-home), creating fertile vapor in the Void. This is Ymer, the frost giant, from which the gods will create worlds: unmanifest worlds and "victory worlds" wherein the rivers of lives will imbody. Ymer is sustained by the four streams of milk flowing in the four directions from the cow Audhumla, symbol of fertility, the still unmanifest seed of life. "Slain" by the gods, Ymer becomes Örgälmer (primal loud noise), the keynote whose overtones vibrate throughout the sleeping shelves of space. Like the Tibetan Fohat which sets the atoms spinning, this graphically describes a first vibration organizing motion in inert protosubstance, creating vortices whose amplitudes and velocities determine the wavelengths and frequencies that make the various ranges of matter. As the Edda has it: "This was the first of aeons when Ymer built. There was no soil, no sea, no

---

1. *The Secret Doctrine*, I, 27.

waves; earth was not, nor heaven. Gaping abyss alone: no growth. Until Bur's sons raised the tables; they who had power to create Midgárd. The sun shone from the south on the stones of the court; then grew green grass in fertile soil."[2]

To paraphrase: Before time began, no elements existed for there were "no waves" — no motion, hence no forms and no time. This graphic description could hardly be improved on. Matter and the whole phenomenal universe are, as we now know, effects of the methodical motion of electrical charges. Organized as atoms with their multitudes of particles they unite to form the many grades of matter that compose suns and planets. In the absence of the organizing forces, the gods, none of these things exist. Space is itself an abstraction, unimaginable, non-existent, yet the sole existence. It is Ginnungagap, the "chasm of Ginn," inexpressible, unspeakable Nonbeing, beyond contemplation and not to be imagined, wherein Ymer, the frost giant, permits of "no growth" until the creative forces "slay" him and from his body fashion the worlds: "raise the tables" whereat they will feast on the mead of life.

The cow Audhumla licks salt from the ice blocks massed in Ginnungagap and uncovers the head of Buri (Space as abstraction, not space having dimensions). Buri corresponds to the "parentless" — the "self-born" of Hindu cosmogony. Audhumla, the primordial seed of life, may be compared with the Hindu *vāc*, the first vibration or sound, also represented as a cow. We find the same idea in the biblical myth, *John* 1:1: "In the beginning was the Word and the Word was with God and the Word was God." The Word (Gk. *logos*) means reason and also contains the concept of sound, vibration. In each case the first thrill of activity has this expression as a first ideation in divine mind, or as a fundamental or keynote whereon is built up a series of overtones, each of which becomes the keynote of a new overtone

---

2. Völuspá, 3, 4.

series. If you have ever listened to a gong's reverberations slowly fading out of hearing, you will have heard the major chord built up on the one deep note. It is conceivably an accurate symbol to describe a big bang whose energic impulses multiply as harmonics to the limits of its progression. By such a proliferation of vibrations the consciousnesses called gods might organize forms to serve them as vehicles, and imbody and dwell in them, be they suns, humans, or subatomic lives.

From the abstract Buri emanates Bur (space as extension) and from this evolves a third, triune logos, composed of Odin, Vile (will), and Ve (sacredness — *awe* in its original sense). These are the noumena or prototypes of the elements which in our sphere we call air, fire, and water: the essence of spirit (breath), vitality (heat), and fluid (mind) — subtle originants of familiar states of matter. There is a suggestive connection between what myths call the "waters of space" — basis of all existence and the common ground of universes — and hydrogen (from the Greek *hydor:* water), when we remember that hydrogen is the simplest, lightest, and most abundant of the elements, and the one which enters into the composition of all known matter. The second arm of the trinity may be sought in the second element, helium, named for *helios*, the sun, where it was first discovered. A connection may also be found between fire and the element oxygen which chemically combines with other elements in combustion. One aspect of the divine fire is Mundilföre, the "lever" or "axis" which turns the "wheels" of galaxies, suns, planets, or atoms. It is the power which initiates rotatory and translatory motion, creating vortices, dynamic entities in the waters of space.

It is striking how the more or less obscure hints found in myths are recognizable in modern science, even in such sophisticated fields as theories on star formation and cosmology. The latter show *how* physical processes take place, the former indicate the causes that bring them about. In chemistry we speak of three conditions of matter — solid, liquid, and gaseous; the myths call these earth, water, and air, adding two more: fire and aether, which were included in ancient science as attributes of the gods.

In the far mythic morning of time, our earth with all its component denizens must still have been in a condition we can only describe as ethereal. The globe had yet to condense from its primordial nebula (*nifl*), born in Niflheim (the primordial cloudhome). We may picture how the divine will-to-be spiraled downward through transcendent, unimaginable realms of spirit, then through levels of ideation and intelligent plan, through ethereal and ever coarser though still intangible substances, forming atoms, organizing molecules, arranging organisms, until all principles and aspects of a world with its appropriate life forms had been breathed forth. From this impulsion the dust of long dead antecedent stars, spread dormant through the fields of sleeping space, received anew the kiss of life and, obeying that creative urge, formed vortices of energy which became the matter of which our worlds were fashioned.

Before our planet became physical, the less solid conditions of matter — fire and aether — were doubtless more in evidence; fire is still found as the vital heat of all living bodies. Even space itself, as much as we know of it, gives such a sign of life: a temperature of $2.7°$ K, while hardly a heatwave, is still evidence of motion however slight, of vitality however faint. Aether is not recognized by that name today, nevertheless euphemisms such as the "interstellar medium" and "intergalactic medium" are used in astrophysics to suggest it. Since that distant past when our globe began to solidify, the ethereal element apparently receded from the range of our perception. In the future, when earth slowly etherealizes, as the theosophic records predict, we shall doubtless rediscover it along with the acceleration of radioactivity.

We have seen how Ymer, the frost giant, is transformed by the divine powers into the substances which make up a world, the primordial protosubstance becoming Örgälmer (the primal noise), keynote of a cosmos, an outpouring of energies so potent that it brings inevitably to mind the phenomenon which scientists call the big bang. The creation of earth in Grimnismál (40–41) is more poetic: "Of Ymer's flesh was the earth formed, the billowing seas of his blood, from his bones the mountains, bushes from his hair, and from his brainpan heaven. With his eyebrows the beneficent powers enclosed Midgárd for the sons of men; but of his brain were surely created all dark skies." The protective eyebrows enclosing the human domain are strikingly suggestive of the arc-shaped, or toroidal, Van Allen belts which trap excessive cosmic radiation.

The creative process of progressive manifestation (called in theosophy the "descending arc" — the Edda's Mjötvidr), marks the fueling or feeding of the Tree of Life, while the subsequent evolution of spirit and decline of matter (theosophy's "ascending arc" and the Edda's Mjötudr), brings the exhaustion of the food that nourishes Yggdrasil. Odin is called Ofner (opener) at the beginning of a phase of life, when he is inseparable from Örgälmer, the keynote whose reverberations multiply into a cosmos. This systolic beat of the cosmic heart should be followed in due time by a diastole when, the expansion consummated, the gods withdraw once more into the heart of Being, and indeed this is confirmed: at the end of life Odin is Svafner (closer), linked with Bärgälmer (the noise of fruition). This matter-giant is "ground on the mill" — homogenized to formlessness, annihilated as matter with remarkable similarity to what science now calls a black hole. He is also said to be "placed on a boatkeel and saved" — an allegory reminiscent of the Noachian flood, which also ensures the renewal of life forms after a dissolution. This may quite possibly be how the funeral custom originated of placing a dead chieftain on his pyre ship and letting the burning vessel drift out to sea.

The rivers of Hvergälmer or diverse classes or kingdoms of

lives pursue their courses of imbodiment through the shelves and mansions of the world systems. They represent the great variety of organisms used by the many kinds of elf-souls, the human of course included. There are the dwarfs and the light elves, and also the dark elves who have not yet "struggled from the hall's stone foundation up to the ramparts" (Völuspá 14).

During the lifetime of a cosmic being Allfather Odin is closely parallel with Trudgälmer (noise of Thor), sustainer of all life. We have seen how Trud (on the cosmic scale), Thor (in the solar system), Lorride (on earth), represent energy in all ranges of the electromagnetic spectrum and how all their appurtenances have the connotation of power in various applications. Thor's hammer, Mjölnir, both creates matter and mills it to extinction; being the agent both of creation and destruction it consecrates marriages and also slays giants, thus officiating at the rites of procreation as well as bringing death by withdrawing consciousness from the spheres of life.

5

Terrestrial Creation

THE CREATION OF OUR PLANET is depicted in several ways. The terrestrial deity is Frey, the valiant. He is the son of Njörd and brother of Freya, and he owns a magic sword which is said to be shorter than the customary weapon but invincible when its wielder is courageous. It must be earned by each of Odin's warriors who would gain Valhalla.

The soul of the earth is Idun, guardian of the apples of immortality which she serves the gods at certain specific times, nor will she yield to any entreaties between meals. Idun is the daughter of the giant Ivalde — "oldest of his younger brood" of children. Nanna, the soul of the moon, one of his "older brood," died of a broken heart on the death of her husband Balder, the sun-god.[1] This may be a way of suggesting that our living planet sees a different sun, another aspect of the solar being, than did its predecessor. The sons of Ivalde are the elements which compose our planet; they are life forces which once formed the dwelling of Nanna but after her death began to form that of Idun. According to the theosophic teachings, each planet, including our own, as well as the sun, comprises several unseen globes along with the one we know; they also regard our earth as the fifth in a series of seven imbodiments of the planetary deity, the moon having been the fourth; our planetary system is therefore one step more advanced than the moon's former composite world.

Many traditions regard the moon as parent of the earth and

---

1. Cf. Vägtamskvädet, p. 258.

say that its substances and vital essences are still being transferred to its successor. Some support is lent to the myths by the fact that the visible moon is slowly diminishing, particularly the side facing the earth. One figure of speech pictures the moon as a mother circling the cradle of her child, the earth. The popular nursery rhyme, Jack and Jill, originated in the Edda where their names are Hjuke and Bil, and they go to the moon to fetch of its substance and bring it back to earth. When they are there, we can see their shapes silhouetted against the lunar disk, much as we see the man in the moon. American Indian traditions refer to the earth as "mother earth" and to the moon as "grand-mother moon," which carries out the same theme of succession.

In one tale, the Edda relates the building of the earth as a contest between two factions: one consisted of two of Ivalde's sons, the dwarfs Sindre and Brock (the vegetable and mineral kingdoms); the other of Dvalin (the unawakened human-animal soul) assisted by Loki (mind). The contest was to determine who could produce the most appropriate gifts for the gods.

Brock and Sindre create for Odin the self-renewing ring, Draupnir, from which eight like itself drop off every ninth night, ensuring the cyclic renewal and perpetuation of life forms. They made for the earth god Frey a golden boar. This symbol for the earth is found also in the Hindu *Purānas*, where Brahmā in the shape of a boar lifted the earth from the waters of space and supports it on his tusks. For Thor the dwarfs fashioned the hammer Mjölnir, the pulverizer. This is the "thunderbolt" in popular versions which, as we have seen, represents electricity and magnetism, hate and love, destruction and creation and, in the form of the svastika, eternal motion. It has the property of always returning to the hand that sent it forth, completing a circuit; in addition to its physical meanings this is one way of expressing the law of justice ruling universal nature on all its "shelves." We readily recognize in it the Oriental doctrine of karma which rules on every level of life, restoring harmony wherever it has been disturbed and, on the grand cosmic scale, causing the cyclic reappearance of worlds. Thor's hammer is somewhat short of shaft, however, for during its forging, Loki disguised himself as a bee and inflicted a vicious sting on the dwarf who was wielding the bellows. The dwarf faltered only an instant but it was sufficient to flaw the gift and accord the victory to Loki and Dvalin. Still, the gifts of the dwarfs are the best that can be produced by the vegetable and mineral kingdoms for the divine (Odin), vital (Thor), planetary spirit (Frey). It is to be noted, however, that these gifts, produced as they are by the minerals and vegetables, are limited to physical properties that concern their creators: Odin's ring clearly denotes the cyclic progression of events with perpetually recurring parallels, whereof the changing seasons are characteristic; Frey's boar with shining golden bristles draws his chariot through the heavens; while the creative and destructive hammer of Thor represents the life force and the powers we associate with the elements — thunder and lightning, seismic stresses and motions, and the interplay of gravitation and magnetic fields.

In competition with these, Dvalin with the aid of Loki creates for Odin the magic spear which never fails its mark when wielded by the pure in heart. This is the evolutionary will, often symbolized by a spear, sometimes by a sword. It is the inborn urge in every living being to grow and progress toward a more advanced condition. There is in this a mystic implication of sacrifice as Odin, transfixed on the Tree of Life, is also pierced by a spear. The spear thrust has been inflicted on other crucified saviors as well.

For Thor, Dvalin and Loki restore the golden hair of Sif, his wife (the harvest), which had been stolen by Loki — human misuse of earth's bounty? — possibly having reference to more than the physical grains of earth. The gift of reseeding and the infinite potential of evolutionary growth on every level of matter and consciousness brings great promise for the world about to be formed. Frey receives as his gift the ship Skidbladnir, which contains all seeds of every kind of life, yet can be "folded together like a kerchief" when its own life is ended.

While the physical, astral, vital, and all other requisites for the new planet are being assembled and re-formed in this manner, the spiritual principles, Lif and Lifthrasir (life and survivor, the latter meaning "hard to kill" or indestructible), are "concealed in the memory hoard of the sun." These are the quasi-immortal part of the planet, the deathless spirit-soul of the human kingdom, the solar essence of humanity which endures throughout the lifetime of the sun. Allegorically we learn in this tale that though the elemental kingdoms produce good and useful gifts for the imbodying deities, human ingenuity is of a superior order and wins the contest.

The name given to our physical planet, Midgárd, means "middle court." This placement of our globe in a central position corresponds strikingly with the theosophic description of our terrestrial home as composed of a series of globes, the central one of them being the sphere we inhabit. The number of its ethereal companions varies in different mythologies; because the highest of them are so spiritual, so far beyond human comprehension as to be unimaginable, they are omitted altogether in some mythic cosmogonies, or else only vaguely suggested. The Edda's twelve enumerated in Grimnismál suggest a pattern where six increasingly material globes culminate in our own, followed by six increasingly spiritual spheres culminating in the divine apex of the terrestrial system. Our globe is the Edda's giant Trym and rests on the most material of the shelves that accommodate and provide the substances for the twelve mansions of the deities.

Like other mythological histories, the Edda has its floods, both universal and terrestrial. We have seen how Bärgälmer, the end-result of a cosmic cycle of activity is "saved on a boat keel" to become a new system of worlds at the beginning of the next period of manifestation. Similar patterns emerge on a smaller scale within the life span of the earth. Here giants succeed one another and, within each gigantic period, a series of briefer but still immense giantesses, their daughters, follow one another, reflecting analogically the greater planetary ages of life.

There are always similarities between the first of one series and the first of a subordinate series, between the second of one and the second of another; sometimes they are given the same name or one that is very similar, which may lead to confusion but which also serves to reveal a design. As an example, there are clear analogies to be drawn between the giants Ymer, Gymer, Hymer, and Rymer, which represent different phases of a series of cosmic events.

As concerns our planet, we know it is subject to gradual changes all the time, in addition to which there occur occasional cataclysms. One reason for this is the depredations of the inhabitants who over a long period violate the laws that govern the ecology; when human destructiveness becomes intolerable, nature rebels, bringing violent change and restoring the balance of forces. This is part of the normal processes of the living earth's restorative system and of its healthy recovery and recuperation.

The greatest upheavals, however, which cause radical alterations in the disposition of continents and seas, are governed by the rhythmic pulse of the planet's own life currents, and they take place at intervals whose length far surpasses any secular histories. During the four and a half billion years of earth's present lifetime to date, only four such major catastrophes are recorded in the theosophic traditions. Lesser events are of course more frequent.

Mythologies unanimously relate stories of floods and the repopulating of the globe after its being all but denuded of human life. Some Amerindian traditions tell of a series of "suns" succeeding one another. Each sun endures while the governing elements, air, fire, and water, are in equilibrium; gradually, however, one or another gains ascendancy causing an increase of stress until a critical point is reached, when violent relaxation restores the balance, radically altering the configuration of land massifs and oceans. The inhabitants of the "new world" see the sun taking a different path in the sky. According to the Nahuatl traditions as well as those of the Hopi, we are now in the fifth sun. The Zuni state with greater detail that we are in the fourth world but with one foot in the fifth. Compare this with the theosophic teachings: that we are in the fourth of seven courses round our earth's series of globes and also in the fourth of the seven globes of the series (called a chain), but in the fifth humanity on this globe.

6

Nature's Kingdoms

WHILE GODS AND GIANTS REPRESENTED complementary poles of divinity and matter on a graded scale extending both spiritward and matterward beyond our perceptions, nature was to the Norse mythographers replete with living beings at all stages of evolution. Every such being represented its god (consciousness-energy), expressed itself in its own appropriate way or soul, and imbodied in a fitting shape, its giant. Our visible, tangible world was one of many — a slender cross section of a vast range of god-giant juxtapositions through which the ripple of life flowed unendingly with scope for infinite kinds of evolutionary change and growth.

The link which both separates and unites the god and its corresponding giant is its *alf* (elf), which, as we know, means river or channel. The elf expresses its godlike qualities through the substantial form to the degree it can. This makes each being a triad: first, the divine consciousness or eternal Odin, the Allfather, immortal root of every being; this animates the giant or body which dies and is ground on the mill, dissolved when the divine life has departed; linking the two is an elf — the actively evolving soul which channels the divine influence to the material world and is itself evolving toward its hamingja, its guardian angel or individual god-self. The elf-soul partakes of both kinds of influence: inspired by its divine nature it becomes progressively more harmonious as it unites little by little with this ennobling source of its being, while its material tendencies, weighted down with the heavy drag of matter, its giant, remain mortal. This is most clearly shown in the lay of Völund, where

the elf-soul, humanity, is held captive by an evil age, yet over-
comes by virtue of spiritual will and determination as well as
ingenuity.

Through the long, slow course of evolution the elves gain
increasingly conscious union with their divine mentors and little
by little become immortal; but until they achieve this state, these
protégés of the gods spend each blissful rest between earth lives
among the deities in the titan Äger's banquet hall (space), but
oblivious of their surroundings. There are numerous classes of
elves at various stages of awareness: light-elves are those who
between lives sleep among the gods at their heavenly banquet,
while dark-elves are drawn toward inferior worlds.

Souls that have not yet reached the human, self-conscious
stage in their evolution are named "dwarfs." These elemental
souls imbody in animals and plants, in the minerals of the globe's
interior, and in the forces of wind and weather. Popular stories
describe them as little people. This is apparently the result of
translating the Icelandic *midr*, the Swedish *mindre*, as "smaller."
This is quite legitimate and has given rise to the notion that
dwarfs are beings smaller in size than humans. However, an
equally valid interpretation and one which makes more sense is
that they are *less* than human — less evolved, less complete in
their development. Judging by their names, they evidently refer
to various animals, plants, and other creatures of the less-than-
human kingdoms, so that more than likely the diminutive refers
to their stage of evolution rather than to physical size.

Among the elemental dwarfs (those belonging to kingdoms
of life less evolved even than the minerals) are *trolls* which are
said to be inimical to humans, and *tomtar* which serve and help
man in many ways. In popular stories the troll is depicted as
a hideous monster, the tomte as an appealing little sprite wearing
a grey suit and a red Phrygian cap. Every farm of old had
its tomte which protected the livestock and the crops, kept
the horses from slipping on the ice in winter, and performed

numerous other services throughout the year. All it demanded in return was a plate of hot rice porridge by the barn door on Christmas Eve. The trolls on the other hand were the allies of sorcerers and not averse to playing pranks of their own on the unsuspecting. It is noteworthy that in all such folklore there was no real exchange between humans and dwarfs on an emotional or mental level. Whether useful or harmful, dwarfs are not intentionally either benevolent or malevolent but simply unthinking nature forces, acting automatically and without amity or malice, so that man's regard for them was a curiously impersonal one. You would not become fond of a tomte though you might well be grateful for his actions.

The classic fairy with gossamer wings, as well as gnomes and pixies and other "little people" in appropriate attire, although their *appearance* is the creation of human fancy, cannot be denied existence altogether. Various ancient legends which tell of these and other "unensouled" denizens of Cloud Cuckoo Land, are echoing a very real knowledge which has become warped and misunderstood in the course of ages: that beneath the minerals on the evolutionary scale are entities and forces which express themselves in the properties of material elements or states of matter. They are beings we would be hard put to define, for we have no conception of the type of "soul" that imbodies in minerals, much less in creatures beneath them on the ladder of evolutionary progression. Classical and medieval stories depict these denizens of the elements as salamanders (of fire), undines (water), sylphs (air), and gnomes (of the earth); the Edda classes them among the dwarfs and ascribes their parentage to the titans or giants of the appropriate elements. As the Greek Oceanus (the "waters" of space) fathered the undines, so in the Norse myths did Äger with his wife Ran, goddess of the sea, bring to birth the nine waves. What we today call laws of nature whose attributes we constantly rely on — all the chemical and physical, automatic and semiautomatic functions of the natural world —

are expressions of elemental forces. Without them we could neither contact the matter we live in, nor could we depend on its behavior. They are the shapers of clouds, the surface tension that defines a dewdrop, they cause flame to rise and water to fall. However, lacking defined sizes and shapes, these beings are generally not recognized as life forms, though they may assume whatever forms are presented by popular imagination. When fairy folk or leprechauns have occasionally been seen by perfectly rational people, their appearance and the attire they wear are due to mental images created by folktales and custom which may be so strong, especially in certain localities, that a sensitive nature, combining hearsay with its own impressions, may perceive them in that way. The image-making faculty is a very real force.

The dwarfs are said to follow in Dvalin's train because the lower kingdoms receive the impulse to growth from Dvalin (the entranced — the human soul which has not yet become awake to its potential). Pictured as Ask and Embla (ash and alder), miniatures of the world tree, Yggdrasil, the human race was still in a vegetating condition, sans thought, sans mind, and growing only as the plants do without consciousness of self, until "the gods looked back and saw their plight." The planet was then still in process of being fashioned by the children of Ivalde, the giant period whose lifetime was our moon's.

The dwarfs in Dvalin's train which are named in Völuspá include such descriptive appellations as Discovery, Doubt, Will, Passion, Failure, Speed, Antlered, and many more. Some names are obscure, others are clearly characteristics of certain plants and animals, "up to Lofar, the handed."

Humanity, whose plight roused the compassion of the gods, became endowed by them with the deities' own qualities, making the human being an *ásmegir* (godmaker), a potential god, in a threefold combination: a dwarf, kin of Dvalin, is his animal nature; in his human self he is an elf, a channel or soul, which links his dwarf nature with the gods; and the spiritual soul is his hamingja, kin of the Norns, his guardian and mentor which never leaves him, unless man himself by persistent unremitting evil severs his link with divinity, forcing the hamingja to abandon her charge.

A more comprehensive classification comes to light as we note that man comprises the gifts of the three creative Aesir, being compounded of their nature: "From one such train [of evolving kingdoms of lives] drew forth in the hall three Aesir, powerful, compassionate. They found on the earth the ash and the alder, of little power, indeterminate. Odin gave them spirit, Höner discernment, Lodur gave them blood and divine light" (Völuspá 17, 18). This makes the human a composite being. In Viktor Rydberg's penetrating analysis, the lowest elements were already combined in the ash and the alder before the advent of the creative gods, whose "gifts" completed man as an ásmegir, a godmaker — an áse in the making — who shares in the divine attributes that endow the universe with form, powers, and organization. On every level a human being is an intrinsic part of the agencies that vitalize the universe. The same idea is found in Genesis: divine essences of universal life breathe into man their own breath and create a human image of themselves, which possesses in latency all that the universal life contains.

The mortal frame may be described as threefold: first, the body, composed of the elements of the earth; second is the formative model which causes any organism to retain its shape throughout life; third is the vegetative growth force in all creatures, the physical vitality or magnetic field. These three ingredients were already present in the ash and alder. To these physical portions the gods add their own properties: Lodur contributes *lá* and *laeti*, literally blood and distinctiveness: blood in the sense of bloodline, hereditary genetic traits, while distinctiveness is evidently what in Sanskrit literature is termed *svabhāva*, self-becoming: the peculiar combination and proportion of qualities that give each entity its uniqueness. These two related gifts constitute the divine light or image furnished by Lodur which, together with the gift of Höner, *odr*, mind or latent intelligence, compose the human elf nature. This, when kindled by a divine . power, becomes an ásmegir, a god-to-be.[1] The highest gift is that of Odin, who endows the humans with his own spiritual essence.

Several unsuccessful attempts had previously been made to people the earth with viable human forms. The Edda describes the mud giant Mockerkalfe who had to be destroyed and superseded. The story is told in the Younger Edda and relates Thor's battle with the giant Rungner:

Rungner was regaled in Ásgárd with ale served in the goblets Thor was wont to drink from, and he drained them all, but he became very drunk and began to boast how he meant to carry off Valhalla to Gianthome, flood Ásgárd and slay all the deities save Freya and Sif, whom he would take with him. As he ranted on, Freya continued to ply him with drink. At length, the gods, weary of his boasting, spoke Thor's name, which instantly brought the Thunderer into the hall with his hammer held high. Thor demanded to know by whose leave Rungner was being entertained in Ásgárd and served by Freya as befits only the gods. The giant claimed to be there at Odin's invitation, which Thor swore he should soon regret having accepted. One word led to another. At last, Thor and Rungner arranged to meet in combat on the border between Ásgárd and Gianthome, and Rungner hastened home to arm himself for the fray.

The whole giant world was alarmed at the forthcoming battle, for they feared evil consequences no matter who should be victorious. So they created a giant of mud nine cubits tall which they named Mockerkalfe. However, they could find no heart large enough to animate the effigy so they gave it the heart of

---

1. Cf. The Lay of Rig, pp. 181, 183.

a mare. "But," says the tale in Snorri's *Edda*, "Rungner's heart is, of course, of stone and it has three corners." His head is likewise of stone and he bears a stone shield and a stone axe.

Accompanied by Mockerkalfe (also named Leirbrimer — muddy water), Rungner awaited the coming of Thor but, seeing the Áse approaching, the mud giant was in such a panic that "he lost his water." Thor's companion, Tjalfe, ran swiftly to Rungner and told him: "You are foolish, holding your shield before you. Thor has seen you and will attack from beneath." So Rungner stood on his shield, wielding his axe with both hands. With flashes of flame and loud thunders, Thor came toward him. At the very same instant Thor hurled his hammer and Rungner his axe, so the weapons clashed in mid-air and the axe broke in pieces; one half scattered over the earth, becoming lodestones; the other half hit Thor in the head so that he fell forward on the ground. But Thor's hammer smashed Rungner's skull and, as the giant went down, his foot fell across Thor's throat.

Tjalfe meanwhile had easily bested the mud giant and now he tried to lift Rungner's foot from Thor's throat but he could not move it. All the Aesir came to help, but they too failed to raise the foot. At this point Thor's three-year-old son, Magne, arrived. His mother was the giantess Järnsaxa (iron shears). Magne lightly tossed the giant's foot aside, apologizing for being late to the rescue, but Thor, proud of his son, "did not hold the delay against him." However, a piece of the stone axe still remained imbedded in Thor's head. The vala Groa (growth) attempted to remove it with magic chants; but as soon as Thor felt it becoming dislodged he set about rewarding her by telling her about his rescue of the former giant Örvandel (Orion) whom he had carried across the icicle waves in a basket. One toe, which stuck out of the basket, became frozen, so Thor broke it off and tossed it to the sky, where it can be seen shining to this day. We call it Sirius. Groa was so enchanted with the tale, however, that she forgot all her charms and the stone axe remains to this day imbedded in Thor's skull.

Like many tales from the Younger Edda, this one contains inklings of thought we may interpret in part, although the tale has probably undergone changes fitting it to Viking humor and character. The three-year-old hero and the iron age which bore him certainly have meaning, as well as the allusion to Sirius. In rough outline the mud giant has parallels in many traditions, such as the Adam of dust in Genesis 2:7. Mankind undoubtedly took millions of years to evolve a form which could survive as a thinking, responsible type of being. Nor did the awakening of mental capacity happen overnight, for this too must have been a very gradual development. The theosophic tradition allots to the awakening of mind several million years. According to the Stanzas of Dzyan the Sons of Mind (mānasaputras), which aroused the thinking faculty in the human race, were unable to imbody in the earliest forms of humans, or even as late as in the early third humanity. These were, they said, "no fit vehicles for us." The curious little "mudheads" found in the Mexican countryside may also represent that phase of our development. Only gradually, as the vehicles became ready, were the third "root race" humans capable of receiving the stimulus of mind from those who had graduated from the human phase of evolution in a previous world cycle. The presently human race will, if successful in completing its evolution as sapient souls, in turn be due to enlighten and inspire those who are now "the dwarfs in Dvalin's train" — in some far-off future aeon on a new and reborn earth, successor to the globe we help comprise today.

7

Rig, Loki, and the Mind

ONE OF THE MOST INSPIRING EVENTS related in every mythology and scripture, though in various ways, is what the Edda calls the coming of Rig. Rig is a ray or personification of Heimdal, the solar essence, which descended to unite with the still unfinished humanity, rousing into activity the mind of the unthinking, semiconscious humans-to-be who were in due time to become as we now are.

In the Lay of Rig[1] the first attempt to produce a humanity gave rise to a race of "thralls," a brutish, primitive type of human. These were born to the "great-grandparents" in a miserable hovel whose door was closed against the entrance of the god. A second effort was more promising: here the door of the cottage was ajar, and the god left with the "grandparents," who dwelt there, his scions who were to become worthy, self-respecting folk and who gave rise to a similar race. At the third attempt, the "parents," who dwelt in a mansion, welcomed the god with the door wide open. This time the divine seeding brought to birth a noble race whose descendants became regal in their own right.

It is a remarkable tale and the symbology is singularly transparent. Each race of semidivine humans refers, if the theosophic keys apply, to immense periods of time. These "races" have of course quite another scope than what we call races today: ethnic groups which inhabit the earth together. These, as we know, vary but little, mainly in coloration. All are one humanity. By contrast, the "dwarf" kingdoms display striking differences

---

1. p. 183.

among themselves: for instance, gold and granite, both minerals, bear only slight resemblance to each other; deodars and dandelions both belong to the vegetable world, while moths and mammoths share the animal realm. Human beings alone are uniformly equipped with nearly identical forms and senses. Our differences are more pronounced in areas of ideas and feelings, talents and opinions.

The time which elapsed since the first attempt was made by the gods to awaken our intelligence until the whole human river had achieved it is not given but we may surmise that it was to be reckoned in millions of years. Myths inevitably telescope their information into the smallest possible compass. The biblical Genesis, for instance, relates the saga of man's awakening mind by saying that "the sons of God saw the daughters of men that they were fair; and they took them wives of all which they chose. . . . There were giants in the earth in those days; and also after that, when the sons of God came in unto the daughters of men, and they bare children to them, the same became mighty men which were of old, men of renown." (Gen. 6:2,4). Another version of the event is also given, when the serpent of Eden urges Eve to partake of the fruit of the Tree of Knowledge of good and evil. He too is the awakener: Lucifer, the bright and most beautiful angel, the light-bringer who defies the *elohim* (gods). In the Greek myths it is Prometheus and in the Norse it is Loki. Both are titans, giants, grown to godhood through evolution. Having themselves surpassed the human stage they bring humanity divine fire from the realm of the gods. The name Loki is related to *liechan* or *liuhan* (enlighten), to the Latin *luc-*, *lux*, to the Old English *lēoht* (light), and the Greek *leukos* (white). The bright star Sirius is named Lokabrenna (the burning of Loki).

The awakening of the capacity to reason, the power of self-knowledge and judgment, was the most crucial event in humanity's evolution. It brought our human river of life to the point where deliberate choices could be made, where reasoning supplants instinct, and where the knowledge of good and evil will be a deciding factor in the further development of the species. The unthinking kingdoms are guided by the built-in monitoring of instinct, which permits only limited freedom, but once the mind becomes active, aware of itself as a separate being, there comes into play a corresponding responsibility and the doer is accountable for everything he does, thinks, feels, and for his responses to the stimuli of the surrounding universe. Thereafter the godmaker cannot turn back. Each moment brings a choice, and every choice produces an endless stream of consequences, each stemming from its predecessor. Through many wrong choices Loki has become the mischief-maker, the instigator of wrongs in many tales, for he represents too often the lower, ratiocinative brain without inspiritment — inspiration. He is, however, the constant companion of the gods and serves as go-between in their dealings with the giants. Perhaps his mischievous nature has been somewhat overemphasized for its naughty appeal to the Viking temperament. It is well to bear in mind too that, while he is often the cause of trouble in Ásgárd, he is also the agent for solving the problems that arise from his own doings.

So acts the mind of man: it causes us no end of difficulties when acting on its own but, when we accept the guidance of Brage, the wise bard who represents poetic inspiration, it resolves them in the end.

8

Human Death and Rebirth

SURVIVAL AFTER DEATH OF THE BODY was clearly taken for granted by the Norse seers, and the adventures of consciousness continue after death without interruption. When a human body dies, the occupant embarks on a journey through the realm of Hel, queen of the dead: she is depicted as half blue, i.e., half dead yet half alive, and she is the daughter of Loki — mind. This interesting point is made in many mythologies, which imply that death came into being following the awakening of intelligence, so that the use of this faculty and of the free will which accompanies it is universally connected with the introduction of death and the opportunity it affords the soul to evaluate and profit by the experiences undergone in life, as well as providing rest and recuperation.

When a human being dies, before embarking on the journey through Hel's domain, the soul is equipped with footgear strictly in accord with its character: a good and kindly person is provided with sturdy shoes whereas the gross and earthbound one is scantily shod or barefoot amid the rocks and brambles it must traverse to reach the well of Urd where its future will be decided. Urd, as we have seen, is Origin — causes created in the past. She waters the soul's individual tree of life as well as the cosmic Yggdrasil: the past determines all one's future condition, in death as well as future lives.

At the spring of Urd the soul is judged by Odin, its inmost Self, "father of the gods" as well as its own "father in heaven." But, although Odin pronounces judgment, he does so according to the prompting of Urd — the soul's past determines the judgment of its inner god and its placement in the many-layered realm of Hel. Following the judgment, the soul seeks its proper habitat and finds the place that is its own by reason of affinity among the endlessly varied regions of the dead. One may enjoy sunlit meadows decked with flowers if this is in accord with its natural inclinations; another, being of evil disposition, may be confined in a venom-soaked cage beneath the nether gates that lead to inferior worlds. The Edda does not specify the duration of these after-life states, but if we may reason from logic as well as from Greek, Tibetan, and other mythical sources, it is safe to assume that each individual remains in this dream world of his own making until its attraction is exhausted. Another description of the after-death condition is given in Loki's Flyting, where the elves are present at the banquet of the gods, but sleepily unaware of their surroundings.

In due course, the Åse-maker is ready to resume its journey through life on earth. Again it visits the well of Urd, who now has the task of selecting a mother for its new birth. Once more we see the past determining the future in an inescapable sequence of cause and effect. We have seen how Bärgälmer, the end result of a cosmos or any world, was ground up and saved for reuse in a subsequent manifestation as Örgälmer. The same law may be applied analogically to human life, which is a universe on a smaller scale. Just as seeds planted in the spring will, after many days and nights, bring forth their fruitage where they were sown, so seeds of thought and action must bear their harvest of good or ill in the field where they originated, even after many deaths and births.

The only true hell in the Edda is Niflhel, the sphere of absolute matter where the material for new worlds is formed out of the dregs of the old, after being ground on the mill, homogenized, reduced to formlessness. It is the caldron of Sinmara which, like the caldron of the Welsh Ceridwen, contains mother-matter. It would seem that only a soul so utterly depraved that it has no mead to contribute to its inner god can know the dread fate of total extinction; having allied its entire being with the giant-side of nature it has lost all trace of spirituality and its hamingja can no longer nurture and inspire its return to the divine spheres that are its home. Such a soul, having passed irretrievably through and beneath the house of Hel with its many halls, both sumptuous and dismal, having no increment whatever of enduring spirit, descends to the Niflhel of absolute extinction. All others visit the well of Urd for her selection of the coming lot in life: the most appropriate and useful conditions for the soul's further growth. The circumstances thus chosen may not always be to our liking, for we have not the wisdom of our divine hamingja to see the precise needs of the soul. It may well be that to one a happy life will bring expanded sympathies and greater awareness, but it is very often suffering which more effectively arouses the knowledge of others' need and the wisdom to supply it aright, mellowing the soul and enabling it to blend with the universal in divine compassion. The right and fitting selection from the well of the past will nevertheless be made.

The Edda, like other traditional classics, takes for granted the reimbodiment of consciousnesses at all levels and the absolute justice of natural law. There is a Christian gloss added at the conclusion of the second lay of Helge Hundingsbane:

> It was the belief in former days that people were reborn after death; but this is now called an old wives' tale. Helge and Sigrun are said to have been born again; he was then named Helge Haddingskate and she Kåra Halfdansdotter, as told in the Lays of the Crow; and she was a Valkyrie.

It is worth observing that it is in the oldest relics of any mythology that we find the largest portion of universal theosophy and the grandest concepts. It seems the intervening millennia have done little but distort the pure versions of prehistory; to reach the pristine ideas we often have to fumble through curtains of ignorant and inhibiting prejudice that have been interposed throughout centuries and that effectively conceal the jewels of thought they contain.

9

Initiation

EACH HUMAN BEING EXPRESSES to a degree the divine conscious-ness which animates all life forms — Odin-Allfather, source of all the gods — and we sense our spiritual link with a greater life, our individual hamingja. Mentally we are intrinsically part of the intelligence that informs and infills the solar system, personified as the Freya principle; emotionally too we draw on the impelling energies of Idun and the ambient world. Our outermost carapace, the physical body, is fashioned from the material which is available in the sphere where we imbody, though it is modeled on patterns we have ourselves shaped in our long past by numberless choices and decisions.

While all the kingdoms of nature comprise the same ingre-dients, the degree to which they manifest the various qualities depends on the stage to which they have developed them. We who make up the human river of lives, while we possess all the faculties we have brought into play in our passage through the dwarf kingdoms, also exhibit the peculiarly human characteris-tics of self-consciousness and intellectual fire and, in our inspired moments, we have an inkling of the spiritual awareness that will be ours in future aeons. So, being human, intelligent to a degree, we are able to pursue our evolution toward godhood with knowl-edge and intent and so accelerate our growth as to earn the greater destiny that awaits us on the next rung of the ladder of conscious life.

In the mythic scriptures, in fairy tales, legends, and folk traditions, surely no tales are more inspiring than those that tell of the heroes who precede us on the pilgrimage we are making through spheres of life, noble souls who have attained a grander perspective, a greater truth, a more enlightened vision than we possess. In all ages and races there have lived outstanding individuals — Buddhas, Bodhisattvas, Avatāras, "One-harriers" (Odin's warriors) — who have "taken the kingdom of heaven by violence," who instead of drifting with the stream in slow meandering growth have gained the goal of human evolution, where "the dewdrop slips into the shining sea," to use Sir Edwin Arnold's inspired phrase.

All mythologies contain some tales of the struggle of a hero, his trials, and either failure or success in overcoming obstacles — the echoes of his own past — to reunite with his divine self. In the West the best known story of initiation is that given in the Christian gospels, which contain many of the recognized symbols attaching to such an event. Another popular mystery tale is the *Bhagavad-Gītā*, wherein the human soul receives the counsel of its divine Self in overcoming the familiar and often fond propensities of the human ego which must be vanquished. The Edda too contains similar tales, one of the most revealing being the beautiful allegory of Svipdag.[1]

Such legends are object lessons for those who desire earnestly to lighten the burden of suffering that afflicts the human race. Those who undertake the rigorous training of self-directed, accelerated evolution must of necessity by so much aid the progress of the whole and by example and encouragement incite a chain reaction of spiritual growth. Therefore those who desire most ardently to help their fellows escape the endless round of error and suffering to which mankind is subject, embark on a path of self-training of their whole nature so that they may aid and encourage the evolution of all.

Those who successfully complete this course, of all human enterprises the most demanding, when known, are universally

---

1. Cf. Verywise's Exchange, p. 231 et seq.

revered as saviors and redeemers for they are the "perfect" who have nothing more to learn in the schoolroom of earth, yet return to help and teach those who lag behind them on the evolutionary ladder. The sagas which relate the trials of the initiant are the most popular and best known of all stories and legends, even in exoteric literature, though seldom recognized as such. In these adventure stories the hero must first become totally fearless for himself; he must wrest from the "dragon" of wisdom the secrets of "birdsong": this means he must know at first hand the structure and functions of the universe; he must be willing to sacrifice all personal ambition, even his own soul's success, to an all-encompassing concern for the welfare of the whole. One who succeeds in attaining such selfless universality becomes a co-worker with the gods, a beneficent force powerfully impelling the evolvement of the world in which he is a component.

The fabled home of the Edda's elect, where the heroes go after being killed in battle, is Valhalla (*val* choice or death + *hall* hall). Popularized chiefly by the Wagner operas, Valhalla is one of the best known but least understood of the Norse allegories. It has become superciliously regarded as a humorous parody of heaven where rough-and-tumble Vikings go to carouse. Brought to this realm of the warrior god Odin by Valkyries, they are regaled with pork and mead each night, and each morning return to the fray only to be slain all over again. Valhalla is protected by many barriers: it is surrounded by a moat, Tund, wherein a werewolf, Tjodvitner, fishes for men. Its gate is secured by magic, and on the door of the hall a wolf hangs transfixed, surmounted by a blood-dripping eagle. In addition it is guarded by Odin's two wolfhounds. To understand the significance of all this we must define the terms used.

Each of the barriers to the Hall of the Elect is symbolic of some weakness that must be conquered. The warrior who would cross the river of time (Tund) and the river of doubt (Ifing) must maintain unwavering purpose and self-direction if he is not to be swept away by the turbulent currents of temporal existence. He must evade the bestial cravings of his animal nature (the lures of Tjodvitner) if he is to gain the other shore. Many scriptures use the allegory of a river. Buddhism, for example, speaks of four stages of progress, beginning with those who have entered the stream, and ending with those who have successfully reached the other shore. All nature is said to rejoice when an aspirant gains his goal.

Next, the candidate seeking Valhalla must overcome the hounds Gere (greed) and Freke (gluttony): he must avoid desire, even the desire for the wisdom he is seeking, if he is to obtain it. To find the secret of the magic gate, he must have strength of aspiration, purity of motive, and inflexible resolve. The wolf and the eagle must be vanquished and transfixed over the entrance to the hall to guard against their intrusion. This means conquering the bestial nature (the wolf), and pride (the eagle) — self-seeking in any guise which, like Proteus of the Greeks, arises in ever new forms to challenge those who approach the realm of the gods. All weapons of offense and of defense must be relinquished and transformed into the constructive materials that form the sacred fane. The walls of Valhalla are built of the warriors' spears, the roof is of their shields. Within the hall even protective armor is discarded: "the benches are strewn with byrnies" (Grimnismál 9).

The surrender of weapons is a hallmark of the Mystery tradition. The candidate for universality cannot, by the very nature of his quest, regard himself as separate from the whole; he can therefore have no use for divisive means of any kind, in thought, word, or deed. First to go are weapons of offense, as harmlessness is cultivated. Thereafter all means of defense are dropped and finally all personal protection of whatever kind. The One-harrier has stepped beyond the notion of separateness. His work lies not in the immediate but in the eternal. He is no longer bounded by a self but extends unlimited; the hero soul has discarded all personal concern, placing complete reliance on the divine law he unconditionally serves.

If these myths had originated among the Vikings who, according to one of their codes, even slept on their shields with sword in hand, this would seem out of character. Rather does it corroborate the theory that the Norse myths far antedate these warriors and stem from the same archaic source as other early traditions. For there is clearly much more than meets the eye in the Edda's poetic enchantment even when it is concealed within its sometimes bawdy anecdotes.

The plain of battle where the warriors each day contend is called Vigridsslätten, which may be translated as "the plain of consecration." It is reminiscent of the *dharmakṣetra* — the field of *dharma* (duty, righteousness) — of the *Bhagavad-Gītā* where the struggle between the forces of light and darkness in human nature takes place. In that classic many of his antagonists are the hero's friends and close relatives whom he must oppose, meaning character traits and habits of which he has become fond and which therefore are difficult to overcome. In both allegories the battlefield is man himself, where are ranged in opposing ranks all the human qualities, which themselves are the reflection of the properties of greater nature. The daily contest profoundly affects the evolutionary course of all beings. From time to time a One-harrier crosses over from the world of men to join the ranks of the gods; such rare forerunners who gain access to "the shining abode" unite their forces with nature's divine intent. The Valkyries, our own inspiring deepest selves, are ever searching the field of consecration for worthy recruits who choose to aid the gods in their unending labors toward the consummation of the cycle when mankind as a whole shall enter into its divine heritage and responsibility.

"The Hall of the Chosen glows golden in Gladhome," according to Grimnismál (8). Here Odin daily crowns the heroes after the battle. Here too, the One-harriers are regaled with ale or mead and are fed the three boars of air, water, and fire, that symbolize different aspects of the earth, for they are the essence of their experience during human life on this planet. The boars that nourish the One-harriers also represent creative powers, the energic aspect of three of nature's elements. Verse 18 in Grimnismál, if we substitute these for the corresponding three boars, would read: "Spirit lets mind be steeped in will and desire." Thus the higher self or spirit of man permits the human ego to be tested in the fires of the soul to prove its integrity. If successful, the man brings to birth his inner god, the mortal earns its immortality, uniting with the indwelling divinity.

Odin, Allfather, is the essence of universal creative consciousness on all levels of existence. The name is a form of *Odr*, universal intelligence (equivalent to the Greek *nous* and the Sanskrit *mahat*), whereof the spiritual soul of man is a child. *Odraerir*, mystic dispenser of Odr, is one of the holy vessels which contain the "blood of Kvasir" — divine wisdom (Greek *theos-sophia*). Kvasir was a "hostage" or avatāra sent by the "wise Vaner" to the Aesir. This is an enlightening hint indicating the descent of divine inspiration from sublime cosmic powers to the god world beneath, which is still far superior to our own. We may infer from this the continuous evolutionary pattern wherein Odin, Allfather to our world and divine root of every living being in our sphere, has risen from a formerly lesser condition and is now progressing toward superior stages, aided by the inspiration of still loftier divinities.

While in a general sense Allfather is implicit in all manifestation, Odin also has his own domain as a planetary spirit: his is the shelf named Gladhome, where is located Valhalla, the Hall of the Elect. Though *Val* means choice it also means death when it applies to Odin's warriors, the "One-harriers." Related to the Greek *koiranos*, "commander," the One-harrier is one who harries, commands, or controls, *one* — himself. Each has moreover elected to die as a personal ego and gained transcendency of consciousness into the nonpersonal, universal, realm of the gods. To put it another way, he has overcome the lesser human self and united with the cosmic purpose of life. This is a continuous process — of growth, hence of change, each change being a "death," a transformation from one state into another, usually from a less to a more perfect condition. The "crowners of the elect" (Valkyries) who bring the heroes to Odin's sacred hall are closely related to the hamingja or guardian angel, the spiritual soul, every human being's protector and tutor.

When Allfather welcomes his heroes to Valhalla, he is named Ropt, "the maligned," and in the Lay of Odin's Corpse, he is Nikar, the "ladler" of misfortune. These mysterious hints become clearer when we recognize that Odin is the initiator who, as well as instructing and inspiring, must subject the human ego to the contending fires of its own complex soul and cannot, may not sway the outcome of the trial. Hence it is only the successful initiate who knows the true nature of Odin, the hierophant, and recognizes the bringer of trials as Ropt.

Valhalla presents yet another aspect which links it with Eastern scriptures of remote antiquity: Odin in Grimnismál tells his pupil that there are "five hundred doors and forty more" to Valhalla; and that eight hundred warriors issue from each when Odin emerges to war with the wolf. Further we are told that there are five hundred and forty halls in bulging Bilskirner (the shining abode), the largest being "my son's" — the solar deity's. Multiplying 540 × 800 we get 432,000 warriors and the same number of halls. In both Babylonian and Indian chronologies this figure occurs in numerous ways. Multiples of it define specific astronomical cycles while, divided by various numbers, it applies to terrestrial events of greater frequency, even down to the pulsebeat of the human heart, generally reckoned as 72 beats per minute. It is itself the length in human years assigned to the Iron Age, in Sanskrit the *kali yuga*, when the forces of darkness are most challenging. Curious that this should be the

number assigned to Odin's champions. It certainly hints vigor-
ously at some common source from which these widely separated
traditions have descended and at some hidden meaning which
makes this figure recur in them.

It is significant that of all the Norse tales, the battles of the
Elect should have gained the greatest popularity: even though
we may be unaware of the hidden meaning, this theme has an
appeal that will not be denied. On the plain of battle, or of
consecration, we all daily meet formidable enemies: weaknesses
of character and habits we have adopted, familiar foibles to
which we have become attached — what the *Gītā* calls our
friends, relatives, and teachers.

For the human race evolution can be defined as developing
awareness, an increasing comprehension of life. This is not
mere knowledge of facts and relationships, nor is it just a growing
understanding of ourselves and others; it entails a very direct
realization and personal discovery of the spiritual unity of beings.
With it comes a self-identification with all, well expressed in the
words, "I am not my brother's keeper; I am my brother." The
self is nonself. In the transition from a restricted inwardness
of ego to all-inclusive self-transcendence, the human soul comes
naturally to identify with all that is. The battle undertaken by
Ygg's heroes, which gains them access to Valhalla, is the constant
exercise of will, firm control of every thought and impulse,
complete selflessness at all times, in all situations. The injunc-
tion, "to live to benefit mankind is the first step,"[2] is tacitly
confirmed in the epics of the Norsemen as is evident in the Song
of Svipdag, where the hero, united with his hamingja — the
Freya of his dreams — returns to perform "the tasks of the years
and the ages." The ally of the gods seeks not merely to do good
when opportunity occurs but to exist throughout with the
paramount purpose of beneficence, constantly cited as character-

---

2. *The Voice of the Silence*, p. 33.

istic of the deities, "the beneficent powers." The One-harriers have in fact died to their personal desires and been "virgin born," to borrow a metaphor from other myths, into universal concern, enabling them to take their natural places in what the theosophic writings call the Hierarchy of Compassion. Odin's heroes do not rest on their laurels but continue to play a vital part in the eternal struggle of life as allies of the gods.

Traditional scriptures hint that, ever since divinities descended among men and taught the early races, there have lived an unbroken succession of spiritual teachers, intermediary between the gods and humans, whose mission is to inspire and aid the human race in its evolution toward perfection. Such adepts in the art of living are the One-harriers. A divine ray may imbody among mankind from time to time as one of these superior men and women who have chosen the lonely road toward merging their human self with the divine essence at the core of being. Even among the highest gods messengers, "hostages," descend among their younger brother deities as avataric rays. Skirner[3] represents such a "hostage" to the human sphere.

Many are the tales linked with this motif, tales that relate how the evolving soul seeks its spiritual self, the Sleeping Beauty, or the Beauty on the Glass Mountain, accessible only to the valiant, pure, and totally selfless hero. He alone can draw from its scabbard, or from the anvil, or the rock, or the tree, the mystic sword of spiritual will placed there by a god. With this magic weapon he conquers the dragon, or serpent (of egoism), and gains inner knowledge, whereupon he understands the language of birds and all nature's voices. He must overcome all weaknesses, all temptations, surmount all fears, to be able, mounted on the steed of his obedient animal nature, to leap the flaming river that separates the world of men from that of the gods. There he gains reunion with his divine hamingja. The godmaker is become a god.

---

3. Cf. Skirnismál, p. 248.

Incidentally, tales wherein the knight slays a firebreathing dragon, rescuing a fair damsel and saving the kingdom, may not all be mere allegory with no basis in physical reality. They are too universally prevalent to be lightly dismissed. While it is certain that they symbolize the hero's overcoming his baser nature and gaining his inmost heart's desire, it is also possible these symbolic tales may be superposed on a historical framework, which seems to be a common practice of myths. We may speculate on the possibility that the earliest human races of our round of life shared the earth with some at least of the giant saurians, whether winged, aquatic, or earthbound, before the latter became extinct. Who knows what lonely relics of once abundant species survived long enough to interact with early humanities? Any encounters with them which may have taken place would certainly have given rise to legends which would persist long after the events themselves were forgotten. If sea serpents qualify as mythic "dragons," we need not look very far back to find their traces; to this day we hear rumors of such "monsters" being spotted in Loch Ness and elsewhere. The mythic Scandinavian dragons are said to have emitted an overpoweringly nauseating odor which defeated many a would-be dragon slayer. Indeed it is daunting to think of facing some gargantuan crocodile with halitosis. But this is by the way.

The universal appeal of myths may stem from a slumbering yearning we all have, to perform valiant deeds of derring-do. Leading what may seem commonplace lives, we have a deep-rooted desire to achieve the conquest implied in the sagas, the inner victory of All-self over myself. The goal of human evolution must be attained eventually with or without our purposeful effort. We can drift along in a slow, unmotivated round of endlessly recurring mistakes and continue to suffer from the inevitable results of our unwisdom. We may also actively oppose nature's beneficent direction and with intense self-centeredness shrink our sphere of interest to a mathematical point and ultimate extinction. A third alternative is that chosen by the heroes who elect to pursue the purposes of the gods. Whichever course is embarked upon will inevitably lead to the moment when a choice must be made: either conscious existence as gods or dissolution in the waters of space as inert frost giant material, becoming ground on the mill of extinction. Skirner, in wooing the giant maiden Gerd on behalf of the god Frey, implies this as he threatens her with Rimgrimner, the icecold (frost giant aspect of) Mimer, ultimate matter-base of all universes. This would mean utter severance from the energic, divine power of the gods. Gerd is apparently a race of humankind who is given the opportunity to decide between immortality and annihilation.

To everyone there come moments when the whispered urgings of divinity are sensed within the silence of the soul. Those who answer the call to serve the gods and help alleviate humanity's future suffering are on the path to becoming One-harriers, heroes who muster the scattered forces of the soul under the single command of universal purpose, and who maintain this tenor through lifetimes of effort. It is simply an acceleration of the godmaker's natural evolution that these heroic souls undertake and by the destruction of personal egoism ally their powers with the long-range work of the gods in our world. It is this message we may find in myths: the initiation of a new kind of living. For initiation means "beginning." It is entering on a new sphere of duty, a more exalted and, to us, godlike arena of life. The "One-harrier" is crowned a warrior of the gods and undertakes to share with them "the tasks of the years and the ages."

PLATES

Photographic reproduction of the first five pages of *Codex Regius*, as it was written down by Saemund the Wise a thousand years ago. Völuspá covers the first four pages and ends on page 5, where Hávamál begins on line 4. Note Bishop Brynjolv's monogram ⅃⅃ (Lupus Loricatus) at the bottom of the first page, and the date when he acquired it, 1643.

Reproduced with permission from the Arna Magnussonar Collections in Reykjavik, Iceland.

...lið oc allar hanðir meiri e mína maunge
hennd... ...viþo ðc ðc vali ... vel ... ... tvía þoru
spioll fira þav e fremst u mꜩa. Ec man iotna roc na
ar um borna þa e forðom mic fadda hofðo. nio mꜳ ek heim
nio ivioir mioꞇ uið mꜳran ꝼ mold neðan. Ar var alda þat
er ymir byggdi vara sandr ne ser ne svalar unnir iꝋð þar ꝛ
eva ne upp himin gap var ginunga en gras hvergi. Aðr burs
syʀ biꝋð u ypðo þr er miðgarð moran scopo. sol scein
sunnan a salar steina þa var grund groin gronom lauki.
Sol varp sunnan sinni mana hendi inni hꙮgri um himin ioður.
Sol þat ne vissi hvar hon sali atti stiornor þat ne visso hvar
þær staði atto mani þat ne vissi hvat hann megins atti. Þa gen
gengo regin oll a rꝍcstola ginnheilog goð oc um þat gettuz
noꞇ oc niþiom nꝍfn um gafo morgin heto oc miðian dag un
dorn oc aptan aron at telia. Hittoz æsir a iða velli þr
er hꜵrg oc hof hatimbroðo. afla lagðo að smiðoðo tang
scopo oc tol gerðo. Tefldo i túni teitir voro þꜵt þeim vettugis
vant oc gulli. unz þriar qvomo þursa meyiar amatkar
mioc or iotun heimom. Þa gengo regin aʀ a rꝍcstola dvergia
drottin scepia oc bmist bloði oc oc blꜳm leggio. þar moð
soꝛ mottr u auðin diga allra þeim durum aꞇ ꝛ þar mꜳꝛ
... ... ꝼ goðo dvgar oc reðo sem durin sagði. Nyi
oc niþi norðri oc suðri austri oc vestri alþiofr dvalin bivꝛ
ꜳvaʀ bavꝛ bꙮmbvꝛ nori an anaʀ ai midvitnir. Veigr
oc gandalfr vindalfr þrain þecꝛ oc þorin þror vitr oc litr
... var oc nyraþ nv hefi ec dvga regin rad svia retꞇ
um talþa. Fili kili fundin nali. hepti. vili hanaʀ svi
oʀ. frar hornbori. fregr oc loni. avrvangr iari eikinꝺ
eikalpa. Þat e dvga i dvalins liði liona kinðo til lofa
er scal. þeir e sotto fra salar steini avrvanga siottr til
iorovalla. Þar var draupnir oc dolgþrasir har hvgspꝛꝩ
hlevangr gloi. scirvir virvir. scafiðr. ai. alfr oc yngvi
eikinscialdi. falar oc frosti finr oc ginnar. þmon vppi

meþ aso [illegible] tal lopars hapat. Unz þriar qvomo
or þvi liþi [illegible] aflgir oc astgir esir at husi. fundo alandi litt
[illegible] emblo orlauglausa. aund þau ne atto oþ þau
[illegible] ne lito goda. Aund gaf oþin oþ
[illegible] lago [illegible] lodvr oc lito goda. Asc veit ec standa
[illegible] yggdrasill harbadmr ausinn hvita auri. þan coma
daggvar þers idala falla stendr e yfir grønn urdar brunni.
Þ þadan coma meyiar margs vitandi þriar or þei se er und
þolli stendr. urd heto eina adra verdandi scaro a scidi. sculd
ena þridio. þer laug laugdo þer lif kuro alda bornom or
laug segia. Þ man hon folc vig fyrst iheimi er gull veig
geiro studdo oc ihaull hars ha brendo. þrysvar brendo
þrysvar borna opt osialdan þo hon enn lifir. Heidi hana
heto hvars til husa com volo vel spa vitti hon ganda seid
hon kvnni seid hon leikinn e var hon angan illrar þrudar.
Þ a.g.r.a.a. hvart scyldo esir afrad gialda eþ scyldo gadin
all gildi eiga. fleygdi odinn oc ifolc um scaut þ var enn folc
vig fyrst iheimi brotinn var bord vegr borgar asa knatto
vanir vigspa vollo sporna. þa.g.r.a. hvir hefdi lopt
allt levi blandit eþ ett iotuns oþs mey gefna. þorr einn
þar var þrunginn modi h sialdan sitr e h slict of fregn. age
ngoz eidar ord oc sert mal aull megin lig er amedal foro.
Ueit ho heimdalar hlioþ um folgit undir heidvonom helgom
badmi. a ser ho ausaz aurgom forsi af vedi valfadrs vitt
op ð e e. h. Ein sat. ho uti þa e inn aldni com yggiongr
asa oc iaugo leit. hvs fregnit mic hvi freistiþ min alt
veit ec odinn hvar þu auga falt iþeim eno mera mimis
brunni dreccr miod mimir morgin hverian af vedi v.v.e.e.h.
Ualþi he herfadir hringa oc men fe spioll spaclig oc spa
ganda sa ho vitt oc um vitt of verold hveria. Sa ho valkyrior
komnar garvar at rida til godþiodar. sculd
hellt scildi enn scaugul aunnor gunnr. hildr gaundul oc geir

scꜵrguli. nu ero talþar nꜵnna hiani gꜵrvar at riþa grvnd
val kyrie. Ec sa baldri blꜵðgo tiva oðins barni ꜵ lꜵg
j olgin stað u varin vollo heri mioc j mioc fagr mistil
tꜵinn g: þei meidr e m synir harmflaug bꜵttlig haufr seni
na seiota. baldrs broðir var oþ bꜵrn snema þa na obis
sonr ein nꜵttr vega. þo h ꜵva hende ne hꜵfi hembbr aþ
a bal u bar baldes aðscota. en frig u gret j en valh uꜵþr
val hallar v. e. e. h. hapt sa hon liggia uid hva lundi le
giarn het loca abeckian. þar sitr sigyn þeygi u sino vey
velglyioð v. þ. e. h. A fellr austan u eitr dala sauro j svꜵþo
þau heit sv. stꜵð fyr norðan a niþa iuollo salr ꜵ gvie sin
dra ettar. en annar stꜵð a okolni bior salr iotuns e sa bru
heit. Sal sa hon standa solo fiarri na strꜵndo a naustr hor
fa dyr. eitr droþar in u lioꜵa la e undin salr ꜵrma
heyfoð. Sa ho þar vaða þunga strauma m snoðð vargar
meins vara j. þau annat glepr eyra runo þar svg nið
hꜵfgr nar j m gengna fleit vargr þa v. e. e. h. Austr sat
in alðna i iarnviði j fꜵddi þar fenris kind. uþ g: þei
ꜵllo eina noccec tungli tiugari trꜵllz hami. fyllz j fiꜵr
vi fꜵigra manna ryþ ragna fiot raðo dreyra svart u þa sol
skin oþ sumꜵr ept veðr ꜵll valynd v. e. h. Sat þar ahauge
j slo harpo gygiar hirðir glaðe ecþer. gol u hꜵno i gagl
viðr fagr rꜵðe hani sa e fialar heit. Gol u aso gul
linkabi sa veckr hꜵlþa at hiarar at hiar aðes. en annat
gelr j iorð neðan sot rauðr hani at salom heliar. Geyr
garmr mioc j gniþa helli fostr mun slitna en fre
ki renna fiolþ veit hon froða fram se ec leng u rag
na rꜵc rꜵmm sigtyva. Broþr muno biar j at bꜵnom
u þa muno systrungar sifiom spilla hart e i heimi hoe
domir mikill scꜵggꜵld scalmꜵld scild ro klofin vindꜵld
vargꜵld aþ vold steypr mun engi maðr ꜵðro þyrma
eica muns syni en miotuðr kyndir at en galla gal

ar heim hat bles heimdallr horn e alopti. melir oðin
við mims hofuð. ... ... aldna tre en iotunn losnar þegar
ymr iþ aldna tre en iotunn losnar. skelfr yggdrasils askr st
andandi. Geyr nu g. Hrymr ekr austan hefiz lind fyr
iþ iormungandr iotunn moði. ormr knyr unn en ari hl
accar. slitr nai nefr folr. nagl fer losnar. Kioll ferr au
stan koma muno muspellz um lǫg lyð en loki styrir. fara
fiflmeg með freka allr þeir er broð byleipz io er. Hvat er
m. aso hvat e m. alfǫ gnyr allir iotnar þeir ekr roa þin
g styria dvergr f. steindurom ves bisf vitar v. e. e. h. Surtr
ferr sunnan m. suiga leyi. skinn af. sverði sol valtiua. griotb i
orgguata en gifr rata troða halir helveg en himin clofn.
a þa hlinar harmr annar fram er oðin ferr við ulf vega
en bani belia biartr at surti þa mun friggiar falla angan
tyr. þa kemr inn mikli maugr sigfauð viðarr vega at valdy
ri. letr hann megi hvedrungs mund um standa hiorr t hiarta
þa e hefnt faður. Þa kemr inn moeri maugr hloðyniar geng
opinn son viðrs ulf vega. drepr hann af moði midgarz veor
muno halir allir heimstað ryðia. gengr fet nio fiorgyniar
bur. neppr fra naðri niðs oqvuðom. Sol tekr sortna
sigr fold imar hverfa af himni heiðar stiornor. geisar eimi
við aldr nara leikr hár hiti við himin sialfan. Geyr. y.
Ser ho upp koma aðro sinni iorð or egi iðia grœna. falla
fors ar. flygr aurn yfir. sa er a fialli fisca ueiðir. fin az
esir iða velli. ok um moldþinur maktan dœma ok a fimbul
tys fornar runar. þar muno eptir undrsamligar gul
nar toflor i grasi finar. þers i ardaga attar hofðo.
Muno osanir acrar uaxa bavtz mun alls batna balðr
m. hꜵð. bua þeir hꜵð ok baldr hroptz sigtoptir vel val
tivar v. e. e. h. þa kna hꜵnir hlutvið kiosa ok byria
byggia brœðra tveggia. vindheim viðan v. e. e. h. Sal ser
hon standa solo fegra gulli þakþan a gimle. þar

Part II

Notes, Translated Lays, and Stories

Völuspá

(The Sibyl's Prophecy)

TRANSLATOR'S NOTES

Among the lays and stories of the *Edda* the place of honor unquestionably belongs to Völuspá. It is the most comprehensive as well as the most enigmatic portion of the Norse scripture. In it are outlined the majestic pageant of worlds in formation, the attributes of the cosmic Tree of Life, its decay and death, and its subsequent renewal and rebirth. To follow the progression of events related by the sibyl we must often resort to other lays and *sagor*[1] which are more explicit, for in Völuspá we see the work of eternities compressed into the wink of an eye, the vastness of a universe in a grain of sand.

The *vala* or *völva*, the sibyl who speaks the poem, represents the indelible record of time, as from a beginningless past events move toward an endless future with universes succeeding one another in surging waves of life. The vala personifies the record of the past: her memory, reaching back through the "foretime," recalls nine former world trees, long since dissolved and now reliving.

Völuspá is the sibyl's response to Odin's search for wisdom. The cosmic record is being consulted by Allfather — conscious, divine intelligence which periodically manifests as a universe, impelled by the urge to gain experience. He is the root of all the lives that compose it, immanent in every portion of its worlds, yet supernal. When the vala addresses Odin as "all ye holy kindred," this not only shows the intimate relationship which links all beings,

---

1. Plural of *saga*, an oral tradition, transmitted by word of mouth, like the Sanskrit *smṛti* and *śruti*, teachings "remembered" and "heard" respectively.

but also identifies them with the questing god. Odin's cited wish to learn of "the origin, life, and end of worlds" is a device to elicit this information on behalf of all the "greater and lesser sons of Heimdal" (1)[2] — all existing forms of life within this solar system, Heimdal's domain — and, incidentally, of the audience.

To those who picture deity as a perfect, omniscient, omnipresent, and unchanging person, it may seem strange to find a god requesting information on anything, especially in worlds beneath his own divine sphere. But in the myths divinities are not static, congealed in divine perfection, but growing, learning intelligences of many degrees. The Völuspá uses a poetic ploy to suggest that consciousness enters worlds of matter in order to learn, grow, and evolve greater understanding, while inspiring by association the matter through which it operates.

The vala "remembers giants born in the foretime" — worlds now dead, whose energizing consciousnesses have long since left them, whereupon their uninspired material reverted to entropy and chaos. She remembers "nine trees of life before this world tree grew from the ground" (2). Elsewhere there is mention of Heimdal's being "born of nine maidens"; also that Odin's vigil when he is mounted on the Tree of Life lasted for "nine whole nights" (Hávamál 137). This all combines to suggest that our earth system is the tenth in a series, following the frost giant Ymer when there was "no soil, no sea, no waves" (3).

Each world tree is an expression of the divine consciousnesses which organize appropriate forms to live in and gain the "mead" of experience. When in due course they withdraw, whatever cannot advance or profit by the association with the gods, that is to say, whatever is unmitigatedly material, becomes the frost giant.

The wise sibyl who tamed wolves, analogous to the cosmic vala, appears to represent the hidden wisdom or occult insight. (It is worth noting that the word "occult" means anything hidden or obscured, just as a star is occulted when it is hidden from our sight by the moon, or any other body. The merest a, b, c, is occult until it is understood.) The vala, Heid, is that hidden knowledge

---

2. Numbers alone refer to verses in the lay named in the chapter title.

which exerts a fascination on the selfish, hence it is "ever sought by evil peoples," although it may be harmlessly acquired by one who is wise and "tames wolves," who is in control of the animal nature and who by self-discipline and service gains access to nature's arcana. The distinction between the two sibyls is clearly made in the poem: "She sees much; I see more" (45). One pertains to human concerns on earth, the other represents an overview of cosmic records.

The skalds distinguished three different kinds of magic: *sejd* or prophecy is the faculty of foreseeing events to come as they follow naturally on those of the past. In most countries there were until quite recently many "wise women" who continued to practice this art, most commonly in trivial matters. Such fortune-tellers are still to be found; many of them trade on public gullibility and prophesy more or less spurious "fortunes" for a fee. A second type of magic is the *galder* — a formula of enchantment purporting to bend the future to one's desire. Such spells, when in any degree successful, are often sorcery, whether performed in good faith and ignorance or, more dangerously, with the impact of knowledge and with will and determination behind them. Inevitably their repercussions complete their circuit and adversely affect the originator as well as associates who may be innocently and ignorantly involved.

A third form of magic is "reading the *runes*" — perusing nature's book of symbols and gaining progressive wisdom. This is the study of Odin himself, as he hangs in the Tree of Life (Hávamál 137–8): "I searched the depths, found runes of wisdom, raised them with song, and fell once more thence" — from the tree.

The vala tells of the end of the golden age of innocence and of the death of the sun-god Balder through the agency of his blind brother Höder — ignorance and darkness — instigated by Loki, the mischievous elf of human intelligence. As in many other tales of the fall from innocence of the early humans, the agent which brought about our knowledge of good and evil and the power to choose between them, has borne the blame for all subsequent ills in the world. The biblical Lucifer, the light-bringer, from "bright and morning star" has been transformed into a devil; the Greek Prometheus who gave mankind the fire of mind was chained to a rock for the duration of the world and will be rescued only when Herakles, the human soul, shall have attained perfection at the end of its labors. Similarly, Loki was bound beneath the nether gates of the underworld to suffer torment until the cycle's completion. In each case the sacrifice brought us humans the inner light needed to illumine our path to godhood, which will be gained through conscious effort and self-conscious regeneration in ultimate reunion with our divine source.

The Völuspá gives a vivid description of Ragnarök. This has been translated as the "age of fire and smoke," probably because *rök* in Swedish means smoke, and students of mythology have regarded this as characteristic of the Norsemen's supposedly doleful temperament, given to doom and gloom. But there is a better interpretation of the word: *ragna*, plural of the Icelandic *regin* (god, ruler) + *rök* (ground, cause, or origin) is the time when the ruling gods return to their root, their ground, at the end of the world. The horrors depicted as accompanying the departure of the gods are indeed chilling, punctuated by the howling of the hound of Hel; however, this is not the end. After the toppling of the world tree, the poem continues to describe the birth of a new world and ends on a note of serene contentment at the dawn of a new and golden age. Many are unaware of this and, having some acquaintance with Wagner's "Ring of the Nibelungen" tacitly ignore the implications of a cosmic rebirth. Yet, the pattern conforms far more closely to the tenor of other profound systems of thought than does the idea of an ultimate end. Such irreversible finality is not found in myths; instead we learn of nature's ceaseless flow into being and back to the unknown source, inevitably followed by a new manifestation — a pattern that better mirrors all we know of nature, and evokes a far grander vision of the eternal pulse of life beating through boundless infinitude and endless duration.

Völuspá

1. Hear me, all ye holy kindred,[3]
   Greater and lesser sons of Heimdal!
   You wish me to tell the ancient tales,
   O Father of seers, the oldest I know.

2. I remember giants born in the foretime,
   They who long ago nurtured me;
   Nine worlds I remember, nine trees of life,
   Before this world tree grew from the ground.

3. This was the first of aeons, when Ymer built.
   There was no soil, no sea, no waves;
   Earth was not, nor heaven;
   Gaping abyss alone: no growth.

4. Until Bur's sons raised the tables;
   They who had power to fashion Midgárd.
   Sun shone from the south on the stones of the
         court;
   Then grew green grass in fertile soil.

5. The sun bore south together with moon.
   On her right hand was the heaven's door.
   Sun knew not what hall she had;
   Stars knew not their places yet.
   Moon knew not his power.

6. The mighty drew to their judgment seats,
   All holy gods to hold council;

---

3. Genera, generations of related beings.

They named night and moon phases, separated
   morn from noon,
Dusk and evening, to tell the years.

7. The Aesir met on the Ida sward,
   Timbered lofty courts and altars;
   They founded forges, smithied gold,
   Fashioned tongs and tempered tools.

8. Goldtable they joyfully played in the court;
   Lacked not abundance of gold;
   Until there came from the giants' home
   Three very immoderate giant maids.

9. The mighty drew to their judgment seats,
   All holy gods to hold council:
   Who should fashion a host of dwarfs
   From Brimer's blood and the limbs of the dead?

10. There was Force-sucker, master of dwarfs
   As *Durin* knows;
   There were fashioned many humanoid dwarfs
      from the earth
   As *Durin* said.

11. Wax and Wane, North and South,
   East and West, All-thief, Coma,
   Bifur, Bafur,[4]
   Bömbur, Nore.

12. *Án, Ánar, Ai,* Mead-witness,
   Path, Magus, Windelf, *Thráin,*
   Yearning, Longing, Wisdom, Color,
   Corpse and New Advice.

---

4. Names in italics are not translated; some may be "nonsense syllables," others may refer to fauna or flora not recognized or perhaps extinct.

13. Slice and Wedge, Discovery, *Nale*,
    Hope and Will, Rooster, *Sviur*,
    Speedy, Antlered,
    Fame, and Lone.

14. It is time the dwarfs of Dvalin's kin
    Be named, up to Lofar, the handed:
    They who have struggled from the hall's
    Stone foundation up to the ramparts.

15. Clarifier, Cycler, Shaver, Channel,
    Sanctuary-of-youth and Oakshield-bearer,
    Fugitive, Frost, and
    Finder and Illusion.

16. While ages endure
    The long, long reach
    Of Lofar's forebears
    Shall be remembered.

17. From one such train drew forth in the hall
    Three Aesir, powerful, compassionate.
    They found on the earth the ash and the alder,
    Of little power, indeterminate.

18. Odin gave them spirit,
    Höner discernment,
    Lodur gave them blood
    And divine light.

19. An ash stands, I know, by name Yggdrasil;
    That tall tree is watered by white icicles daily;
    Thence comes the dew that drops in the dells;
    It stands ever green above Urd's well.

20. Thence come maidens who know much,
    Three from that hall beneath the tree:

One was named Origin, the second Becoming.
These two fashioned the third, named Debt.

21. They established law,
    They selected lives
    For the children of ages,
    And the fates of men.

22. She remembers the first slaying in the world,
    When Gullveig[5] was hoist on a spear;
    Thrice was she burned and thrice reborn,
    Again and again — yet still she lives.

23. Heid was her name.
    To whatever house she came
    She prophesied well and was versed in spells.
    She was much sought by evil peoples.

24. The mighty drew to their judgment seats,
    All holy gods to hold council;
    Should the Aesir alone atone the wrong,
    Or all the gods make reparation?

25. Odin hurled his spear among the throng.
    This became the first war in the world.
    The ramparts were rent in the Aesir's
        stronghold;
    Victorious Vaner strode the field.

26. The mighty drew to their judgment seats,
    All holy gods to hold council:
    Who had mingled the air with evil
    Or given Od's maid to the giant race?

27. Thor struck out in mighty wrath;
    He stays not quiet when such he learns;

---

5. "Thirst for gold." Cf. p. 42.

Oaths were broken, words and promises,
Mighty pacts were broken then.

28. She knows where Heimdal's horn is hid
Under the sacred sun-drench'd tree;
She sees ladled a stream mixed with icicle
torrent
From Allfather's forfeit. Know you as yet,
or what?[6]

29. She sat outside alone when the Old One came;
The fearsome Áse looked her in the eye:
"What ask you of me? Why do you tempt me?
I know all, Odin. I know where you hid your
eye —

30. "In the redoubtable Mimer's well.
Mimer quaffs mead each morning
From Allfather's forfeit."
Know you as yet, or what?

31. The Father of Hosts gave her rings
And gems to gain
Wisdom and lore from her.
Far and wide she scanned the worlds.

32. *She* saw Valkyries ready to ride: Debt bore
armor.
So also did War, Battle, and Spearwound.
Thus are the Hero's maidens named,
Valkyries mounted to ride over earth.

33. *I* saw the fate determined for Balder,
The gentle god, Odin's child.
High above the field there grew,
Slender and fair, the mistletoe bough.

---

6. This cryptic recurring phrase is translated verbatim.

34. The sprig that I saw was to become
    A threatening sorrow-dart shot by Höder.
    Balder's brother, born before his time,
    But one night of age, Odin's son rode to battle.

35. He laved not his hands nor combed he his hair
    Ere he bore Balder's foe on the funeral pyre.
    Frigga bewept in her watery palace
    Valhalla's woe.
    Know you as yet, or what?

36. She saw the one bound beneath the court,
    Where the caldron is kept.
    The wretch resembles Loki.
    Unhappy Sigyn remains by her spouse.
    Know you as yet, or what?

37. A torrent of daggers and swords
    Runs from the East
    Through vales of venom.
    Her name is Scabbard.

38. On low northern fields stood a golden hall
    Belonging to Sindre's race.
    Another one stood on the Unfreezing Ocean,
    The giant Brimer's brewhall.

39. A hall she sees standing far from the sun
    On the shores of death, with its door to
          the north.
    Venomous drops fall in through the weave,
    For that hall is woven of serpents.

40. Therein wading the streams she saw
    Oathbreakers, murderers, adulterers.
    There Nidhögg[7] sucks cadavers,

---

7. The serpent undermining Yggdrasil's roots.

Wolves tear men.
Know you as yet, or what?

41. Eastward in the Ironwood the Old One sat
Fostering Fenrer's offspring.
Of them all shall come a certain something
That in troll's guise shall take the moon.

42. It feeds on the life of those who die,
And blood-red it colors the dwelling of powers.
The sun shall be dark the summers thereafter,
All winds be odious.
Know you as yet, or what?

43. There in the field, playing the harp,
Carefree Egt sits, watching the sword maids;
There crowd for him in the human world
Fjalar, the fair red rooster of spring.

44. For the Aesir crowed the goldcomb-adorned,
Who wakens the warriors in Hostfather's hall;
But another crows beneath the earth:
A soot-red cock in the halls of Hel.

45. Garm howls at the Gnipa-hollow of Hel.
What is fast loosens, and Freke runs free.
She grasps much; I see more:
To Ragnarök, the Victory-gods' hard death
      struggle.

46. Brothers shall battle and slay one another.
Blood ties of sisters' sons shall be sundered.
Harsh is the world. Fornication is rife,
Luring to faithlessness spouses of others.

47. Axe time, sword time, shields shall be cloven;
Wind time, wolf time, ere the world wanes.
Din on the fields, trolls in full flight;
No man shall then spare another.

48. Mimer's sons arise. The dying world tree
    flares
    At the sound of the shrill trump of doom.
    Loud blows Heimdal, the horn held high.
    Odin confers with Mimer's head.

49. With a roaring in the ancient tree
    The giant is loosened.
    The ash, Yggdrasil,
    Quakes where it stands.

50. Garm howls at the Gnipa-hollow of Hel.
    What was fast loosens, and Freke runs free.

51. Rymer steers westward; the tree is o'erturned;
    In titanic rage
    Iörmungandr[8] writhes,
    Whipping the waves to froth.

52. The eagle shrieks loudly;
    Bleknäbb[9] tears corpses.
    Nagelfar[10] casts off.

53. Comes a keel from the east. From over the
    waters
    Come Muspell's folk with Loki at the helm.
    Monsters fare with Freke.
    Such is the train of Byleist's[11] brother.

54. How is it with Aesir? How is it with elves?
    The giant world roars; the Aesir hold council.
    Dwarfs groan before their stone portals,
    Masters of mountains.
    Know you as yet, or what?

---

8. The world serpent: the equator, ecliptic, or Milky Way.
9. "Palebeak": the eagle Räsvälg.
10. "Nailfarer," ship of death, built of dead men's nails.
11. "Wildfire": the adverse side of Loki.

55. Fire fares from south with flaring flames.
    The embattled gods' sun is skewered on
        the sword.
    Mountains burst open. Hags hurry hence.
    Men tread Hel's road; the heavens are sundered.

56. Then comes Lin's[12] second life sorrow,
    As Odin emerges to war with the wolf.
    The bane of Bele[13] flashes forth against Fire:
    There shall Frigga's hero fall.

57. Victory-father's son, Vidar the mighty,
    Comes forth to battle the beast of death.
    He plunges his sword from mouth to heart
    Of the Son of Completion. The Sire is avenged.

58. Approaches the shining scion of Earth:
    Odin's son meets with the wolf.
    In raging wrath he slays Midgárd's woe.
    Then do all men turn homeward.

59. Nine steps only away from the monster
    Staggers the son of Earth.
    The sun grows dim; earth sinks in the waters;
    The sparkling stars fall from the firmament.
    Fire entwines the Life-supporter;[14]
    Heat rises high to the heavens.

60. Garm howls at the Gnipa-hollow of Hel.
    What was fast loosens, and Freke runs free.

                    .   .   .

61. She sees rising another earth from the sea,
    Once more turning green.

---

12. Frigga, Odin's spouse.
13. The sword of Frey.
14. Yggdrasil, the Tree of Life.

Torrents tumble, eagle soars
From the mountains, seeking fish.

62. The Aesir met on the Ida sward
To judge of the mighty Soil-mulcher;[15]
There to recall their former feats
And the runes of Fimbultyr.[16]

63. There are found in the grass
The wondrous golden tablets;
Them in days of yore
The races had owned.

64. Harvests shall grow on unsown fields,
All ills be redressed, and Balder shall come.
With him Höder shall build on Ropt's sacred soil·
As gentle gods of the Chosen.
Know you as yet, or what?

65. Then Höner may freely seek his destiny,
Shake the divining rods, read the omens;
And the two brothers shall build their dwelling
In wide Windhome.
Know you as yet, or what?

66. She sees a hall more fair than the sun,
Gilded, glowing on Gimle.[17]
There shall the virtuous hosts abide
And joy in serenity during long ages.

67. Then comes the dragon of darkness flying,
Might from beneath,
From the mountains of night.
He soars o'er the fields in a featherguise.

---

15. Yggdrasil.   16. The "god of secret wisdom."
17. A superior shelf of existence, home of the new earth and sun.

Gylfaginning
(The Apotheosis of Gylfe[1])

TRANSLATOR'S NOTES

The title of this tale, Gylfaginning, is usually given as "The Mocking of Gylfe" for the verb *ginna* means to mock or to fool in Icelandic. This may, however, be another instance of semantic misunderstanding, like that which makes dwarfs into little people instead of unevolved souls. In Icelandic there is a noun *ginn* which has a very lofty meaning indeed. It is the word for the inexpressible divine principle, or essence, beyond the Aesir, beyond the Vaner, beyond all possible manifestation, however exalted. It corresponds most nearly to the Sanskrit *tat* which means simply "THAT" — an abstraction too sacred to be belittled by being named. It is the ONE — All-being — the self-existent void which is all-fullness, not to be comprehended by finite mind, and it is the concept expressed by the word Ginnungagap — "chasm of ginn."

The story then becomes self-consistent and may be interpreted. The Ásgárd of the tale has evidently been depicted as an earthly locality harboring advanced, though human, beings, yet it retains an air of remoteness and is situated in a hall so large that the roof can barely be seen. The juggler at the entrance to the hall may be supposed to represent a stage of proficiency in magic — an element which never fails to make an impression but which is given small importance here: the performer exhibits his marvels outside the precincts. He shows the visiting king into the sanctuary where three hierophants are enthroned. Their names, or lack of names, in themselves pose an interesting enigma, suggesting that while there

---

1. From the Younger Edda.

are differences in standing, there is no differentiation made in rank.

No sooner has the neophyte entered than the door closes behind him — a revealing detail and true to life. Thereupon he is treated to the long poem Hávamál which, as we shall see, is directed to three stages of spiritual growth.

Having obtained from the triad of divine kings all the wisdom he could receive from them, King Gylfe "returned to his country and told these tidings he had heard and seen," thus fulfilling the destiny of a true spiritual student-teacher.

Gylfaginning

King Gylfe was a wise and knowledgeable man. He wondered how the Ása-people were so knowing that all went according to their wishes. He considered that this was caused either by the people's own nature or was brought about by the gods to whom they sacrificed. He determined to find this out and prepared to travel to Ásgárd in all secrecy, disguised as an old man. But the Ása-people were wiser. They saw his journey before he came and caused him to be beset by illusions. When he arrived at the court he saw a hall so high that he could barely see the top of it. Its roof was covered with golden shields as other roofs might be with shingles.

At the entrance to the hall he saw a man juggling seven small swords at once. Gylfe was asked his name and gave it as Gángläre (wandering learner), said he had come by watery ways (by sea) and wished to find lodging here. He then asked whose hall it was. The juggler replied it belonged to the king, "and I shall take you to see him," he said, "so that you yourself can ask his name."

The man walked into the hall; Gylfe followed. At once the door closed behind him. He saw many rooms and many people, some at games, some at drink, others with weapons at swordplay.

He saw three high seats, one above the other, with three figures seated, one on each. He asked what names these chieftains had and his conductor replied that he who sat in the lowest high seat was a king named The High One; the one above him was named As High, and the uppermost was named Third.

The High One asked the stranger his errand; and at his disposal were food and drink as for all in the High One's hall.

Gylfe said he first wanted to know if there was any wise man to be found. The High One replied that he would not leave the place whole were he not the wiser, and initiated the interrogation:

> Step forward as you question.
> Seated shall be the respondent.

[Here follows the poem Hávamál, whereby the postulant is taught the ancient wisdom. The conclusion of *Gylfaginning* follows *Hávamál*. See next chapter.]

12

Hávamál

(The High One's Words)

The Song of the High One is something of an enigma. It has three quite distinct and very different styles, each with its internally consistent character. Scholars have been understandably perplexed by the incongruous juxtaposition of the parts of this lengthy poem.

The first and longest portion appears to be a book of elementary etiquette, a sort of rustic Emily Post. It lays down rules of propriety for social intercourse and for maintaining friendships; explains the duties of a host and of a guest at the festive board; outlines some simple home remedies for common ailments, prescribes appropriate drinking habits for maintaining a sane and reasonable outlook (and avoiding a hangover) and gives other pieces of mundane advice and practical wisdom worded to suit a semibarbaric people learning to adapt to community life.

The second division, formally introduced in verse 111, is directed to the dwarf Loddfáfner. Here the emphasis is on right and honorable action, on consideration for others and kindly conduct. Loddfáfner is clearly one step ahead of the populace who need directives for preserving the barest amenities, but he is still a dwarf because as a soul he has not yet developed his humanity to any marked extent. This section would have applicability to most of us and Loddfáfner may at this stage be regarded as Everyman. Gradually, by following the precepts of the god, the dwarf nature can evolve into full humanity. A soul that has awakened to some degree and is striving to improve its condition, Loddfáfner in the end is addressed as a pupil or disciple in the third and final section which is in a wholly different vein. Its symbolism defies analysis while it orients the inward eye to vistas of inexpressible grandeur. The brief, laconic verses hint at concepts so luminous and insights so vast they may well be the substance pondered by the elect in pursuit of divine wisdom.

Clearly the Song of the High One is intended for three very different audiences: the early part is for the public — a coarse-grained people, responsive only to the simplest advice applying to their daily pursuits; next, the plain ethics of any exoteric school or church, common practices for decent living. The third is the mystical evocation of the reaching soul in a disciple who has dedicated his life to serving the divine purpose; it is directed to those individuals who are capable of emulating the god's commitment and who lend their strength and determination to the divine labor of "raising the runes" (138) by Odin, the inner god of all.

The same three natural divisions may be discerned in any system of thought or religion. There are always large numbers who are uninspired and self-centered, content to make the most of their circumstances and enjoy life. They generally adhere to conventional norms, demanding and presenting an appearance of respectability. There is a second, fairly numerous group who enjoy speculating on the unseen causes of observed phenomena and who may dabble in a variety of superstitious practices. Among them are many who yearn for greater knowledge and recognize that the universe holds mysteries to be discovered, but they often lack the needed insight and perseverance which is achieved by self-discipline.

The third group has little popular appeal. It is composed of those who have penetrated the sanctuary of their soul and at first hand verified some measure of truth. These are the elect, the few who work for spiritual nature, indifferent to praise or blame, and without regard for their own ends, knowing that these are bound up with the larger, universal destiny. There is for them no pandering to personal satisfaction though, paradoxically, their altruism forms the backbone and stamina of the human evolutionary impulse for all mankind, the advancement of which must bring the greatest satisfaction of all.

It has always been necessary for teachers of wisdom to make a distinction among their followers: those who are irrevocably committed to the noble work of the gods receive a greater share of knowledge and, with it, a far more onerous responsibility. Jesus told his disciples this: "To you it is given to know the mystery of the kingdom of God: but to them that are without, all these things are done in parables" (Mark 4:11). Gautama, the Buddha, also had an esoteric school where worthy Arhats were given advanced instruction and training; so did Pythagoras and numerous other guides and spiritual preceptors through the ages.

The Song of the High One shows the different audiences to whom it is directed both by the manner of address and, even more, by its substance. The portion wherein the teacher is speaking to a general public ends with a parable which tells of Odin's former quest for wisdom. Verses 104–110 relate in somewhat obscure language how with the aid of the squirrel Rate (which can also mean a drill), Odin bored a hole in the giant's mountain and entered in the guise of a serpent. He persuaded the giant's daughter to give him a draught from the well of wisdom secreted there by the giant. Through the story are twined numerous symbols, each with several meanings — a typical example of the method used in myths to relate truths. Rate, the drill or rodent, like the squirrel in the Tree of Life, represents consciousness which gives access to the depths of the matter-world where Odin earns wisdom, as well as to the heights of its crown. Gunnlöd, the giant's daughter — unable to ascend to heights of divinity, was left behind in tears, though the "precious mead of Odraerir" — vessel of inspiration — was carried upward one step on the ladder of existence, raised to our own "earth's ancient shrine." The question is asked by the frost giants, whether the god had emerged victorious or been overcome by the giant Suttung (earth's previous imbodiment). Odin was able to give assurance that he had indeed returned unscathed to the realm of the gods.

Gunnlöd, "the good woman," personifies an age when, amid the mountainous materialism of her father — the greater cycle — at least a portion of it welcomed the deity and was able to supply a draught of wisdom. It is suggestive too that "Odraerir now has come up here to earth's ancient shrine" in view of the theosophic teaching that our planet (which furnishes the sacred mead) has itself progressed upward by one stage since its former imbodiment on an inferior, more material, shelf, and that what was then the astral model of the moon is our present, solidly physical, satellite. This implies of course that mankind has progressed upward by one stage. The "ancient shrine" refers to a still earlier phase, on the "downward arc" toward matter.

Among the early divine teachers of humankind are many who have left no trace of their passage; it would seem that Odin was one of this progression, for in *The Secret Doctrine* H. P. Blavatsky states that

> the day when much, if not all, of that which is given here from the archaic records, will be found correct, is not far distant. Then the modern symbologists will acquire the certitude that even Odin, . . . is one of these thirty-five Buddhas; one of the earliest, indeed, for the continent to which he and his race belonged, is also one of the earliest.
> — II, 423

Whether the final portion of Hávamál has been preserved since so great an antiquity or was reconstructed and dispensed in its present form by later teachers is impossible for us now to determine. We may recognize in these verses the very essence of esoteric cosmogony and feel a profound reverence and gratitude as we contemplate the divine sacrifice of the cosmic spirit inherent in the Tree of Life. This divine imbodiment takes place throughout any world's existence as conscious energy impels the world to be and energic consciousness absorbs its draught from the well of wisdom guarded by the giant Mimer, the matter of which the worlds are formed.

Verses 137–42 give a remarkably concise expression to some fundamental tenets of the ancient wisdom, and explain the periodicity of manifested life and the karmic action which on every level of existence leads from each event, word, and deed, to the next. The seventeenth *galder* (spell) relates also that these instructions are given under a seal of secrecy, while the final verse shows clearly why this must be so: it is not possible to grasp the meaning of the teachings unless the nature is sufficiently matured in understanding. They are "useful to children of men, but useless to sons of giants" (163): only the spiritual intelligence is capable of receiving the inner message; the temporal, uninspired, giant-nature is not, for it lacks the insight to discern it. For this reason very little is known of the Mystery schools of the ancient world — or for that matter of the modern — beyond the bare fact of their existence from very remote times. The knowledge they imparted *could not* be divulged to any unqualified person due not just to actual prohibition but, more effectively, to the need for a developed faculty of understanding; this comprehension (the word literally means embracing) within one's own sphere of sympathy and love must be naturally active before the deeper teachings could be received. It follows that to betray the Mysteries in any significant degree must be as impossible as to explain higher mathematics to a beetle. Nevertheless, a breach of faith is a serious defect in the offender and adds to the adverse karma of the race. Still, as much as may be understood is "brought back" by the enlightened sage and shared with those who are able to profit by what he has to give. King Gylfe as Gánglāre performed this task, relating the things he had learned, which subsequently were passed on from one to another.*

It will be noted that, like other mystical poems, Hávamál in part assumes the form of a love song, reminiscent of the Rubaiyat or the Song of Solomon, perhaps because this form is the nearest expression man can devise for the poignant ecstasy of union with the divine self, the inner god, as there exists nothing comparable in material experience. The full and intimate expansion of human consciousness belongs naturally only to those whose entire nature is subject to, and mirrors the god within, that is, to the One-harriers of Odin, named thus because of being in total control of "one" — their own personal ego.

---

*Conclusion of Gylfaginning, p. 130.

Hávamál

1. Scrutinize an entrance before passing through;
   Uncertain it is where foes may be seated.

2. Hail, generous ones! A guest has arrived. Show
   him a seat.
   He has haste who must prove himself at the fire.

3. Warmth is needed by one who comes in from the
   cold;
   Food and drink needs the man who comes in from
   the mountains.

4. Water needs he who comes to his host, a towel and
   greeting;
   A kindly reception for one who seeks words and
   a friendly hearing.

5. Wit needs the wanderer in foreign lands. At home
   all is easy.
   Boast not your deeds among those who are wise.

6. Display not your cleverness; have a care; the wise
   man is silent
   On another's ground, and arouses no anger. Better
   friend has no man than good sense.

7. The wary guest at the feast keeps silent when there
   is whispering;
   He heeds with his ears, seeks with his eyes; so the
   wise man observes.

8. Happy the man who gains honor and esteem;
   But uncertain the gain borne in another's breast.

9. Happy is he who has himself honor and wisdom
   in living;
   Others' advice is often bad counsel.

10. No better burden can a man bear than good sense
    and manners;
    Better than gold it serves, a strong support in need.

11. No better burden can a man bear than good sense
    and manners;
    And no worse provender is borne than an excess
    of ale.

12. Ale is not so good as they say for the race of men;
    The more a man drinks the less he knows how to
    keep his wits about him.

13. In raving delirium is one who noises in his cups; it
    steals his senses;
    By that bird's feathers was I fettered in Gunnlöd's
    court.

14. Drunk was I, senseless drunk, in the hall of peaceful
    Fjalar;
    Best is that ale feast when each goes home retaining
    sense and reason.

15. Agreeable and cheerful shall be a son of man, and
    valiant in battle;
    Gay and friendly a man shall be as he awaits his bane.

16. A coward thinks he may live forever if he avoids
    the fight;
    Yet old age will not spare him, though he be spared
    by spears.

17. A fool at a feast sits staring and mumbling to
        himself;
    But if he takes a drink his mind stands stark revealed.

18. He who is well traveled
    Expresses each thought well.

19. Keep not the tankard long,[1] drink moderately,
        speak sense or hold your peace;
    None will hold you uncivil if you retire early to bed.

20. A greedy man without manners will make himself
        ill;
    A boor's stomach becomes the butt of jokes in clever
        company.

21. Cattle know when to leave the pasture and go home;
    But a fool knows not the measure of his stomach.

22. The wretch of mean disposition derides everything;
    He knows not, as he should, that he lacks not faults
        himself.

23. A fool lies awake nights worrying over many things;
    Feeble is he when morning breaks, and matters are
        still as before.

24. The fool believes all who smile at him are his friends;
    He knows not how they speak about him.

25. The fool believes all who smile at him are his friends;
    He finds out only in court, when few will speak
        for him.

26. A fool thinks himself all-wise in a sheltered corner;
    He knows not what to say when tested by strong
        men.

---

1. The tankard was often a cow's or ram's horn, and it was passed round
the table from one to another. Such a horn could not be put down until empty.

27. A fool among the elders should hold his peace;
    No one knows how little he understands if he keeps
        silent.

28. He seems wise who makes questions and answers;
    But no fault on earth can be hidden.

29. He who speaks much says ill-chosen words;
    A tongue unreined speaks its own undoing.

30. Mock not another who comes among your kin;
    Many feel wise on their own mountain.

31. He thinks himself smart when leaving, the guest
        who has mocked another;
    Who pokes fun at table sees not the anger around
        him.

32. Often friends will bicker and tease at the board;
    This may rouse contention of guest against guest.

33. One should eat each meal at due time and not go
        hungry as guest;
    Else he may sit choking, with no question to ask.

34. It's a long detour to a faithless friend, though he
        live by the road;
    But to a good friend, however distant, there are
        many shortcuts.

35. A guest shall leave betimes and not stay too long;
    Pleasure palls if he lingers too long at another's
        board.

36. Better your own home where each is his own master;
    Two goats and a thatch are better than begging
        abroad.

37. Better your own home where each is his own master;
    The heart bleeds in one who must beg for his food
        at each meal.

38. Weapons should never be left more than a step away
    on the field;
    Uncertain it is how soon a man may have need of
    his spear.

39. I saw none so lavish that he declined what was
    offered;
    Nor any so generous that wage was unwanted when
    earned.

40. He who has money does not suffer need;
    But saving is a virtue that can be carried to a fault.

41. With weapons and garments friends please one
    another;
    Gifts to and fro help a friendship endure.

42. To a friend be a friend and give gift for gift;
    Jest should be taken with jest, wile with wile.

43. To a friend be a friend, both to him and his friend;
    But to enemy's friend, be not bound by friendship.

44. If you know a friend, believe in him and desire his
    goodwill,
    Go share his tastes, and gifts exchange; go often
    seek him out.

45. If you know one who evil thinks but you desire his
    goodwill,
    Speak him fair though you falsely feel; repay lies
    with cunning.

46. This also applies to one you distrust, whose mind
    is uncertain;
    Meet him with smiles, choose your words well;
    repay gifts in kind.

47. When I was young I traveled alone and wandered
    away from the road;
    I thought myself rich when I met with a man, for
    a man is good company.

48. Noble, courageous men live best; they seldom
    harbor sorrow.
    A foolish man fears many things and begrudges
    every gift.

49. I gave of my clothes to two wooden men in a field;
    They felt in fine fettle, robed in rags; naked, a man
    suffers shame.

50. The fir tree withers on a dry knoll without shelter
    of bark or needles;
    So too does a man whom no one loves; why should
    he live for long?

51. Hotter than fire may be the love of a peaceful man
    for his faithless friend
    For five days; but on the sixth his friendship dies.

52. Not much it takes to give a man, oft praise is bought
    with little;
    With half a bread, a draught from the stein, I won
    a faithful comrade.

53. Small piles of sand and tiny streams, small are the
    minds of men;
    All are not equally strong in wisdom; each age is of
    two kinds.

54. Wise in moderation should each one be — not
    overwise;
    Life smiles the fairest on him who well knows what
    he knows.

55. Wise in moderation should each one be — not overwise;
For a wise man's heart loses gladness if he thinks himself all-wise.

56. Wise in moderation should each one be — not overwise;
His fate beforehand no one knows; the soul is thus carefree.

57. Fire is lit by fire till it dies, and flame is lit by flame;
Man knows man by his speech, the speechless by his silence.

58. Early to rise is one who seeks another's life or possessions;
The sleeping wolf rarely gets a bone or a sleeping man victory.

59. Early to rise is one who has few laborers and himself goes to work;
Much is neglected by one who sleeps late; the prompt is half rich.

60. Of kindling and roofbark a man knows the measure;
Likewise of firewood how much suffices for a whole or half a season.

61. Clean and fed shall he ride to the Ting,[2] even though poorly clad;
None need feel shame over patches on shoes nor over inferior mount.

62. Question and answer were made with forethought by one who would be called wise;

---

2. Ting, or Thing, the governing assembly — parliament — in which all must participate.

Take one only into your confidence; what three
know the world knows.

63. He studies and stares when he wanders the wave,
an ern on the ancient sea;
So too does the man who comes into a crowd where
few will speak for him.

64. A wise man keeps within proper bounds his right
and authority;
In concourse of warriors he will find none the most
valiant.

65. For every word he speaks
A man will pay in kind.

66. To many a place I came too soon, to others much
too late;
The ale was drunk, or not yet brewed; ill guest
comes ill-timed.

67. In some places I would have been invited if I needed
no food;
If two hams hung at my friend's where I had just
eaten.

68. Among children of men, fire is the best and the
shining sun,
If man may have the gift of health, and live without
vice.

69. No man is unhappy in all things though his health
be poor: one is blessed with sons,
Another with friends, a third with full barns,
a fourth with good deeds.

70. Better to live and live happy; a good man can get
a cow;
I saw the fire die out in a rich man's house; death
stood at the door.

71. A lame man can ride; a handless herd cattle, a deaf
    may be a fine warrior;
    Better blind than burn on the pyre; no one needs
    a corpse.

72. A son is better even though born late when his
    father's life is ended;
    Memorials are seldom raised unless by kin.

73. The two are companions-in-arms, but the tongue
    is the bane of the head;
    Beneath each fur I expect a fist.

74. One night may you trust to your provender but
    short are ship's biscuits, and quickly changes
    an autumn night;
    The weather shifts much in the course of five days,
    much more in a month.

75. He knows not who little knows that many are fools
    to others;
    One may be rich, another poor. No blame attaches
    to this.

76. Cattle die; kinsmen die; you likewise must die;
    But the voice of honor never dies for him who has
    earned a good name.

77. Cattle die; kinsmen die; you must likewise die;
    One thing I know that never dies: a dead man's
    reputation.

78. Full sheepfolds I saw at the rich man's sons; they
    now bear the beggar's staff;
    Riches are like the wink of an eye, the most fickle
    of friends.

79. When a fool gains goods or a woman's favor, his
    pride grows but not his sense;
    He walks in a fool's blindness.

80. This then is known: when you ask for runes known
    but to the ruling powers;
    About those that were scribed by the bard of secret
    wisdom he had better be silent.

81. Day may be praised by night, a woman on her pyre,
    sword's edge when tested;
    Maiden when wed, ice when the crossing is over,
    ale when it has been drunk.

82. Trees should be felled when the wind blows, sail
    when the breeze is fair;
    In darkness dally with maiden, for many eyes see
    by day;
    You need speed from a ship, protection from a shield,
    blows from a blade, kiss from a maid.

83. By fire drink ale, on ice score with skates, buy a
    horse when it's lean, and a blade when it's rusty.
    The horse you fatten and the hound you train.

84. Trust not a maid's words, nor a wife's,
    For on a whirling wheel were born their hearts and
    fickleness fixed in their breast.

85. Trust not breaking bow, flaring flame, gaping wolf,
    carping crow,
    Bellowing boar, rootless willow, waxing wave,
    bubbling caldron.

86. Airborn arrow, breaking wave, night-old ice, coiled
    snake,
    Bride's words in bed, broken sword or playful bear,
    nor the children of a king;

87. Sick calf, stubborn thrall, sibyl's fair words, newly
    killed whale,[3]
    Such may no man trust to appearances.

---

3. Walrus?

88. Depend not on a new-sown field, nor too soon on
    a son;
    Nor on a brother's bane, even on a wide road;

89. Nor on a house half burnt, a horse swift as the wind
    (he would be useless with a broken leg);
    No man is so confident he trusts in these.

90. So is the love of women, fickle ones, like riding on
    slippery ice with uncleated horse,
    A lively two-year-old, ill trained, or rudderless
    sailing in violent storm, or like a lame man's
    reindeer chase on bare slippery rock.

91. Openly I declare, for I know both, how treacherous
    is man's mind toward women;
    When we speak most fair we think most false;
    this traps even the cunning.

92. You shall speak fair and offer gifts if you desire
    maid's love;
    Devote praise to the fair one's beauty, a young
    wooer shall get his wish.

93. For his love shall no man blame another!
    Often a wise man, not a fool, is beguiled by a pretty
    face.

94. Nor shall one man censure another for what befalls
    many a man;
    A sage is often made a fool by overwhelming desire.

95. Mind only knows what lies near the heart, it alone
    sees the depth of the soul;
    No worse ill assails the wise than to live without
    inner peace.

96. This I learned, crouched in the reeds, waiting for
    my love,
    My body and my soul seemed wise to me. Yet I
    have her not.

97. Billing's maid[4] was found by me, white as the sun,
    asleep;
    All princely joy seemed naught to me beside life
    with her beauty.

98. "Toward evening, Odin, shall you come, if you
    would win the maid;
    It would be unfitting if we alone knew not of this."

99. Back I ran and deemed myself lucky, went to learn
    the wise one's wish;
    I had hoped to have her tenderness and joy.

100. When I returned all the gallant warrior band was
    awake;
    With blazing torches and high borne lights, the
    road was perilous to me.

101. I returned in the morning, the watchers were asleep;
    I found a dog bound by the holy woman's bed.

102. Many a sweet maid, if you seek, is unfaithful;
    This I learned when the clever maiden I had hoped
    to lure with wile made a mockery of me; I
    gained not the lovely wife.

103. A man glad in his home, gay among guests, shall
    always take a wise stand;
    Of good memory and easy speech, if he would be
    wise and speak sagely;
    An idiot has naught to say, this is the sign of a fool.

---

4. Billing's maiden: the white snow-covered earth, also named Rind.

104. I sought the old giant, now am I returned; little did I there gain by silence;
    Many words won me success in Suttung's halls.

105. Gunnlöd on the golden throne gave me a draught of the precious mead;
    Ill did I repay her for her pains.

106. Rate's mouth made room for me, gnawed through the rock;
    Over and under me ran giants' roads. Great was my peril.

107. A well-earned draught I enjoyed; the wise lack little;
    Odraerir now has come up here to earth's ancient shrine.

108. I doubt I had even yet escaped from the giants' dwelling
    Had I not Gunnlöd, the good woman, held in my arms.

109. The following day, frost giants went to hear Odin's counsel in the High Hall;
    They asked after Bölverk,
    Whether he had begged his freedom, or been vanquished by Suttung.
    Odin, I mind, gave oath on a ring that he had overcome.

110. How may his troth be trusted?
    Suttung bereft of his mead, Gunnlöd in tears!

                .   .   .

111. It is time to speak
    From the speaker's chair
    By the well of Urd;
    I saw and kept silent,
    I watched and I thought,

I listened to what was said;
I heard runes discussed,
There was no lack of knowledge
In the High Hall.
In the High Hall
I heard it said.

112. I tell you, Loddfáfner, heed you the counsel:
You will gain if you keep it, benefit if you follow it.
Do not rise in the night unless something occurs
Or you must visit the outhouse!

113. I tell you, Loddfáfner, obey you the counsel:
Do not sleep locked in the limbs of a sorceress;
She can contrive that you do not go to the Ting
or assembly;
Food will not please you, nor human company; you
will go sadly to sleep.

114. I tell you, Loddfáfner, heed you the counsel:
Never lure another's wife with soft words.

115. I tell you, Loddfáfner, heed you the counsel:
If you expect danger on mountain or fjord, supply
yourself well with provisions.

116. I tell you, Loddfáfner, obey you the counsel:
Let no evil man see your misfortunes; from a man
of ill will you receive no thanks for your trust.

117. I saw a man hurt by a treacherous woman's words;
Her poisonous tongue wounded him to death and
without truth.

118. I tell you, Loddfáfner, heed you the counsel:
If you know a friend you trust, go often seek him
out;
Brambles and grass grow high on untrodden paths.

119. I tell you, Loddfáfner, heed you the counsel:
Attract good-natured men to you with happy runes,
sing songs of joy while you live.

120. I tell you, Loddfáfner, heed you the counsel:
Be not quick to break the bond of love for your
friend;
Sorrow will rend the heart
If you dare not tell another your whole mind.

121. I tell you, Loddfáfner, heed you the counsel:
Exchange not words with a fool,

122. For from ill-minded man you will have no good
return,
But a noble man may honor you with his nobility.

123. A friendship is firm when each can speak his mind
to the other;
All is better than broken bonds; no friend is he
who flatters.

124. I tell you, Loddfáfner, heed you the counsel:
Waste not three words in quarrel with a villain:
Oft the better man cedes
While the worse deals blows.

125. I tell you, Loddfáfner, heed you the counsel:
Make your own shoes and the shaft of your spear.
A shoe may be ill formed, a spear may be warped
If the maker wills you ill.

126. I tell you, Loddfáfner, heed you the counsel:
When you meet anger take it as meant for you;
Give your foe no peace.

127. I tell you, Loddfáfner, heed you the counsel:
Never rejoice over evil revealed, but always rejoice
over good.

128. I tell you, Loddfáfner, heed you the counsel:
     Gaze not in the air during battle — humans may
          walk like boars —
     Lest you lose your wits.

129. I tell you, Loddfáfner, heed you the counsel:
     If you wish to bind a good woman in wedlock and
          win her favor,
     You must promise handsomely and keep your word;
     None wearies of a good gift.

130. I tell you, Loddfáfner, heed you the counsel:
     I bid you be wary; be most careful with ale,
     With other man's wife and, third,
     Be on guard against thieves.

131. I tell you, Loddfáfner, heed you the counsel:
     Never mock a wandering man or a guest.

132. They who are seated often know not what manner
          of man enters;
     None is so good he lacks all fault, none so wretched
          he lacks all virtue.

133. I tell you, Loddfáfner, heed you the counsel:
     Smile not at the graying storyteller;
     Often is good what the old ones sing;
     Wrinkled lips may speak choice words
     From him whose head droops, whose skin sags, and
          who limps between canes.

134. I tell you, Loddfáfner, heed you the counsel:
     Abuse no guest nor turn any away; the poor do you
          well receive.

135. It takes a strong hinge to keep the door open to all;
     Yet give of your alms lest one wish you ill.

136. I tell you, Loddfáfner, heed you the counsel:
When you drink ale, seek the aid of earth's force,
Because earth counteracts it, as fire does disease;
Oak is a laxative, grains against sorcery,
The home against bickering, the moon against hate,
Biting helps snakebite, runes against ill designs,
Field of dirt makes flood abate.

        .   .   .

137. I know that I hung in the windtorn tree
Nine whole nights, spear-pierced,
Consecrated to Odin, myself to my Self above me
    in the tree,
Whose root no one knows whence it sprang.

138. None brought me bread, none served me drink;
I searched the depths, spied runes of wisdom;
Raised them with song, and fell once more thence.

139. Nine powerful chants I learned
From the wise son of Böltorn, Bestla's father;
A draught I drank of precious mead
Ladled from Odraerir.[5]

140. I began to thrive, to grow wise,
To grow greater, and enjoy;
For me words led from words to new words;
For me deeds led from deeds to new deeds.

141. Runes shall you know and rightly read staves,
Very great staves, powerful staves,

---

5. Böltorn is apparently the Trudgälmer, sustaining life force, of a previous cycle of life; Bestla is sister of Bärgälmer, wife of Bur, and is the female counterpart of the karmic seeds of the previous life and of the initial impetus of the present one; Odraerir is the well of Mimer, source of the wisdom sought by the gods in manifestation.

Drawn by the mighty one who speaks,
Made by wise Vaner, carved by the highest rulers.

142. Odin among Aesir, Dvalin[6] among elves,
Dáin[7] among dwarfs,
Allvitter[8] among giants.
I myself have also carved some.

143. Know you how to write?
Know you how to interpret?
Know you how to understand?
Know you how to test?
Know you how to pray?
Know you how to sacrifice?
Know you how to transmit?
Know you how to atone?

144. Better not to pray than to sacrifice in excess,
gift always tends to return.
Better send naught than waste too much.
Thus wrote Tund[9] for the passage of years,
Where he arose,
Where he came again.

145. I know songs unknown to the wife of the king
or to any son of man;
Aid is one, and it can help you
In sadness and sorrow and difficult trouble.

146. A second I know that should be known
By those who would be healers.

147. A third I know, if need be,
That can fetter any foe.
I can dull their blades so that sword
Or deceit cannot harm.

---

6. Sleeper.   7. Dead.   8. Allknowing.   9. A cycle of time.

148. A fourth I know: if warriors place links of chain on
       my limbs;
     I can sing a charm that will make me free.
     Fetters fall from my feet and the hasp from my hands.

149. A fifth I know: if I see hurled
     Arrows hard at my horde;
     Though rapid their flight I arrest them in air
     If I see them clearly.

150. A sixth song I sing: if a man does me harm
     With the roots of wild weeds,
     Or a Hel-man hates me, he brings harm to himself,
     Not to me.

151. The seventh I sing: if a fearsome fire
     Flames in the hall where the warriors sit;
     So broad burns he not that I cannot quench him;
     This charm is one I can chant.

152. The eighth I sing is for every one
     The most fortunate lore he can learn:
     When hatred is harbored by children of chiefs,
     This I can hastily heal.

153. The ninth that I know, if need there should be
     To save my boat on the billow,
     The wind I can lay to rest on the wave,
     And still the stormiest sea.

154. A tenth I am able, when witches do ride
     High aloft in the air;
     I can lead them astray, out of their forms,
     Out of their minds.

155. Eleventh I can, if forth into war,
     Old friends into battle I lead:
     I sing below shields so that they draw with force

Whole into the fight,
Whole out of the fight,
Whole wheresoever they go.

156. Twelfth I am able, if I see a tree
With a hanged man hovering high,
I can carve and draw runes, so that he that is hanged,
Hastens to speak to me.

157. Thirteenth I know, if they wish me to sluice
With water a citizen's son,
He shall not fall, though outnumbered he be,
He shall not fall by a sword.

158. Fourteenth I can name to the warriors' horde
The names of beneficent gods;
The Aesir and elves, I can all distinguish
As an unwise man cannot.

159. Fifteenth I know what the Setter-in-motion
Sang at the doors of Dawn;
He sang power to Aesir, progress to elves,
Mind-force to the god of the gods.

160. Sixteenth I can chant, if I desire
The wise maid's joy and favor,
The white-armed woman's love I can win,
And turn her mind to me.

161. Seventeenth I sing that not soon may be parted
From me the beloved maid.
For a long, long time shall you, Loddfáfner,
Be lacking these lays.
It were good that you keep them concealed,
You are fortunate to learn them,
It were useful to heed them well.

162. The eighteenth I sing as I never have sung
     To a maid, or to any man's mate.
     All that is best is known only to One,
     She who embraced me as a sister.
     This is the end of the song.

163. Now is sung the High One's song in the High One's
     Hall:
     Useful to children of men; useless to sons of giants.
     Hail Him who sang! Hail Him who knows!
     Happy is he who receives it!

(Conclusion of Gylfaginning)

[King Gylfe, calling himself Gángläre, heard all these things.]

At length the High One spoke: "If you can ask still further, I know not whence you find the questions, for I never heard further forward the destinies of ages told. Enjoy therefore what you have learned."

Gángläre then heard a powerful thunder from all sides and looked out through the door; and as he looked about him he found himself on a level plain with no court or hall in sight.

So he returned to his country and told these tidings he had heard and seen. And after him, these sayings were passed on from one to another.

13

Vaftrudnismál

(*The Lay of Illusion*)

This is one of several lays and stories that treat of the illusory nature of the worlds of matter wherein consciousness is deceived. Vaftrudnir means "he who enwraps in riddles." It is a theme which recognizes the fallibility of our sense perceptions. Hindu scriptures also emphasize the deceptive nature of matter. In Sanskrit, illusion is called *māyā*, a word derived from *mā*, which means to measure, hence it refers to anything that is limited, that can be measured, however large or small. This applies to both space and time and to all things existing in space-time. Only infinite space in eternal duration, beginningless, endless, boundless, and unimaginable, can in truth be called Reality. The seeming duality of space-time is itself illusory — an inescapable phenomenon pertaining to finite existence however vast in scope and however much we try to reach beyond it in consciousness.

It is important to realize that illusion does not mean nonexistence. Illusion exists; illusory things exist; we are surrounded by illusions and in fact are very much a part of the illusory universe. So accustomed are we to taking certain fallacies for reality that we are hardly aware of them. For instance, science tells us that matter is mostly holes — minute particles moving rapidly in proportionately large volumes of seemingly empty space. Our senses disagree with this knowledge as a stubbed toe will readily confirm, yet we do not doubt the structure of matter built of atoms we have never seen. We see a beautiful sunset and watch the redgold globe of light disappear beneath the horizon, though we are aware it had already disappeared eight minutes earlier because the light we see took eight minutes to reach us across some 93 million miles of space. We see a red flower because it absorbs *all but* the red rays of light; what we see are the colors the petals have rejected. We also perceive things differently one from another. Since the senses report to the mind and feelings of a personality, their report is largely dependent on the attitudes, moods, understanding, and predisposing experience of the individual. Because of our differences in outlook, someone who knows more than we do — a specialist in any field unfamiliar to us — appears to perform feats of magic.

Nonetheless truth must exist: the universe exists, hence knowledge about it also exists. In the Lay of Illusion, the god-self, Odin, the searching, probing consciousness, enters worlds of matter, descending through cosmic shelves of substantial existence to face the giant Vaftrudnir and "see how his hall is furnished," for it is by traversing spheres of matter that divine consciousness gains the mead of wisdom which nourishes the gods. But Odin refuses to settle on the bench in the hall of Illusion. Consciousness is not at home in this sphere.

During the first half of the tale (11–19) it is Vaftrudnir who questions the god: matter is being informed, inspirited, is growing and learning from the entering consciousness who here calls himself Gagnrád (gainful counsel). In the latter portion it is Odin who learns, questioning the giant until at the final dénouement the visitor reveals himself as Allfather. This is essentially the course of events related in many scriptures: first, the spiritual giving its energies and impulses to the material, organizing and building forms for its habitation and imbodying in them. Thereafter it is matter which is drawn inward, as it were, lending substance to the growing, perfecting, and enlarging of spiritual nature. Thus the two sides of existence are forever related and paired, with the tendency being first one way, then the other. The consciousness which has entered the realm of the giant, even though it may temporarily be captivated by the webs of illusion, will, as Vaftrudnir says of Njörd, "in the fullness of ages . . . return home with the wisdom of woe" (39). So shall we all.

Vaftrudnir is taught, and we are reminded, that the grounds of the gods and those of the giants are separated only by the everflowing stream called Doubt, whereon no ice-bridge can ever form; also that the eternal battlefield (life), where the destructive and the beneficent forces do battle in man and nature, exists for that very purpose. The god is here indicating the course of evolution of beings whereby the matter-side of existence can earn access to the "ground of the beneficent gods."

Thereafter the giant world cedes its wisdom as Odin elicits the story of the past creation from his host. Verse 23 gives Mundilföre as the parent of sun and moon and indicates their use as a measure of years. Mundilföre is the "lever," or axis, that rotates the galactic sphere, the central power that imparts motion to our Milky Way. The next response, in verse 25, speaks not only of the terrestrial day and night but also of the moon's phases, which are named also in Völuspá. It is a small hint, but we may surmise without undue temerity that the bards possessed some knowledge of astronomy and of seasonal events sufficiently important to be included in the time capsule of the myths. Verse 42 is remarkably revealing when we consider that this is the giant responding: the matter of nine worlds is he, stemming from the "hells below Niflhel" — the rootless root of matter.

In contrast with this, the spiritual human element "Life and Survivor . . . lie concealed in the memory hoard of the sun" during the long Fimbulvetr, the cold winter of inactivity when life is gone with the gods (44) from our ecosystem. They will be fed morning dew and bring to birth the ages to come. Here again we see a new life following the death of the present system of worlds. Those who are now Aesir will be succeeded by their offspring, a new Thor and a new Odin (in his son Vidar), who will "avenge the death" of the Father of Ages.

At last Odin reveals his identity by asking the unanswerable question — unanswerable by anyone but the deity himself: What had Odin whispered in the dead sun-god's ear? Well may we wonder what secret was perpetuated beyond the realm of death by the Allfather of past and future worlds.

Vaftrudnismál

1. ODIN: Advise me, Frigg, as I wish to journey
Vaftrudnir, the riddler,[1] to seek in his hall!
I crave to sound the ancient wisdom
Of him, the all-wise titan.

2. FRIGG: At home would I rather see Hostfather
tarry,
In the courts of the gods;
For no other giant I know has the equal
Of Vaftrudnir's power.

3. ODIN: Much have I traveled, much have I tested;
Much from the various powers I learned.
Now I will study in Vaftrudnir's hall
How that one is furnished.

4. FRIGG: Fortune go with you, and then, in
returning,
May happiness be on the roads that
you take!
Nor fail you your wits, oh, Father of Ages,
When you Vaftrudnir engage in debate.

5. *Hence journeyed Odin to probe by a discourse*
The wisdom and wit of the all-knowing titan:
Arrived at the hall of the father of Im,
Forthwith the Thinker entered therein.

---

1. Vaftrudnir: weaver of the webs of illusion.

6. ODIN:

Hail thee, Vaftrudnir, here am I come
In your own hall to see you.
First would I know if it's wise you are
Or all-knowing, giant?

7. VAFTRUDNIR:

Who is this man, who in my hall
Hurls such words at me?
Never shall you leave this place
If you are not the wiser.

8. ODIN:

Gagnrád[2] is my name. I am come on foot
And athirst to your hall;
I have wandered afar and need a welcome
And your hospitality, giant.

9. VAFTRUDNIR:

Why stand you, then, Gagnrád, and speak
    from the floor?
Step forward and sit in the hall.
Then shall we measure whether the
    stranger
Or this old bard is more knowing.

10. GAGNRÁD:

A poor man who comes to a rich man's
    house
Should be silent or wisely speak;
Idle talk serves him ill
Who comes to a cold-ribbed[3] host.

11. VAFTRUDNIR:

Tell me then, Gagnrád, as you from
    the floor
Will try your success:
What name has that steed that draws each
    day
Over the sons of the ages?

---

2. Gainful counsel.   3. Cunning.

12. GAGNRÁD: Brightmane is he; the rose-colored one
               Draws the day over the sons of ages;
               Held the most excellent steed by the
                    people;
               His mane ever radiates sunlight.

13. VAFTRUDNIR: Tell me, then, Gagnrád, as you from the
                    floor
                Will try your success:
                What name has that steed that draws from
                    the east
                The night over useful powers?

14. GAGNRÁD: Frostmane is the steed that draws in space
               Each night over useful powers;
               Each morning the froth falls from his bridle:
               Thence drops the dew in the dells.

15. VAFTRUDNIR: Tell me Gagnrád, as you from the floor
                Will try your success:
                What name has that stream that is shared
                    and divides
                The grounds of the gods and the titans?

16. GAGNRÁD: Doubt is the stream that is shared and
                    divides
               The grounds of the gods and the titans;
               He shall run free and open forever;
               No ice ever forms on that river.

17. VAFTRUDNIR: Tell me, then, Gagnrád, as you from the
                    floor
                Will try your success:
                What name has that plain where the battle
                    is fought
                Between Surt and the beneficent gods?

18. GAGNRÁD: Vigrid is the plain where the battle is fought
                Between Surt and the beneficent gods.
                One hundred days' journey on every side,
                That plain is created for them.

19. VAFTRUDNIR: Wise are you, guest. Go to the bench
                  And let us speak, seated together.
                  Our heads we shall wager here in the hall
                  On our wisdom and wit, Guest.

                  CAPITULUM

20. GAGNRÁD: Tell me first, if your wit suffices,
                And, Vaftrudnir, if you know it:
                Whence came the earth or the heaven
                    above it,
                First, thou knowing giant?

21. VAFTRUDNIR: Of Ymer's flesh was the earth formed,
                  The mountains were built of his bones;
                  Of the frost-cold giant's brainpan heaven,
                  And the billowing seas of his blood.

22. GAGNRÁD: Tell me second, if your wit suffices,
                And, Vaftrudnir, if you know it:
                Whence came the moon that over men
                    wanders,
                Or likewise the sun?

23. VAFTRUDNIR: Mundilföre is father of moon
                  And equally so of the sun;
                  Both are borne across heaven each day
                  To measure the years for man.

24. GAGNRÁD: Tell me thirdly, as you are called knowing,
                Vaftrudnir, if you know it:

Whence comes the day that moves
over men
And the night with its dark of waning?

25. VAFTRUDNIR: Dawn it is that fathers the Day,
While Night is the daughter of Dusk.
Waxing and Waning the useful powers
Made for man's measure of ages.

26. GAGNRÁD: Tell me fourthly, as you are named forewise,
Vaftrudnir, if you know it:
Whence came the winter or the warm
summer
First to the forewise powers?

27. VAFTRUDNIR: Windcool is named the father of Winter
But Mild is the summer's sire;[4]

28. GAGNRÁD: Tell me fifthly, as you are named pastwise,
Vaftrudnir, if you know it:
Who first of the Aesir's or Ymer's kin
Arose in the times of old?

29. VAFTRUDNIR: Unnumbered winters ere earth was formed
Was Bärgälmer born;
His father, it's said, was Trudgälmer;
Örgälmer his father's sire.

30. GAGNRÁD: Tell me sixthly, as you are named knowing,
Vaftrudnir, if you know it:
Whence came Örgälmer first among
giant-sons
In the dawn of time, wise giant?

31. VAFTRUDNIR: From Elivágor[5] sprang drops of venom,
Until they became a giant;[6]

---

4. The rest of the verse is missing in Codex Regius.   5. Icicle waves.
6. The rest of the verse is missing in Codex Regius.

32. GAGNRÁD: Tell me seventhly, as you are named skillful,
Vaftrudnir, if you know it:
How begat offspring the bold giant,
As he had known no giantess?

33. VAFTRUDNIR: By degrees from the word of the frostgiant
grew
Man and maid together;
Foot mated with foot and bore to the giant
A many-headed son.

34. GAGNRÁD: Tell me eighthly, as you are named pastwise,
Vaftrudnir, if you know it:
What is the first you remember or earliest
know,
Thou all-wise giant?

35. VAFTRUDNIR: Unnumbered winters ere earth was formed,
Bärgälmer was born;
The first I remember, the forewise giant
Was laid in the flour-bin.[7]

36. GAGNRÁD: Tell me ninthly, as you are called clever,
Vaftrudnir, if you know it:
Whence comes the wind that wafts on the
wave,
Though himself unseen?

37. VAFTRUDNIR: Räsvälg is perched at the end of the heavens,
A giant in eagle guise;
From his wings are wafted the wandering
winds
That howl o'er the human host.

38. GAGNRÁD: Tell me tenthly, as the gods' fates thou
knowest,
Vaftrudnir, to the full:

---

7. Mill: dissolver and creator of matter.

Whence came Njörd to the Ása-sons? He reigns over courts
And sanctuaries, begotten of Ása-stock.

39. VAFTRUDNIR: In the home of the Vaner wise powers created
And sent him as hostage to the gods;
In the fullness of ages he shall return
Home with the wisdom of woe.

40. GAGNRÁD: Tell me eleventhly, where the heroes
Each day slay one another:

VAFTRUDNIR: They select the Chosen, ride from the battle,
Then sit reconciled together.

41. GAGNRÁD: Tell me twelfthly, Vaftrudnir, how the endless reach
You know of the gods' destiny.
Of eons' runes and of the gods'
You say what is truest, allwise giant.

42. VAFTRUDNIR: Of giants' runes as well as of gods'
The truth I tell;
For I have come into nine worlds, from hells below
Deepest Niflhel.

43. GAGNRÁD: Much have I traveled, much have I tested,
Much from the various powers I learned:
What humans live when for man has expired
The dread Fimbul-winter?

44. VAFTRUDNIR: Life and Survivor, but they lie concealed
In the memory-hoard of the sun.
Morning dew is their food, and from them will be born
Ages to come.

45. GAGNRÁD:	Much have I traveled, much have I tested, Much from the various powers I learned: Whence will come the sun on a trackless sky When Fenris has overtaken this one?
46. VAFTRUDNIR:	One daughter only the Elf-wheel bears Before Fenris o'ertakes her; The radiant maid shall ride her mother's roads When the gods are gone.
47. GAGNRÁD:	Much have I traveled, much have I tested, Much from the various powers I learned: Who are the maids who, o'er watery waste Unerringly find the way?
48. VAFTRUDNIR:	Three mighty rivers flow through the lands Of the maids of the son-in-law seeker:[8] They are hamingjor in their own right Though they were fostered by giants.
49. GAGNRÁD:	Much have I traveled, much have I tested, Much from the various powers I learned: Which of the Aesir remain as gods When the flames of Surt have subsided?
50. VAFTRUDNIR:	Vidar and Vale shall dwell in the shrines of the gods When the flames of Surt have subsided. Mode and Magne shall then have Mjölnir And do Vingner's[9] work.
51. GAGNRÁD:	Much have I traveled, much have I tested, Much from the various powers I learned: What shall become of Odin the aged, When the rulers' reign is riven?

8. Or kin-seeker.   9. Thor.

52. VAFTRUDNIR: The wolf shall devour the Father of Ages,
                  But Vidar shall come to avenge him;
                  Vidar shall cleave the icy jaws
                  With Vingner's sacred weapon.[10]

53. GAGNRÁD: Much have I traveled, much have I tested,
                  Much from the various powers I learned:
                  What whispered Odin in the ear of his
                      son,[11]
                  As the latter was borne on the pyre?

54. VAFTRUDNIR: None knows what *you* in the foretime spoke
                  At the pyre in the ear of your son.
                  With the lips of one dead have I told my
                      tale,
                  Runes of old and of Ragnarök.

---

10. Mjölnir, Thor's Hammer.   11. Balder.

14

Thor and Loki in Jotunheim*
(Gianthome)

TRANSLATOR'S NOTES

This entertaining episode must have afforded much amusement
to an audience of simple people. It is apparently an event in the
history of our globe, when freezing winds accompanied the lowering
of the water level as the polar ice caps spread over the continents,
absorbing more of the globe's water. At the same time there was
a shift in the position of the Midgárd serpent — the equator, or
perhaps the arc of the Milky Way. There is no doubt the events
denote a period of glaciation but which ice age is open to question.

This lay bears a striking resemblance in one particular to the
gods' search for the caldron which is related in the Lay of Hymer
(which follows it). In both tales Loki instigated a forbidden act
which was to bring down the wrath of Thor on the luckless perpe-
trator, but here it is the farmer's son — a lesser cycle — who breaks
the bone.

Like Vaftrudnismál (the Lay of Illusion), Thor's and Loki's visit
to the giant world illustrates the misperceptions to which consciousness is subject in the worlds of the giants. We do not perceive
things as they really are; all consciousnesses, even the gods, it
seems, are beset by the illusion which marks existence in matter.

---

*A tale from the Younger Edda.

Thor and Loki in Jotunheim

Once an icy age drew over the lands, destroying crops and killing men and beasts. Thor, accompanied by Loki, set out to remonstrate with the giant Räsvälg who, in eagle guise, fanned freezing winds over Midgård. They had of course to take a roundabout route because, as noted earlier, Thor's chariot cannot cross the rainbow bridge Bifrost which connects the worlds of men and gods: its lightnings would set the bridge afire. So they forded the river Ifing (doubt) which marks the boundary between those worlds.

At Midgård they received the hospitality of a poor farmer who had two children, Tjalfe and Röskva. To supplement the meager fare, Thor slaughtered the two goats which pull his chariot, Tandgniostr and Tandgrisnir (toothgnasher and toothcrusher). He instructed his companions to lay the bones unbroken carefully in their skins. During the feast, Loki whispered to the farmer's son that he should taste the marrow which, he said, had magic properties, and the boy cracked a bone to do so. In the morning, Thor revived the animals with a blow of his hammer on each of the skins, only to find that one of his goats was lame. In a towering rage the Thunderer threatened to destroy the farmer and all his family, but the old man appeased the god by offering his two children to be Thor's servants. Thereupon Tjalfe (speed) joined the gods on their excursion while Röskva (work) stayed to await their return.

One night on their journey they sheltered in a curiously shaped structure containing two rooms, one very large, the other small. Disturbed and alarmed by a loud roaring noise, the travelers hid in the smaller of the two chambers. Emerging in the morning they found a monstrous giant asleep nearby: the house was his mitten, the roars were his snores. Beside him lay his sack of provender. Being hungry the two gods tried to open the satchel but even Thor was unable to undo the knots, so he set about trying to waken the giant. Three times he struck his hammer against the giant's skull, which caused the sleeper to stir and mutter something about flies, but failed to rouse him. The gods went hungry. However, to this day there are three valleys cleaving the mountain where the giant slept.

Eventually the two Aesir and Tjalfe reached the home of the king of the giants, whose name Utgárdaloki means Loki-of-the-outermost-court. Here the gods were challenged to a series of contests. First, Tjalfe ran a race against the giants' champion but was ignominiously outdistanced. Then Loki, who by this time was ravenously hungry, offered to out-eat any giant. He too failed for, though the two finished together, the giant had consumed the platter as well as the food. Thor offered to drain any drinking-horn but, when he was handed a gigantic vessel, failed to lower the level more than a little. He was then asked to lift the giant's cat. Mortified by so simple a task, he nevertheless found himself unable to do more than raise one of its paws. He thereupon undertook to wrestle any giant and was laughingly faced with the giants' elderly nurse, who easily brought the Thunderer to one knee.

After these undignified defeats the gods left to return to their own sphere, accompanied part of the way by their host, who — once they were safely off the premises — proceeded to explain the illusions to which they had been prey. Though Tjalfe had the speed of lightning, his opponent in the race had been Thought, which easily outdistanced him. Loki's opponent was Logi (flame), which consumed not only the food but also the wooden platter. The horn Thor failed to drain had its tip in the ocean's depths; the whole giant world had quaked with fear as the level of the waters was considerably lowered. The cat was really the Midgárd serpent Iörmungandr, which Thor had moved to an alarming degree. As for the giants' elderly nurse, Elli, she was in reality old age, which brings everyone, even the gods, low in due time.

When Thor in a mighty rage raised his hammer to avenge these defeats by trickery, neither his host nor any city was to be seen on the flat plain that reached endlessly in all directions.

15

Hymiskvädet

(Hymer's Lay)

Our solar system has its home in a portion of space from which we see certain configurations of stars. Our earth rotates on its axis so that each side is irradiated with sunlight half the time and is in shadow the other half of the time as we travel along the almost circular path of its orbit. The stars we see are those on the shadow-side of our planet, that is to say those outside the solar system in the direction we face at night. This direction changes, of course, with the seasons, so that in the course of a year, one revolution round the sun, we have faced by night all the stars that surround us in our solar neighborhood. Those stars that are close to being on a level with our orbit, called the plane of the ecliptic, have been grouped into 30 degree arcs and these groups are called the twelve constellations of the zodiac. Together they make a complete circle (360 degrees). Our sun, which is situated in one arm of a spiral galaxy we call the Milky Way, is thus surrounded by the twelve "animals" (i.e., animate beings) of the celestial "zoo."

We need to have a clear picture of this scenario in order to see how the tale of the giant Hymer suggests the prelude to a new imbodiment, possibly of our sun, perhaps of a planet such as the earth. According to the theosophic teachings a planet lives a number of lives with intervals of rest, comparable to death, during the lifetime of the sun. It also undergoes shorter periods of repose comparable to sleep, within its own lifetime. The pattern is analogous to that of human and other types of life which include sleeping and waking as well as death and birth.

Hymer is evidently a preliminary stage in the formation of a celestial body. His nine daughters, or aeons, are the nine mothers of the god Heimdal, god of beginnings, who, as we have seen, is a solar deity. He has a particular affinity with the constellation Aries, the ram, marker of beginnings: of the year at the vernal equinox, of the zodiacal year (25,920 terrestrial years), and of each lifetime of our planet. He is personified as the wind which, like the ram, butts, or blows, or pushes, with its head. As parent of Heimdal's nine mothers, Hymer apparently represents the beginning of the present imbodiment of our solar system within the encompassing pattern of stars where our sun has its habitat. At the end of life he is named Rymer. Both names are suggestive of Ymer, a universal concept here applied to a particular case.

An interesting sidelight may be mentioned here: in the biblical story in Genesis 17 occurs a transformation with the addition of the letter H, the aspirate, which symbolizes breath, spirit, the principle of life: Abram becomes Abraham, and his wife Sarai becomes Sarah. It is possible that the Norse used the same convention to indicate the in-spiration, in-breathing, of life into matter when Ymer becomes Hymer with the inbreathing of the divine power which endows our world with life.

In the tale of Hymer, the gods had learned by divination that the titan Äger — space — could supply the mead of experience whereby they are nourished, for he "possessed this mead in plenty." But when Thor commanded Äger to make feast for the gods, the giant replied: "Bring me first a caldron to contain it. Then shall I make feast for the gods."

As there was no vessel large enough to hold the mead, the gods were at a loss until Tyr[1] recalled that his kinsman Hymer owned such a caldron. Thor and Tyr set out to find Hymer and acquire the caldron "by cunning if need be." On their way through Midgárd they met Egil, the "mountain farmer, son of the dim-eyed one" — of

---

1. Tyr, "animate being" hence "god," means specifically Mars who is closely linked with Aries of the zodiac, and with Heimdal, as well as with the energic impulse of Thor. As such, he symbolizes will and desire. Here we again see the progression from giants to gods, as Hymer, a giant, represents a parent or a past condition of Tyr, a god.

Tjasse, the previous period of evolution. Egil was entrusted with the care of the two goats which draw the Thunderer's chariot, and the gods proceeded on foot.

At the giant's home they were greeted by the wife who advised them to hide before Hymer should arrive in fierce ill-humor. It was late in the evening when "misshapen, harsh Hymer" came home from the hunt; we are treated to a delightful kenning which describes how "icicles rattled as he stepped in, for his face forest was frozen" (10). The wife tried to soften his mood before breaking the news that their young kinsman Tyr had come to the hall bringing with him "a noble foe named Vior.[2]" This emphasizes the reluctance of the matter-giant to entertain the god-energy in a way which brings to mind Newton's first law of motion: "A body remains at rest or continues to move with the same speed in the same direction, unless it is acted on by a net force."

At the giant's glare the ridgepole broke in two and eight kettles fell down, only one remaining unbroken. With customary (mandatory) hospitality Hymer ordered three bullocks slaughtered for the evening meal. Thor devoured two of them so that the following morning the giant and the Thunderer needs must set out to catch fish for food. Vior offered to row if the giant would provide bait, so Hymer, with tongue in cheek, invited Thor to take one of his herd of oxen, knowing this to be an all but impossible task. Thor, however, accomplished the feat without difficulty. At sea, "Hymer drew aboard two whales together" (21). Thor hooked the Midgárd serpent Iörmungandr with the result that icebergs shook, volcanoes erupted, and the whole world trembled, until Thor restored the monster to the deep.

In this story several interpretations overlap, and the descriptions may apply to terrestrial, solar-systemic, or cosmic events. The Midgárd serpent we know represents the equator, displaced again and again throughout our earth's history; it may also refer to the plane of the ecliptic which is the sun's apparent path across the sky; or it may be the Milky Way which seems to writhe round the

---

2. Vior is, as we have seen, Thor in his capacity as the life force, the vitality of any organism.

sky with the seasons like an immense ribbon of stars immersed in the "waters" of space. The serpent is one of Loki's three dread offspring; the other two are Fenris, the wolf who will devour the sun at the end of its lifetime, and Hel, the cold, half blue queen of the realms of death.

Hymer was displeased with the god's success; for a long time he spoke no word but he "turned the helm in the wrong direction" (25). This may indicate a change in the configurations of observed stars, caused either by the introduction of a new body or the destruction of a former planet; it may also mean simply a change in inclination of the earth's polar axis — something that is known to have taken place many times, leaving traces in the magnetic alignment of rocks. There is no mention of a further change of direction, yet the boat shortly reached its landing. Hymer requested the god to "either bear home the whales to the village or bind the water goat fast at the shore" (26).

Thus far we have had our attention drawn to a very curious set of objects: we see juxtaposed a "water goat," a man rowing, fish, the ram, the ox or bull, and the "two whales together." Translated into the ancient customary descriptions of the zodiacal constellations we recognize in them respectively Capricorn, Aquarius, Pisces, Aries, Taurus, and Gemini, all conjoined with the disturbing of the Midgárd serpent. The implication is unmistakable as we realize that these six consecutive constellations cover 180 degrees of sky, that is, a half circle, or as much as may be seen at one time. Can this be mere coincidence?

Back at the giant's home, Thor was challenged to break a drinking vessel, but though he hurled it against a pillar with all his might, the chalice remained whole, whereas the pillar broke in two. When the giant's woman whispered to Thor that he should break the goblet against his host's skull, than which there exists no harder substance, the Áse did so with the result that "whole was the giant's helmet-holder; the wine cup's rim split into two" (31). Thereafter the gods were free to bear off the caldron, though not without having first to overcome the gigantic horde which pursued them. This was of course accomplished by Mjölnir, Thor's hammer.

When they reached the place where Egil, the innocent, was

tending Thor's goats, one of the animals was lame, just as in the previous tale. Loki had persuaded the farmer to break a marrow-bone. Here too the Thunderer's rage was appeased only when Egil offered his two children to be Thor's servants. Thenceforth, whenever Lorride, the terrestrial aspect of Thor, is found on earth, he is accompanied by Tjalfe (speed) and Röskva (work), the children of Egil, the "innocent mountain farmer," who serve him as elemental agents of vital electricity.

The search for the caldron of Hymer, with all its details and seeming trivia, is one lay that can be read many and many a time without "ringing a bell" of understanding. Not until we apply the key of the ageless cosmogonies do we discern what may have been a method of conveying the idea that the gods are seeking the appropriate place for a star or planet to reimbody. The caldron seems to represent a specific volume of space which satisfies certain requirements. A solar or planetary consciousness about to come into life must find its proper home, and this is defined as the place from which the surrounding stars present a certain appearance. There is, when you think about it, only one way to define a particular location in space, and that is to describe its surroundings. The caldron of Hymer is here pinpointed by naming six consecutive constellations of the zodiac, spanning one hemisphere or half the sky, as it appears from our solar system.

So Hymer's lay apparently tells of a celestial being preparing to enter into a new manifestation: it seeks by desire for life (Tyr) and electromagnetic life force (Thor) its own ancient habitat (caldron). This most ingenious device demonstrates again and well the technique used by the sages to perpetuate their knowledge by means of tradition. People who themselves were quite incapable of grasping any but the simplest anecdotes could thus be used as unwitting transmitters of scientific fact. The breaking of the ridgepole at the giant's fierce glare and the destruction of all but one kettle hanging from that pole no doubt struck many of them as hilarious, but within the joke may be secured the record of an astronomical event of awe-inspiring proportions, when the polar axis of rotation of a global or universal system was overturned, leaving only one "kettle" or container unbroken: the location where a globe is reborn in the space it had formerly occupied. Thor's capture and release of the Midgárd serpent confirms the same pattern of events.

In Ásgárd the gods were awaiting the capacious vessel when "to the Ting of the gods came victorious Thor bearing with him the caldron of Hymer." Now the gods drink grandly with Äger each fall "when the golden grain is garnered," as translated in some versions. It goes without saying that the harvest is the culmination of any period of activity, whether it is a day, a year, a life, or an aeon. It is then that the gods absorb the mystic mead which has been brewed in the space where a world has lived and died.

Hymiskvädet

1. The Gods of Choice[3] had good hunting,
   But thirsted much ere they were filled;
   They shook the divining-rods, studied the signs,
   And found that Äger had ample fare.

2. The mountain farmer sat outside, child-happy,
   Seeming the son of the dim-eyed one;
   The son of Ygg[4] looked him in the eye:
   "You shall often make feast for the Aesir."

3. Anxiety assailed the giant at the harsh-worded
       warrior;
   He plotted revenge against the gods;
   He asked Sif's husband[4] to bring him the caldron,
   "Then shall I brew your ale."

4. But nowhere did the noble gods
   Or wise Vaner know of any;
   At length, faithful Tyr gave Lorride[4]
   This friendly advice:

5. "There lives to the east of the Eli-waves,
   Many-wise Hymer at the end of the sky:
   My battle-loving father owns such a kettle,
   A capacious brewing vessel miles deep."

6. "Think you we might that sap cooker get?"
   "If we use guile."

---

3. Aesir.   4. Thor.

7. That day they traveled a long day's journey
   Forth from Ásgárd to reach Egil;
   He was to guard the horned goats,
   As they hied onward to Hymer's hall.

8. The son[5] found his mother's mother,
   The hideous one with 900 heads;
   But forth came another, gold-adorned woman
   With fair brow to bring her son mead.

9. The wife: "Offspring of Titans,
   I will cover you with a caldron, ye noble twain;
   Often my husband is grouchy toward guests
   And of ill humor."

10. Late that evening came
    Misshapen, harsh Hymer home from the hunt;
    Icicles rattled as he stepped in,
    For the man's face forest was frozen.

11. "Hail, Hymer, be mild of mind!
    The scion is come to your halls;
    Him whom we awaited from far away;
    With him comes a noble foe, friend of warriors,
        Vior[6] by name.

12. "See them under the gable,
    Sheltering, fearful, behind the post."
    At the giant's mere glance, the pillar collapsed
    And above it the roof-ridge broke in two.

13. Eight kettles fell from the ridgepole down;
    Only one, hard-tempered, remained unbroken.
    The guests stepped forth as the grim old giant
    With glowering glare followed his foe.

---

5. Tyr.   6. Thor, as vitality.

14. No good he boded
    As forth on the floor
    He saw standing the terror of giants.
    He ordered three bullocks taken and cooked.

15. Each of the three was made a head shorter
    And borne to be broiled; Sif's husband alone
    Ate, before going to sleep,
    Two of Hymer's oxen withal.

16. Rungner's ancient kinsman[7] thought
    Lorride's meal abundantly meted.
    "Tomorrow we three must, I believe,
    Find fish food to eat."

17. Vior was willing to row on the wave
    If the bold giant provided the bait.
    "Go to my herd, if you have a mind,
    You mountain-giant-crusher, to take bait!
    I expect though you will not find it easy
    To take bait of my oxen."

18. The god gaily hastened forth to the forest,
    Where all-black oxen stood;
    The thurses' bane[8] broke from the bull
    The highfort above, both of its horns.

19. Spake Hymer: "You, chariot-master,[8] are terrible
    When you are still;
    Your works are far worse."

20. The flashing goats' master[8] bade the ape's kinsman
    To row farther out,
    But the giant had no desire
    Farther to row.

---

7. Hymer.   8. Thor.

21. Mighty Hymer drew on board ship
    A pair of whales together;
    But in the stern Sif's Vior
    Cunningly readied a line.

22. The savior of peoples, the serpent's bane,
    Now heaved the ox's head on the hook;
    There gaped at the bait the one whom gods hate,
    That is curled in the depths round all lands.[9]

23. Then doughty Thor courageously drew
    The venomous snake aboard ship;
    He hit with his hammer disdainfully down
    On the crown of the head of the wolf's[10] fell brother.

24. Mountains roared,
    The fields shrieked aloud;
    So collapsed the former world;
    The slimy serpent sank in the sea.

25. Unhappy was Hymer
    As they rowed homeward;
    Long time the giant spoke no word;
    He turned the helm in the wrong direction.

26. Spake Hymer: "Do you share the work
    Equally with me:
    Bear you home the whales to the village,
    Or bind the water goat fast at the shore."

27. Lorride[11] gripped the prow and drew the sea-horse[12]
            up on the shore
    With sprit, oars, and bailer;
    The giant's billow-boar[12] he bore to the village
    Through dark forest paths.

---

9. Iörmungandr, the Midgárd serpent.
10. Fenris.   11. Thor.   12. Boat.

28. But still the giant of obstinate habit
    Vied with the god;
    Said the man was not strong, though a mighty
        oarsman,
    If he could not break a drinking vessel.

29. Lorride hurled the chalice at once,
    The stone pillar cracked, but the goblet was whole;
    Seated, he broke the hall's pillars through,
    Yet whole was the cup he handed his host.

30. At length the giant's concubine, friendly woman,
    Gave this advice, all that she knew:
    "Hit Hymer's skull with it;
    It is harder than any chalice."

31. Thor sprang up, braced himself,
    Gathered his Ása-strength:
    Whole was the giant's helmet-holder;
    The wine cup's rim split into two.

32. Quoth Hymer: "I have lost the precious treasure,
    Seeing the chalice, crushed, fall from my lap;
    This word I can never unsay.
    This draught was too bitter.

33. "You are free to take the caldron
    Away from our court, if you can."
    Twice Tyr tried to move it,
    But it stood firm and steady.

34. Mode's father[13] grasped the rim
    With such force that his foot broke the floor.
    Sif's husband heaved it over his head;
    The handles rattled against his heels.

---

13. Thor.

35. They had not gone far
    When Odin's son looked back;
    He saw Hymer's hordes approaching
    From eastern hollows, hundreds of heads.

36. He lowered the kettle, put it down,
    And turned on the murderous mass with Mjölnir,
    Slaying the terrible whales of stone
    That hastened behind him with Hymer.

37. Not long did they travel ere Lorride's goat
    Staggered and fell half dead before them;
    The loping beast was lame of leg;
    This had been caused by Loki.

38. But ye have heard, whoever is learned
    In god-spells may readily see,
    The wage he earned from the tiller of soil,
    Who forfeited both his children.

39. To the Ting of the gods came defiant Thor,
    And brought with him the caldron of Hymer;
    Now the gods drink grandly with Äger each fall,
    When the golden grain is garnered.

16

Grimnismál

(Grimner's Lay)

This may be the most explicit esoteric instruction concerning the composition of worlds to be found in any extant mythology. It compares well with the descriptions of the inward nature of our universe found in other sources, such as the Qabbālāh and the Persian and Hindu scriptures; indeed, if we have *The Secret Doctrine* as a touchstone, Grimner's teaching is startlingly outspoken.

Odin in disguise (Grimner means hooded, disguised) explains to his pupil Agnar the construction of our universe from the loftiest levels of divinity to the basest matter worlds, rounding out the sketchy picture drawn in Völuspá regarding the creative and destructive processes that go on in a universe. The astrology of the myths is not concerned with birth charts and personal predictions. It deals with the properties of living worlds, with the character and functions of their planetary deities and the interrelationships and vital forces that circulate through and among the heavenly bodies.

In Grimnismál we find the earth's two earliest races growing under direct divine supervision, Agnar, the elder, being trained by Frigga, mother of the Aesir, and Geirröd, the younger, by Odin. Allfather causes Geirröd to usurp Agnar's place — the second humanity to supersede the first. There is an exact parallel in the Old Testament where Rebekah is told: "two nations are in thy womb and two manner of people. . . . one people shall be stronger than the other people; and the elder shall serve the younger" (Gen. 25:23). Then follows the familiar story of Esau who sold his birthright to his younger twin.

The third humanity is symbolized by the son of Geirröd, also named Agnar, who is instructed by Grimner, now named Väratyr (God of Being or God-that-is). The lad, having earned this privilege by an act of kindness, is taught of the formation and composition of the solar system: its "shelves" of substances, seen and unseen — "planes" of theosophic literature — and the courts, halls, or mansions which are the dwellings of their respective gods. The characteristics of these mansions of divine powers are very ingeniously suggested, though no words could give an adequate understanding of their properties: human awareness simply does not include the rates of vibration that fall, whether near or far, outside the range of our sense perceptions. Until we develop the appropriate senses to cognize such substances we must be content to regard the spheres as apt homes for the powers that use them.

The first world named is Trudheim — "a holy land, near to the Aesir and the elves" (4). Its god, Trudgälmer, is that aspect of the triune deity which corresponds to Vishnu, the sustaining power of the Hindu *trimūrti*[1] or divine triad. The other two are Örgälmer which, like the Hindu Brahmā, is the outpouring, expansive force, the "creator," while the third, Bärgälmer, fruitage of a life, parallels Siva, the destroyer-regenerator. The three are clearly inseparable, being the three aspects of the motive force, whether in a universe or any other entity, which expresses itself as constant change. The descriptions of the twelve homes of the gods are subject to many interpretations; they can apply to the twelve directions in space which are most commonly designated as zodiacal influences, and also to the planetary powers through whose modifying characters these influences are filtered before we receive them; they may also refer to the unseen traits of our terrestrial deity, which correspond to all of the above and are modified by them. Analogy is a valid guide to understanding myths, provided it is not distorted or carried to extremes. As the twelve deities named in Grimnismál vary greatly in their attributes, it is not surprising to find included such diverse characters as Ull and Trym, respectively the highest, most spiritual sphere of life in our terrestrial system, and the one most deeply sunk in matter, the globe we at present inhabit.

---

1. Literally "three faces."

It is well to remind ourselves that we are dealing with qualitative forces having infinitely diverse characteristics, not personages, however magnified. Perhaps if we could study cosmic processes and their dynamic powers on their own levels we might so perceive them, but from our human, microcosmic viewpoint they can be only dimly imagined as principles belonging to the solar universe. The figures in the myths are anthropomorphized — even by merely being named — and can give us only the vaguest approximation of their true characters and functions. Just so does the zodiacal symbology supply only the dimmest suggestions as to the various fields of influence that dominate the different directions in space. We simply are not equipped to distinguish them.

The lays are not always sequentially clear, and we find ourselves suddenly plunged into a sketchy mention of Valhalla where Odin's warriors are fed the three boars — the results of their conquests on the earth which, as we have seen, is symbolized by a boar in the Norse as well as other mythologies. Their names, Andrimner, Särimner, and Eldrimner, respectively breath (air, spirit), sea (water, mind), and fire (heat, desire and will), constitute a symbol within a symbol as these characteristics apply to the composition both of nature and of man. When verse 18 is paraphrased: "spirit lets mind be steeped in desire and free will; few know what nourishes the One-harriers," the deduction is that the conquerors of self are nourished by a progressive and purposeful sublimation of the desires and will. This is psychology of a high order. It gives substance and purpose to human evolution as progressive change, and affords a powerful incentive for growth to the human soul. Far beyond the notion that evolution pertains merely to bodies, there is here a realization that what evolves is the consciousness of beings, and that in the human kingdom free will plays a significant part in this process. The instruction and training of Agnar has as its practical application the promoting of an understanding of the role he — the human soul — has to play in the cosmic drama.

Odin describes his two hounds, Gere and Freke (19), his constant companions. He feeds them, Greed and Gluttony, though he himself lives on wine alone, wine or mead being used to denote wisdom. Thus the god supports and uses animal nature, though

himself sustained by wisdom alone. The New Testament affords
a parallel in the familiar story of the wedding in Cana, where Jesus
transformed water (ritual observances) into wine (spiritual teaching).
Odin's ravens, Hugin and Munin, also describe aspects of consciousness essential for gaining experience. Hugin means mind in all the
many connotations in which that word is commonly used: mental
proficiency is only one of its meanings; it can also be used for
purpose, intent, mood, attitude, disposition — all of which apply
to Hugin. Munin too has many meanings, memory being chief of
these. Without memory there would be no modification of the
mind. It is on such modification caused by cumulative experience
that intelligence feeds and proficiency is gained, character is altered,
and evolution proceeds. We are always building on the awareness
of events gone by. But more than that: Munin also determines
motivation, the primary factor in directing the mind and subsequent
action. It is Hugin that is in danger of entrapment on its excursions,
but the fear for Munin is eternal.

Allfather speaks of Tund, the river of time, which forms the
moat surrounding Valhalla. Therein cavorts Tjodvitner's fish —
humanity. Tjodvitner is one of the names of Fenris, the wolf sired
by Loki, all the brutish spawn of the undisciplined mind. It is the
werewolf that is forever fishing for human souls to draw them astray.
Those who succeed in crossing the river are faced with the "Gate of
Choice" or "Gate of Death," whose latch can be opened by few and
which, as we have seen, leads to the Hall of the Elect — Valhalla.

Grimner then explains to his disciple how the Tree of Life is
constituted and the perils to which it is subject. There has been
no attempt to translate the names of all the rivers of lives. Suffice
it that among them are such appellations as Waywise and War (in
several forms), which suggest the characteristics of the various
kingdoms of beings and their standing on the evolutionary scale.
Only a few of the clearer meanings are proposed. Untranslated
names, except those explained elsewhere, are rendered in italics.
Then follow the names of the steeds of the gods.

The final "blessing of Ull on him who first touches the fire"
implies a promise of human perfectibility. It is a reminder that the
unmanifest world of Ull — the acme of divinity in the system to

which our earth belongs — is accessible. The "fire" of this un-created "cold" world of pure consciousness can hardly be explained in terms that would be comprehensible in our existence, but the words give us an inkling of the reaches our essential self may attain.

The final verses of Grimnismál need no explanation. In them the father of gods and men reveals his many names, culminating with the telling words: "the Opener and the Closer. all are one in me."

Grimnismál

King Rödung had two sons; one was named Agnar, the other Geirröd. Agnar was then ten winters old, Geirröd eight. Both rowed a boat and were fishing when the wind blew them out to sea. In the darkness they ran aground, went ashore, and met a poor farmer, who gave them lodging for the winter. The wife reared Agnar, but the man taught Geirröd. When spring came, the man gave them a vessel, but when he and his wife brought them to the beach, the man spoke privately to Geirröd.

They had favorable wind and soon came to their father's landing. Geirröd was in the prow; he jumped ashore but pushed the boat away and said: "Go where the trolls may take you!" The vessel drifted out to sea.

Geirröd went up to the home and was well received. His father was then dead and Geirröd became king in his stead and a famous man.

Odin and Frigga sat upon Lidskjälf[2] and looked out over all the worlds. Odin said: "Do you see Agnar, your foster son, how he begets children with a giantess in a cave? But Geirröd, my foster child, is a king and rules over lands." Frigga replied: "He is so stingy, he starves his guests, if they are too numerous." Odin said this was a great lie; they made a wager on this dispute. Frigga sent her handmaiden Fulla[3] to Geirröd to warn him that a sorcerer arriving by night

---

2. See note on p. 13. *Lidskjälf* may have other meanings, but the most probable would seem to be "shelf of compassion."

3. Fulla and Bil are names for phases of the moon.

would be his undoing, and she added the sign that no hound, however fierce, would attack the man. It was the greatest calumny to say that King Geirröd lacked hospitality, but he caused this man, over whom hounds had no power, to be taken prisoner. The man was clad in a blue fur coat and called himself Grimner.[4] He would tell no more about himself however much they questioned him. The king had him tortured and placed between two fires. There he remained for eight nights.

King Geirröd had a son, ten winters old, whom he had named Agnar after his brother. The lad went to Grimner, gave him a horn filled with drink and said his father was wrong to torture an innocent man. Grimner drained the horn. By then his coat was on fire. He spoke:

1. "Hot are you, Fire, and all too strong!
   Farther may we part, Flame!
   The pelt-lining chars, though I draw the skirts up,
   The coat starts to burn.

2. Eight nights I sat between fires here
   With none to bring me food;
   Agnar only, who alone shall rule,
   Geirröd's son, in the land of the Goths.

3. Hail to thee, Agnar, in all things
   Väratyr[5] bids you be fortunate!
   For but one drink shall you never
   Receive greater recompense.

4. A holy land I see placed
   Near to the Aesir, near to the elves;
   But in Trudheim Thor shall dwell
   Till the rulers' reign be rent.

---

4. Literally "hooded"; disguised.
5. God of Being.

5. Raindales they name those dells
   Where Ull[6] has arranged his hall;
   Elfhome the gods gave to Frey
   As a teething-gift in the morning of time.

6. There is a third dwelling where gentle powers
   Covered the hall with silver;
   Shelf of the Chosen was built for himself
   In the dawn of time, out of wisdom, by the Áse.

7. Deep River is fourth;
   Thence cool waves surge;
   There Odin and Saga forever
   Quaff out of golden goblets.

8. Gladhome is fifth, where golden glows
   The Hall of the Chosen.
   There Odin, the Maligned, daily crowns
   Those killed in battle.

9. Recognized clearly by those who come
   To Odin is this hall;
   Its frame is of spears, roofed over with shields,
   The benches are strewn with byrnies.

10. Recognized clearly by those who come
    To Odin is this hall;
    Wolf hangs on western door,
    Blood-dripping eagle above.

11. Sixth is Trymheim where Tjasse lived,
    The mighty giant of old;
    Now Skade builds, the slender god-bride,
    On her father's former grounds.

12. Broadview is seventh, where Balder
    Disposed his halls;

---

6. Winter, a "cold" or unformed world.

On that land I know
Are the fewest harmful runes.

13. Heavenmount is the eighth, where Heimdal
Is said to rule the sanctuaries;
The watcher of the gods with joy
Quaffs good mead in this happy house.

14. Folkvang is ninth. Freya rules there,
Assigning the seats in the hall;
Daily she salutes half the chosen.
Odin owns the other.

15. The Shining is tenth, supported on golden pillars
And roofed with silver.
Forsete there lives out his days
And wisely judges causes.

16. Ships' Haven is eleventh,
Where Njörd furnished his hall;
The man-ruler, the harmless,
Reigns over high-timbered holiness.

17. Hidden in thickets and tall reeds
Is the wide land of Vidar;
There shall my son dismount
To avenge his father.

18. Andrimner lets Särimner
Be steeped in Eldrimner[7]
The best of meat!
Few know what the One-harriers eat!

19. Gere and Freke are nurtured
By battlewont father of hosts;
But on wine alone lives ever
Odin, the weapon-adorned.

---

7. The "boars" that feed the gods: air, water, and fire.

20. Hugin and Munin fly each day
    Over the battlefield Earth.
    I am anxious for Hugin that he returns not
    But I fear more for Munin.

21. Tund[8] howls and Tjodvitner's fish[9]
    Plays in the stream;
    The flowing river seems all too big
    For the celebrants to ford.

22. The Gate of Choice is in the wall,
    Holy, before the holy doors;
    Fine is that gate, and but few know
    How it is locked.

23. Five hundred floors and forty more
    Are there in bulging Bilskirner;
    Of all roofed halls it seems to me
    The largest is my son's.

24. Five hundred doors and forty more
    I know there are to Valhall;
    Eight hundred One-harriers emerge at once
    From each, when they go to bear witness.[10]

25. Heidrun is the goat in Hostfather's hall,
    That nibbles the Shadegiver's boughs;
    She fills the cup of creation with fine mead full,
    Drink that never runs dry.

---

8. "River of fire," the moat around Valhalla.

9. Tjodvitner — the werewolf, Fenrer or Fenris, son of Loki, who fishes for men. Hence Tjodvitner's fish is the human race.

10. $540 \times 800 = 432,000$, the cycle named in the Purānas which is used in a pattern like the Pythagorean tetraktys to form greater cycles, multiples of this one. The "golden age" is the longest of the four "yugas" or $1,728,000$ years which is $4 \times 432,000$: "The largest of these is my son's," Balder's, or the golden age.

26. Eiktyrner is the hart in Hostfather's hall,
    That nibbles the Shadegiver's boughs;
    Drops from his antlers in Hvergälmer fall,
    Whence all waters spring.[11]

27. *Sid* and *Vid, Säkin, Äkin, Sval* and *Gunntro,*[12]
    Fjörm and *Fimbultul;*
    Rin and *Rinnande, Gipul, Göpul, Gammal,* and
        Geirvimmel,
    Which wind round the dwellings of the gods;
    Tyn and *Vin, Töll* and *Höll, Grat* and *Gunntorin.*

28. *Vina* is one, another *Vägsvinn,* a third *Tjodnuma.*
    Nyt and *Nöt, Nönn* and *Rönn, Slid* and *Rid,*
    Sylg and *Ylg, Vid* and *Vand,* and *Strand,*
    Göll and *Leiptr,* which flow close to mankind
    And stream down to Hel below.

29. *Körmt* and *Örmt,* and *Karlögar* twain, where
    Thor wades each day on his way to the judgment
    'Neath Yggdrasil's ash; else would the Aesir's bridge
    Burst into flames and the holy waters boil.

30. *Glad* and *Gyller, Gler* and *Skidbrimer,*
    Silvertopp and *Siner, Gisl* and *Falhofner,*
    Gulltopp and *Lättfot;* them the high gods ride each day
    On their way to the judgment 'neath Yggdrasil's ash.[13]

31. Three are the roots that run three ways
    Under Yggdrasil's ash:

---

11. From Hvergälmer run all the rivers of lives which inhabit or animate the kingdoms of nature.

12. Italicized names are not translated.

13. The names are symbolic and descriptive: the steeds of the gods translated are: Glad (Frey's), Gilt (Brage's), Glazed (Njörd's), Running River (Ull's), Silvertop (Forsete's), Sensations (Tyr's), Hostage (Balder's), Hollowhoof (Höder's), Goldtop (Heimdal's), and Lightfoot (Höner's).

One harbors Hel, under one are the frost-giants;
The third, humanity's men.

32. Ratatosk is the squirrel that runs
        in Yggdrasil's ash:
    The words of the eagle above in the crown
    He bears to the Gnawer below.

33. Four are the stags with necks gracefully arched,
    That gnaw on the limbs.
    Dáin and *Dvalin*,
    Dunör and *Duratror.*

34. There are more serpents 'neath Yggdrasil's tree
    Than an unwise ape can imagine;
    Goin and *Moin*, the sons of Grave-witness,
        the dragon Grayback, Ghost;
    The Opener and Closer, which I believe tear
        the tree's twigs.

35. Yggdrasil's ash must endure more than humans can
        know;
    The stag gnaws above,
    The bole of it rots,
    And below gnaws the serpent Nidhögg.

36. *Rist* and *Mist* bring me the horn, *Skäggjöld* and *Skögul*,
        Hild and *Trud*,
    Löck and *Härfjätter, Göll* and *Geirönul*,
    Randgrid, Rádgrid, and *Reginleif*,
    These bring the One-victors mead.

37. *Árvak* and *Allsvinn* shall up and away
    Draw the supple sun;
    But under their flanks the merciful powers
    Have hidden the Ironcold.

38. Svalin[14] is he that stands before,
    Shielding the shining god;
    Mountain and billow would burn away
    Should he fall aside.

39. *Sköll* is the wolf that pursues the shining god
    To the sheltering woods;
    The other, *Hate*, son of Rodvitnir,[15] precedes
    The heaven-bride.

40. From Ymer's flesh was the earth formed,
    The billowing seas of his blood;
    From his bones the mountains, bushes from his hair,
    And from his brainpan heaven.

41. With his eyebrows beneficent powers enclosed
    Midgárd for the sons of men;
    But from his brain were surely created
    All dark skies.

42. The blessing of Ull and of all the gods
    Is his who first touches the fire;
    For worlds are opened round sons of the Aesir
    When caldrons are heaved from the hearth.

43. Ivalde's sons went in the foretime
    To build Skidbladnir,
    The best of ships for gentle Frey,
    Njörd's beneficent son.

---

14. "The cool one," that protects the planets from those wavelengths of solar radiation which would destroy them, is a myth held in common with those of other parts of the world; also the "sundogs" in the following verse (39), an optical phenomenon seen at northern latitudes as a dual reflection on the horizon, when the sun is rising or setting.

15. Red-witness — red skies at dawn and sunset which bear witness to a mystery.

44. The ash Yggdrasil is the noblest of trees,
    Skidbladnir of ships,
    Odin of Aesir, and Sleipnir of steeds,
    Bilrast[16] of bridges, Brage of bards, Hábrok
       of hawks,
    And of hounds, Garm.

45. Now have I shown my face to the victorious gods,
    To arouse good will;
    All Aesir are called to the cruel one's benches,
    The cruel one's feast.

46. I called myself *Grim*, I called myself *Gángläre*,
    Härjan and *Hjälmbäre*,[17]
    Tack and Third, *Tunn* and *Unn*,
    Helblind and *Hár;*

47. *Sann* and *Svipal* and *Sangetal* am I,
    Härteit and *Nikar*,
    Bilögd, *Bálögd*, *Bölverk*, *Fjölnir*,
    Grim and *Grimne*, *Glapsvinn*, and *Fjölsvinn;*

48. Broadbrim, and Broadbeard, Father of Victory,
    Nikud, Allfather, Father of death;
    Atrid and *Farmatyr*.   Never I called myself
    Twice the same since I fared among men.

49. *Grimne* was I at Geirröd's, but at Ásmund's *Jalk*,
    And *Kjalar* when I drew a toboggan,[18]
    Tro at the Ting, *Oske* and *Ome*,
    Jafnhár and *Bäflinde*, *Göndle* and *Hárbard* among gods.

---

16. Bifrost, the rainbow bridge.

17. Odin's names designating different guises and functions: Hood or Mask, Wandering Learner (cf. the Apotheosis of Gylfe, where the name is that adopted by the postulant), Harrier and Helmet-bearer, etc.

18. The myth wherein Odin as Kjalar drew a toboggan has been lost and only indirect references to it remain.

50. *Svidur* and *Svidrer* I was when I baited
    The aged giant;
    When I became the only bane
    Of *Midvitner's* son.

51. Drunk are you, Geirröd, and out of your senses;
    Much have you lost
    When you forfeited all One-harriers'
    And Odin's favor.

52. Vainly was it spoken, for it avails you naught,
    Friends fool and trick you;
    I see my friend's sword lying
    Dripping with blood.

53. Ygg gains the fallen, your life is elapsed;
    The protectors are angered;
    Here you see Odin,
    Approach if you can!

54. Odin am I now, Ygg was I before,
    Tund before that:
    Vak and *Skilfing, Vafud* and *Roptatyr,*
    Opener and Closer: all are one in me."

King Geirröd sat holding his sword athwart his knees
but, when he heard that Odin was come, he started up to
move him [Grimner: Odin] from between the fires. His sword
slipped from his hands and fell on its hilt just as the king
tripped and fell forward, and his own sword ran him through.
He met his bane. Odin vanished then. Agnar was king for
a long time thereafter.

17

Trymskvädet
(The Theft of Thor's Hammer)

TRANSLATOR'S NOTES

Long ago, before humanity became thinking and responsible, the hammer of Thor was stolen by the giant Trym. Thor's hammer represents power not only of destruction but also of creation, including the power to procreate: hence Mjölnir is the symbol of marriage. Loki, agent of the gods and spokesman for the giants, is sent by Thor to find the hammer and forthwith borrows Freya's "feather-guise" and sets out to locate the irreplaceable emblem of creation. He returns with the tidings that Trym has indeed stolen Mjölnir and hidden it deep in the earth. In exchange for its return the matter giant demands that Freya become his bride. Freya, besides being the indwelling spirit of Venus, and sister of Frey, the earth deity, represents, as we have seen, the higher intelligence of our humanity; she guides and protects our human race which is her Brisinga-jewel.

Hearing Trym's outrageous demand, the goddess snorted with such vehemence that the precious gem was shattered. Indeed, all the gods, meeting to deal with this emergency, greeted the giant's ultimatum with consternation. During their deliberations, Heimdal proposed that Thor disguise himself as Freya in bridal attire so that he might himself retrieve his property. His futile protests are overruled by the assembled deities, and Thor reluctantly submits to the indignity of being garbed in fine linen and, wearing two rounded stones on his bosom, journeys to the hall of Trym, accompanied by Loki attired as a bridesmaid.

During the nuptial festivities the giant is appalled by the bride's prodigious appetite and thirst. Only Loki's ready wit saves the situation as he explains that Freya has fasted long in anticipation of this happy event. When Trym bent to kiss his bride and, raising the veil, met the Thundergod's lightning glare, he reeled back the length of the hall from the impact. Again Loki intervened with an explanation which fortunately satisfied the giant (who evidently was a bit dimwitted).

Trym ordered Mjölnir to be brought and laid on the bride's lap to consecrate the marriage. And so it was that the power of Thor was restored to the god after its misuse in the sphere of matter by a race not yet awake to its responsibility as a humanity. It may not be out of place here to note that our own hedonistic age is apparently not the first to misuse creative and destructive power. The creativity symbolized by Thor's hammer — the power to set in motion vortices of action to contain life and organize forms for gods to occupy — can obviously be applied on many levels of existence. Our earth provides analogous examples: from the proliferation of mineral crystals through the many ingenious devices plants have for disseminating spores and seeds; through the seasonable mating of animals to human sexuality, each stage of development opens up more opportunities than the last for creativity. We humans are not limited to the physical world in our creations; we enjoy greater freedom of creativity than at any previous stage of progress: our versatile intelligence and exclusively human intuition are gateways to worlds of science and art, to reaches of inspiration and philosophic and spiritual ideals not available to "the dwarfs in Dvalin's train." This places us in a position of responsibility for the governance of our earth and the kingdoms beneath the human which follow our lead.

It should be mentioned that theosophic history records that, since the age when the creative power came to earth from the realm of the gods, the planet has undergone even grosser materiality than that which prevailed when Thor's hammer was stolen, at which time it was comparable to its present condition. We have since then descended even further and begun the reascent. At the midpoint of its life, the earth's heaviest atoms began to radiate away their substance, i.e., radioactivity began. This was millions of years ago, though it was only recently discovered. The planet should continue to refine its matter (with intervals of consolidation that should become progressively briefer) until it eventually dies. We are, according to Brahmanic and theosophic chronology, past the nadir or turning point when we began to wend our slow steps once more upward in spiritual growth. The tale of Völund relates how the most material humanity fared in that, the planet's darkest hour (pp. 202–210).

Trymskvädet

Wroth was Wing-Thor when he awoke and missed his hammer. He shook his beard and tore his hair. Son-of-Earth groped about him and his first words were:

THOR: Hear me, Loki. What I have to say no one knows, neither on earth nor in the heavens: the hammer has been stolen from the Áse.

They went to the court of beautiful Freya and his first words were:

THOR: Lend me, Freya, your featherguise, that I may find my hammer.

FREYA: I would give it to you though it were of gold. I would give it though it were silver.

Loki flew, the featherguise whirred; he left the Aesir's courts and entered the giant world, where Trym the thurse[1] prince sat on the high seat twining golden collars for his hounds and braiding the manes of his horses.

TRYM: How is it with Aesir? How is it with elves? Why are you come to the giant world?

LOKI: Ill is it with Aesir. Have you hidden Lorride's[2] hammer?

---

1. Uninspired matter giant.   2. Thor.

TRYM: I have hidden Lorride's hammer eight days' journey
        beneath the ground; no man shall fetch him back again
        unless he bring me Freya to wife.

Away flew Loki, the featherguise whirred; he left the giant
world and entered the Aesir's courts; there Thor met him in
the middle of the court, and his first words were:

THOR: Did you make the errand as well as the effort? Give
        air to the message from afar. Seated, a speaker oft
        digresses; reclining he may lie.

LOKI: I have completed the effort and also the errand: Trym,
        the thurse prince, has your hammer. No man shall
        fetch it back again unless he bring the giant Freya to
        wife.

They sought out fair Freya, and these words he at once
spoke:

THOR: Array yourself, Freya, in bridal gown. We two shall
        fare to the giant world.

Wroth was Freya. She snorted with rage so that all the
Aesir's halls shook. The Brisingamen was shattered.

FREYA: I should truly be man-crazy to go with you to the
        giant world.

All the gods and goddesses met in council; the mighty
Aesir conferred on how to regain Lorride's hammer. Quoth
then Heimdal, the whitest of Aesir, wisely foreknowing as
are the Vaner:

HEIMDAL: Let us dress Thor in a bridal gown and let him
        wear the Brisingamen! Let him wear a bunch of rat-
        tling keys, a woman's garb falling about his knees,

upon his breast broad rounded stones, and bridal linen upon his head!

THOR: Aesir might call me unmanly if I let myself be arrayed in bridal linen.

LOKI, SON OF LÖFÖ[3]: Quiet, Thor! Such words! Soon the
. giants will settle in Ásgárd if you do not fetch your hammer.

They adorned Thor in bridal linen and with the great Brisinga-jewel; from his waist dangled keys and a woman's skirt fell about his knees; on his chest two rounded stones. They veiled his head in costly linen. Quoth Löfö's son:

LOKI: I shall go as your bridesmaid. We two shall journey to the giant world.

Quoth the thurse king:

TRYM: Arise, giants. Strew the benches. They are bringing me Freya to wife, the daughter of Njörd from Noatun! Bring me golden-horned cows and all-black oxen to please this giant; treasures I have aplenty, gems aplenty; Freya alone is lacking.

Toward evening came guests; ale was served for the giants. Sif's man[4] alone ate one whole ox, eight salmon, and all the dainties meant for the women; and he drank three kegs of mead.

TRYM: When did you ever see a bride with a broader bite? Never saw I a bride bite sharper, or a maiden drink more mead.

Between them sat crafty Loki, who retorted to the giant's words:

---

3. "Leafy isle": earth.   4. Thor.

LOKI: Freya ate naught for eight whole days, such was her longing for the giant world.

Trym bent beneath the veil to kiss the bride; he staggered back the length of the hall.

TRYM: Why are Freya's glances so fierce? Her eyes burn like fire.

Between them sat crafty Loki, who retorted to the giant's words:

LOKI: Freya slept not for eight whole nights, such was her longing for the giant world.

There entered the giant's sister to ask for a bridal gift. She begged:

TRYM'S SISTER: Give me the redgold rings from your hands if you would win my love and my favor.

TRYM: Bring in the hammer to consecrate the bride. Lay Mjölnir in the maiden's lap; join our hands with the wedding band.

Then smiled the heart in Lorride's breast, as the hard-headed hammer he felt. First he slew Trym, the thurse king, then lamed all of his kin. He slew the aged giant sister who had dared to ask a bride's gift; blows she received, not rings and coins, hammerblows instead of gems.

Thus came the hammer once more to Odin's son.

18

Kvädet om Rig
(The Lay of Rig)

Long, long ago, the human race had not yet acquired the abilities which distinguish us from the beasts today: the powers of speech, of abstract thought, of artistry, creativity, and empathy. This is the tale of our awakening into rudimentary humanhood, initiating the process of training, honing, and perfecting the human instrument — something which is still continuing today.

Rig[1] is a ray of Heimdal, "the whitest Åse," a solar influence. Symbolically he is allied with Tyr, the god of beginnings, and with the zodiacal constellation Aries. The lay relates how the descent of this godlike influence into the humanity of that early time took place in three stages. Humanity was still dumb, lacking mental power, and vegetated aimlessly, drifting with infinite slowness along the evolutionary way without incentive or desire for growth, when the compassionate gods looked back and saw their plight. And so "fared along green paths the mighty, mature, wise Åse, powerful, manly, wandering Rig" (1). He descended among mankind to aid in awakening man to his potential as an ásmegir, a godmaker.

The first attempt was unsuccessful: the door of the human abode, a miserable hovel, was closed (2). At the second descent, the god found man in a comfortable homestead, whose door was ajar (13) — partially receptive; the third venture found man dwelling in a mansion whose "door stood open" (23): these human forms were fit to receive the divine influx of self-conscious mind.

---

1. Rig means a "descent" or an "involvement."

From that time forward the human race became self-aware, able to determine its destiny. With thought came freedom of will and with choice came responsibility. The human being was now accountable for his thoughts and actions on moral and intellectual levels as well as on merely physical grounds, as before.

It is noteworthy that the progeny of the god in the third dwelling was taught by his divine father, given runes of wisdom, and successfully gained for himself the title "Rig." This race gave rise to succeeding humanities, whereof the youngest, King, was proficient in healing and "learned birdsong," meaning he could understand the languages of nature, possessed insight and understanding.

In the lay's abrupt and unexpected conclusion, King is warned by a crow to pursue more manly objectives than hunting birds: he should "ride a horse, hew with sword, and fell the foe" — symbols for learning to control the animal nature, to grasp the sword of will or knowledge, and to slay the enemy of human progress — egoism. The warning could be a premonition of the ensuing race's perversion of its divine endowments. The tale of Rig is often taken to lend support to the caste system that exists in most societies, whether openly or unrecognized. Be that as it may, it holds far greater import as well. We must bear in mind the structure of myths, which may repeatedly disclose deeper layers of meaning to the limit of our individual understanding. If we regard evolution primarily as the unfolding of consciousness, with forms and personalities following suit, we see the divine compassion in the descent of Rig, our divine parent, who came to endow us with the specifically human qualities which, after many a winding of the course of our lives, will bring the perfection of our species.

Kvädet om Rig

In former times men say that a certain one of the Aesir named Heimdal arose and rode along a seashore, came to a homestead, and named himself Rig. From that story comes this lay.

1. Began to stride along green lanes
The strong, mature, wise Áse,
Powerful, manly, wandering Rig.

2. Continued along the middle of the road,
He came to a cabin whose door was closed
And entered. There was fire on the floor,
Seated by the hearth a grayhaired couple,
Áe and Edda[2] in an ancient kerchief.

3. Rig knew how to advise them,
Seated himself in the middle seat
With the hall's folk on either side.

4. Edda served him simple fare,
A loaf, heavy and thick, of coarse grain;
Then brought more food to the table,
Soup in the bowl was placed on the board,
Simmered veal, the best of fare.

5. Rig knew how to advise them,
Then rose and prepared for rest;
He lay in the middle of the bed
The hall's folk on either side.

---

2. Great-grandfather and great-grandmother.

6. Three nights he dwelt with them together,
   Then strode away down the straight road.
   Nine months went by.

7. A son bore Edda, he was water-sluiced,
   Had swarthy skin and was named Thrall.

8. His skin was wrinkled, his hands were rough,
   With knobby knuckles and broken nails;
   The fingers were thick, the face unsightly,
   His back was bent, his heels were long.

9. He grew and flourished, exerted his strength
   To bind osiers, prepare burdens, and hauled wood all day.

10. There came to the homestead a wandering wench
    With scarred soles, sunburnt arms and downbent nose.
    Her name was Tir.

11. She sat in the middle of the bench;
    With her sat the son of the house.
    They whispered and giggled, prepared a bed,
    Thrall and Tir in burdensome days.

12. Contented they dwelt and bore children. . . .

    [Here follow the names of their twelve sons and ten daughters.]

    They laid out farms, fertilized fields, bred swine,
    Herded goats, dug peat.
    From them are descended the race of thralls.

13. Rig strode along the middle of the road,
    Came to a hall where the door was ajar;
    He entered in, there was fire on the floor,
    At their tasks were seated the dwellers.

14. Afve and Amma[3] owned the house.
    The man was whittling a tree bole for a loom,

    _____
    3. Grandfather and Grandmother.

Wore a trim beard and his hair combed down,
A fitted shirt. A chest stood in the corner.

15. The wife spun yarn at a whirring wheel,
Spread her arms and built a weft,
Wore a kerchief round her hair,
A scarf at her bosom,
And brooches on her shoulders.

16. Rig knew how to advise them,
Sat between them on the bench
With the folk on either side. . . .

[Here a part of the lay is missing.]

17. Rig knew how to advise them,
Rose from the table, prepared for sleep;
Lay in the center of the bed with the local folk on either
side.

18. Three nights he remained,
Then strode on down the middle of the road;
Nine months went by.

19. A child bore Amma, it was water-sluiced and named Karl;[4]
The lad was diapered, pink and pretty, with sparkling
eyes.

20. He grew and flourished;
Tamed oxen, made plows,
Timbered houses and tall barns,
Crafted carts and drove a plow.

21. To the home was brought a bride with dangling keys,
In a kidskin skirt, and was wed to Karl.
Alert was her name, she was adorned with a veil.

---

4. Man.

> They built together, united their possessions,
> Erected a home and made their bed.

22. Content they lived. . . .

> [Their children are named: twelve boys, ten girls.]

From these all free men's races had their source.

23. Thence went Rig along the middle of the road,
Came to a hall with the door to the south,
And the door was open, a ring at the post.

24. He entered. The floor was strewn;
There were seated, exchanging friendly glances,
Fader and Moder,[5] their fingers entwined.

25. The man twined string, bent an elmwood bow
And fletched arrows, while the wife
Eagerly pressed linen and starched sleeves
To cover her arms.

26. She wore a tall headdress, a gem on her breast,
Blue-adorned blouse and trailing skirt;
Her brow was brighter, her breast lighter,
Her throat whiter than sparkling snow.

27. Rig knew how to advise them,
Seated himself on the middle of the bench,
With the hall's folk on either hand.

28. Moder set the table with the broidered cloth,
Brought thin white slices of wheaten bread.
She placed platters of wrought silver
Full of garnish on the table:
Fish and pork, and fried wild fowl,
Wine in a decanter, costly cups.
They drank and pleasured till the day was done.

_____
5. Father and Mother.

29. Rig knew how to advise them,
    Rose and prepared for sleep.
    He lay in the middle of the bed
    With the hall's folk on either side.

30. He there abode with them three nights;
    Strode down the middle of the road.
    Nine months went by.

31. A son bore Moder. He was swathed in silk,
    Was wetted with water and named Jarl.[6]
    His hair was fair, his cheeks were rosy.
    His eyes sparkled like a young snake's.

32. Jarl grew up on the floor of that hall.
    He soon swung shield, twined string, bent bow,
    Shafted arrows, hurled spear, swung lance,
    Harried hounds, rode horses, wielded sword, and swam
       the wave.

33. From the concealing woods came wandering Rig, came
       striding Rig.
    He taught him runes, gave him *his* name and called him
       son,
    Gave him inheritance, possessions, farmlands,
    Farmlands and ancient cities.

34. Mighty Jarl rode through dense woods,
    Over snowcapped mountains to a distant hall;
    Hurled his spear, shook his shield,
    Spurred his steed, hewed with sword,
    Roused to battle, to bloody field,
    To choose to fall, won himself land.

35. Alone he ruled over eighteen farms,
    Shifted goods and gave to all

---

6. Earl.

Gems, precious stones, agile horses,
Shared his rings, cut the red gold.[7]

36. Messengers went forth over damp roads,
Arrived at the hall where Härse lived.
A maid had he, soft-fingered, white-skinned,
Nobleminded. Her name was Ärna.[8]

37. They won her and sent her home.
She wore bridal linen and was wed to Jarl.
Together they built and were content,
Increased their race and gained old age.

38. [Here follow the names of their children.]

Kon[9] was the youngest.
There grew Jarl's sons, tamed horses, arched shields,
Cut arrows and shook lances.

39. But Kon, the young, knew runes,
Eternal runes and ageless runes.
Mighty was he to rescue men,
Soothing swords and swelling seas.

40. He learned birdsong, to quench flames,
To still pain and heal sorrows,
Had eight men's strength and clear vision.

41. Jarl contested with Rig over runes,
Performed feats and did the better.
He gained that which was his lot:
To be named Rig and to know runes.

42. Rode Kon, the young, through marsh and woods,
Let flying dart crown him a bird.
So sang a crow on a twig one day:

---

7. In Viking times spiral gold rings worn round the upper arm served as money, a piece of an arm-ring being cut off as payment when needed.

    8. Aspire.   9. King.

43. "Why, Kon the young, do you slay birds?
    Better you should ride a horse,
    Hew with sword and fell the foe.

44. "Other kings have costly mansions and better farms
    Than you possess;
    Well do they ride a keel, bloody a sword's edge
    And draw wounds."

19

Loki Steals the Brisinga-Gem

TRANSLATOR'S NOTES

Here is an instance where the naughtiness of Loki sets in motion a train of events vitally connected with the course of human evolution. At the instigation of Odin, once more in his role as destiny, karma, the trickster Loki gains possession of Freya's precious "gem of fire" — human intelligence. We have seen that Freya represents the higher, spiritual faculty of intelligence and is, as the planetary deity of Venus, the sponsor and protectress of her brother Frey's intelligent kingdom, the human race of the planet earth.

When Freya confronts Odin and asks for her gem, the god imposes a condition which is profoundly meaningful: she must incite a struggle between the world's two most powerful kings, one not to be resolved by the victory of either but by the ultimate slaying of both "by a Christian man." This phrase of course reflects the attitude of an age when Christian missionaries were militantly spreading the gospels of the Prince of Peace over the lands of northern Europe and Iceland. However, the crux is the eternal opposition of the forces of light and darkness: there can be no existence and certainly no progress without the tension between pairs of opposites which denotes life. It is a significant philosophical concept which passes almost unnoticed, lost in the levity of Loki's wiles. In a more farseeing frame, it becomes evident that Freya's battle continues for the duration of existence, alleviated from time to time as another human heart is moved to overcome the opposing armies in himself, to gain, and to give, the peace that passeth understanding. This must lend added luster to Freya's precious gem.

*Loki Steals the Brisinga-Gem**

It is said that Loki discovered that Freya had obtained the gem from the dwarfs. He related this to Odin. Odin then demanded that Loki should bring him the gem. Loki objected that this was not to be obtained and gave as his reason that no one could enter Freya's home against her will. Odin said that he was to leave and not return until he had obtained the gem. Loki slunk away complaining loudly. He went to Freya's house and found it locked; he tried to enter but could not. It was very cold outside and he soon became frozen. He then transformed himself into a fly and flew around to all the locks searching for a crack but could nowhere find a hole big enough to enter. Finally at the rooftree, under the rafters he found a hole no larger than could accommodate a needle. Through this hole he entered. Once in, he looked about to see if anyone was awake but he found that all were sleeping. He entered Freya's bed and discovered that she was wearing the gem around her neck, but that the lock was turned downward. Loki transformed himself into a flea, sat on her cheek and stung her, whereupon she woke up, turned over, and once more fell asleep. Abandoning his flea disguise he took the gem, opened the house, went away, and gave the gem to Odin.

When Freya awoke in the morning and saw that all the doors were open without having been forced, and that the

---

*From *Sörla Tháttr*, folktale. The Icelandic *tháttr*, like the Sanskrit *sūtra*, means a strand (in a rope).

precious gem was gone, she felt certain she knew what had happened. She went to the hall, to King Odin, just as she was, and told him that he had done ill to let the gem be stolen from her. She requested that he return it. Odin said that as she once had received this gem, so would she never receive it again; "unless" he added, "you can cause two kings, the greatest in the world, who each rule over ten others, to battle each other under the condition that both shall fight, living or dead, until some Christian man were so brave and possess so much fortune that he dare to tackle both these men and kill them. Only then shall their misfortune cease, when the same hero shall release them from the need and trouble of their perilous paths."

Freya agreed and received back her gem.

20

Grottasöngr
(The Song of the Mill)

TRANSLATOR'S NOTES

Though the mills of God grind slowly, yet they
grind exceeding small.   — LONGFELLOW

Included here are two myths which seem to allude to the fourth
(Atlantean) humanity on our globe. Both are the subject of numerous sagas. One is the lay of Grotte, the magic mill, as it applies
to a terrestrial cycle, though, as we have seen, it also has a more
universal application. The other tale is that of Völund, the smith.
This relates how in the fourth great age humanity's soul — Völund
— was enslaved by evil — King Nidud — the most material age of
earth's and mankind's evolution.

These events in humanity's history took place some millions of
years ago according to the chronology of theosophy, at a time when
the human race had made the greatest material advances, surpassing
in physical skills, technology, even our present age. But it was a
one-sided prodigy, for man had already forgotten the spiritual values
that had been given the race in earlier periods when divine influences
imbodied among the first humanities and taught and guided our
human infancy.

Among the myths that can claim descent from the wisdom-
tradition of antiquity the tales of the magic mill are perhaps the most
universally known, the most consistent and, in certain particulars,
the most mysterious. It has never been satisfactorily explained
why people on every continent in ancient times made a particular
point of the magical properties of this implement: they endowed it
not only with its accepted capacity to grind flour but credited it

with grinding every possible substance for the gods. For this was no ordinary tool of man. It was an instrument of divine forces which supplied not only food but health, wealth, salt, happiness, peace, prosperity — of mind as well as of body; it ground up continents on earth and dying worlds on the cosmic scale, and it spewed out homogeneous protosubstance from which new worlds could be formed. In the Finnish *Kalevala*, the celestial smith after several failures in the beginning of time successfully formed the mill Sampo, and its work of destruction and creation goes on for as long as worlds die and are born. The Maya people of Middle America to this day perform rites of the sacred mill, echoing some long lost lore. In the Edda its name, Grotte, means growth and is semantically connected with evolution.

The mysterious mill of all sacred traditions is featured in fairy tales as a remarkable instrument which was the producer of every-thing, faculties and properties of beings as well as matter. It was formed by divine agency for the manifestation of life and its suste-nance. It was also its destroyer.

In one Edda story, two giant maidens are forced to take turns grinding riches and comforts for King Frode (his name means pros-perity) during the early aeons of peace and joy known as the golden age. They work without ceasing to produce endless delights for the king's pleasure. As time goes on the monarch grows greedy for more gold and greater pleasures until he gives the maids only so much time to rest as it takes for a cock to crow or a cuckoo's call. Thus he prepares his own undoing. Inexorably, the tireless giantesses grind their ponderous revenge. Their ceaseless singing, accompanied by the creak of the millstones, grinds forth an army which, under the sea king Mysing, overruns and conquers Frode's lands.

King Mysing takes with him the mill of growth and in time he too falls victim to greed as the magic mill supplies his wants: his continent sinks beneath the waters — the classic tale of the flood which is told world wide.

As in the biblical account and other mythic tales, the king or principal personage represents a nation or race of people over an undetermined period of time, giving us in capsule form the history of ages. The flood, at once so common and so controversial, is featured in every comprehensive tradition, for it is an experience common to all mankind. Myths relate in story form the periodic rising and sinking of continental land massifs — both as rapid cataclysmic events and as the prolonged erosion and slow emergence with which we are familiar. Whether the sudden deluge they depict represents a singular happening or one that is periodically repeated, it undoubtedly made a sufficiently deep impression on human consciousness to have justified being part of the scriptural heritage of every people on the globe.

In the light of present-day science the divine mill suggests something even more universally significant than a device to describe seismology on earth. In its versatility, in its being used to produce all kinds of things — not only physical matter but also other substances — we see a clue to its character as an implement of creation. In this respect it closely parallels the hammer of Thor, Mjölnir (which means "miller"). Mjölnir is the pulverizer of giant worlds, which reduces matter to homogeneity. It is also the agent of creation: we have seen that Thor and his hammer officiate at weddings to insure continued generation and reproduction.

The possibility of an astronomical black hole being depicted as the mill of the gods is a tempting one, for with each gain in astrophysical science regarding these intriguing phenomena we seem to come closer to a description of the mythic mill. As the whirlpool sucked King Mysing's world into the eye of the millstone, so does the vortex surrounding a rotating black hole draw all matter within reach of its insatiable gravitational field into its event horizon, where it disappears from the perceivable universe. In addition, the mysterious quasars, which emit seemingly impossible quantities of radiation at all detectable wavelengths, from infrared to X-rays, are thought to coexist with black holes in the centers of galaxies. It is an interesting sidelight worth noting that in *The Mahatma Letters* (p. 47), which was published half a century before black holes were conjectured — the substances of dead worlds were said to be "ground over in the workshop of nature."

Such divine mills apply on the cosmic scale. As for the terrestrial Grotte, the mill of growth or evolution whose massive wheels are turned by the giantesses of earthly ages, it produces the result of whatever grist is supplied by the current "king" or race of humanity. It can do nothing else. Thus each civilization or wave of characteristic properties must bring its own consequences. During King Frode's early days of peace and plenty, a gold ring lay unclaimed at a busy crossroads for ages, it is said. When it disappeared the golden age was ended. A new age succeeded it — King Mysing — who in his turn was overcome by the deluge as his lands sank beneath the waves, an event which may have reference to the sinking of the so-called Atlantean continent and its cultures. In the theosophic records, these marked the midpoint of our planet's lifetime, the most material age of all — humanity's midnight.

Significantly it was midnight when the giant maids asked of King Mysing if he had enough of salt. It was a moment of decision: to continue the creation of matter, the downward trend of the past age, or turn the evolutionary current toward spiritual growth. The king's choice brought its inevitable result: the deluge sank his ships and drew the cycle of his reign to a close. The fourth age had brought on itself its own destruction by inundation — an event which offered humanity the opportunity to rise once more toward the divine source from which it had originally descended.

ʿProem to Grottasöngr

Sköld (shield) was the son of Odin. He had one son named Fridleif (lover of peace), whose son was named Frode (prosperity).

During the age when Frode was king, the world was filled with peace and harmony. No man would harm any other; there were no thieves or robbers. For ages a golden ring was left lying openly at a crossroads, untouched. King Frode bought two thralls, two giantesses named Fenja and Menja. They were big and strong, able to set in motion the cumbrous mill which none other could move. This mill possessed the property of being capable of producing whatever was demanded of it. Its name was Grotte.

King Frode had the giant maids brought to the mill and he bade them grind gold and peace and fortune for him. He gave them no rest lasting longer than the cuckoo took to sing its song. It is said that the two mighty maidens sang the Song of the Mill and that, before they stopped singing, taking turns at the quernstone, they had ground out an army against Frode, so that there came a sea king by night who slew Frode and took much booty. This ended the Peace of Frode.

The conqueror, King Mysing, took with him the quern and the miller maidens. He bade them grind salt. At midnight they asked him if he yet had enough salt, but he bade them continue. They milled further, until, after a time his ships sank. There came to be a whirlpool in the sea where the waters pour into the eye of the millstone. The ocean foams as the mill turns, and this makes the sea salty.

Grottasöngr

1. Now are come to the palace the foreknowing pair,
      Fenja and Menja;
   They are at Frode's, the son of Fridleif, mighty maidens
      Held as helots.

2. Forth to the mill bench were they brought
      To set the grey stone in motion;
   He gave them no rest nor peace,
      Attentive to the creak of the mill.

3. Their song was a howl,
      Shattering silence;
   "Lower the bin and lighten the stones!"
      Yet he would have them grind more.

4. They sang as they swung and spun the stone
      While most of the men were sleeping;
   Then sang Menja, her turn at the mill,
      The hardminded maid with thunderous voice:

5. "Goods we grind Frode, milling out fortune,
      Full fare of riches on the mill of delights;
   He shall sit upon gold; he shall sleep upon down,
      And wake with a will, then is it well ground.

6. "Here shall none harm another, nor harbor malice,
      Nor bring to bane,
   Nor cut with sharp sword, even should he find
      His brother's bane bound!"

7. The hands stopped, resting; the quern was quiet;
    Then called the king his ancient plaint:
   "Sleep no more than the cock is silent, rest no more
     Than the words I speak!"

8. "Frode, you were not wholly wise, oh, friend of man,
     When you bought these thralls;
   You chose us for strength and bearing,
     Not heeding of what race we are born.

9. "Hard was Rungner, hard his father;
     Tjasse was greater than both;
   Ide and Örner, sires of our race, brothers of mountain
       giants,
     These are our forebears.

10. "Grotte had never risen from the grey mountain
      Earth's hard bedrock,
    Nor would be grinding the mountain-maid,
      Did anyone know her kind.

11. "Nine winters lasted our playing-time,
      Beneath the earth matured our power;
    Great works performed we constantly;
      We moved the very mountains.

12. "From giants' fields we tore out boulders;
      So the earth trembled, subsided, and quaked;
    We rolled from thence the singing stone,
      The heavy slab, for men to take.

13. "In the land of Svitjod, foresighted,
      We two joined the people;
    Hunted bears, broke shields,
      Marched through the ranks of grey.

14. "We destroyed one prince, supported another,
      The good Gothorm we helped with his horde;

No peace there was till we conquered Knue
There we were stopped and captured.

15. "Such was our progress in former times,
     Well known were we among warriors;
Then we cut heroes with sharpened spears,
     Wounded and reddened with fire.

16. "Now we are come to the house of the king,
     In thralldom, with mercy from none;
Grit tears our feet, frost freezes our forms as we turn the
          peace mill.
     It is dreary at Frode's.

17. "Hands shall rest; the stone shall stop;
     I have milled my whole life's aim.
Yet the hand may not stay until Frode feels
     All has been fully milled.

18. "The hands shall hold handles hard, bloodstained
          weapons.
     Wake up, Frode!
Wake up, Frode, if you would hear our songs and
     Our sayings of long ago.

19. "Fire I see burning east of the fort;
     Call up the couriers, call for the beacons!
A warrior horde shall o'errun this place
     And burn the Budlung's[1] dwelling.

20. "You shall not retain the throne of Leidre,
     Your redgold rings, or your quern of riches;
Grasp the shaft more firmly, sister!
     We are not warmed by the blood of the whale!

---

1. King.

21. "Surely my father's maid mightily milled,
      For she saw many men go to their death;
   The mill's great props, though cased in iron,
      Burst asunder — yet more we milled.

22. "Yet still more we milled! May Yrsa's son, scion of
      Halfdan,
      Avenge him on Frode;
   He may be held her son, and also her brother.
      We both know this."

23. The maids they milled with might and main,
      Young they were, in giant-wrath;
   The rafters quivered, the boom was lowered,
      With deafening din the boulder burst.

24. So collapsed the former world.
      Chanted the mountain-giant's bride:
   "We have ground for you, Frode, as we were forced.
      At the quern the women remained till the end!"

21

Völundskvädet
(The Lay of Völund)

TRANSLATOR'S NOTES

Völund's is a tale of the degradation of the fourth humanity's soul. The three brothers and their Valkyrie-wives apparently represent the first three ages of the fourth humanity. Oldest was Egil, the innocent, whose children became the servants of Thor. The second was named Slagfinn, the hunter; the third, which in the tale gave the seed of the fourth great age, was Völund, the elf-king — the soul of humanity during that phase. There may as usual be an analogy drawn with shorter cycles having to do with different types of cultures: first, Egil, the innocent — the primitive phase; next, the hunter-gatherer stage, and third the technologically skilled. These early races were still under the semidivine guidance of their Valkyries, who serve directly under Odin as divine protectors: the spiritual soul, radiance of the divine source of consciousness. They withdrew from contact with their human spouses, as this tale relates.

Völund is a smith, skilled in the use of metals. He is captured, hamstrung, and imprisoned by King Nidud (*nid:* evil, treachery) and is compelled to forge treasures for the king. Secretly he forges also the magic sword (spiritual will) which figures in so many hero tales, and the marvelous ring (of cyclic renewal) which reproduces itself — analogous with the one the dwarfs wrought for Odin. During his forced labor, Völund plots a terrible revenge and in the ripeness of time his opportunity presents itself. He seduces Nidud's daughter and slays his two sons, whom in one version he serves the unsuspecting king at a feast. This cannibalism of the king establishes him as a period of time, for Time devours all his children: all that time brings to birth comes to an end in time. There is a parallel in the Greek myths, where Chronos (who also stands for Time) devours his children. In this version Völund sells the ruler his sons' skulls plated with silver.

Völund thereupon escapes in a "wingwain," a winged wagon of his own making, bearing with him the magic sword and ring, the qualities of determination to grow and the ever-recurring opportunities for renewal; with these priceless treasures of our human race "smiling Völund rose in the air; Nidud, sorrowing, stayed where he sat" (38). Völund is also called "Rungner (roar) of the featherblade." This too suggests that aviation was known and used by the race Völund represents. (Other traditions as well record that select members of humanity escaped the sinking fourth continent which, as noted, has generally been called Atlantis, some leaving it in flying machines,[1] and settled on rising lands where they brought forth the races that belong to our present, fifth, humanity.) The evil king who was left behind was evidently a period when technology reigned, while spiritual values were almost entirely lacking.

---

1. Sanskrit *vimāna*, "celestial car" mentioned in *Rig-Veda*, *Atharva-veda*, and the *Mahābhārata*. Has also been translated "chariot of the gods."

Völundskvädet

Nidud was the name of a king in Svitjod; he had two sons, and a daughter named Bödvild. There were three brothers, sons of the Finn-king; one was Slagfinn, one Egil, the third Völund. They hunted on skis. They came to the Wolfdale and built themselves houses; there is a water, Wolfsea.

Early one morning they found three women on the shore spinning flax, and beside them lay their swan-disguises, for they were Valkyries. Two of them were daughters of King Lödver (Njörd), namely Ladgun-Swanwhite and Hervör-Allvitter, while the third, Ölrun, was the daughter of Kjar of Valland. The three brothers took them home with them. Egil got Ölrun, Slagfinn got Swanwhite, and Völund got Allvitter.[2]

For seven years they lived together; then the women flew away to seek battles, and did not return. Egil ran on skis to find Ölrun, Slagfinn sought Swanwhite, but Völund sat in the Wolfdale. He was, according to legend, the cleverest artificer men know of. King Nidud had him captured, as the song tells.

I.　　　　The maids flew south through the dark woods,
　　　　Allvitter the young, to fulfill her fate;
　　　　They sat down to rest by the edge of the sea,
　　　　These spirits of the south who spun precious flax.

---

2. Allknowing, science.

2.
> One Egil took to wife, the lovely maid
> With finefleshed bosom; the other Swanwhite
> Who had swan's wings; but the third sister
> Embraced Völund's white neck.

3.
> They remained seven winters, but in the eighth
> A yearning claimed them, and in the ninth
> Necessity parted them; the maids longed for
>   the somber woods;
> Allvitter, the young, to fulfill her fate.

4.
> Came from the chase the waywise hunters;
> Slagfinn and Egil found their halls void,
> Searched all about: Egil skied east after Ölrun,
> Slagfinn went south after Swanwhite.

5.
> Völund waited alone in the Wolfdale,
> Hammered the red-glowing gold at the forge,
> Letting each arm-ring lock a divine link,
> Biding his bright-browed bride's return.

6.
> Then learns Nidud, king of the Njars,
> That Völund alone in the Wolfdale waits;
> By night there came men in mailed byrnies;
> Their shields shone bright by the sickle moon.

7.
> They dismounted from their saddles at the gable
> And, entering, marched the length of the hall.
> Rings they saw threaded on ribbons and straw,
> Seven hundred, all owned by the smith.

8.
> They took them off, they threaded them on,
> Except one only, which they left off.
> Came from the chase the hunter suspicious,
> Völund had wandered a very long way.

9.
> Quickly he went to brown the bear-meat,
> High burned the kindling of dried fir wood,

The windsere wood,
Before Völund.

10.   He sat on the bearskin and counted the links,
The ruler of elves. One link was missing;
He thought that Lödver's daughter had taken it,
That Allvitter, the young, had returned again.

11.   Long he sat thus, until sleep overcame him.
Awakened to sorrow:
His hands were heavy with hard fetters
    chained,
On his feet was a shackle laid.

12. VÖLUND: "What men are they
Who have bound with bonds
The tamer of winds,
Who have tied me up?"

13.   Now called Nidud, the king of the Njars: "How
    did you,
Völund, wise elf, find our noble gold in the
    Wolfdale?
There was no gold on Grane's road;
Our land is far from the mountain lode."

14. VÖLUND: "I remember we had greater treasure, when all
Together we were at home.
Ladgun and Hervör, children of Lödver,
Ölrun was daughter of Kjar.

15.   "She entered and strode the length of the hall,
Stood still and quietly said:
'Now evil comes out of the woods.'"

King Nidud gave his daughter Bödvild the ring that was
taken from the chain in Völund's hall; but he himself bore
the sword of Völund. The queen spoke:

16.   "See how he bares his teeth when he sees the
            sword
        And the ring borne by Bödvild.
        His eyes gleam like serpents' eyes.
        Cut his sinews' strength and place him
        In the ships' harbor."

This was done and he was hamstrung and placed in the
Sävarstad (harbor). There he smithied treasures for the king.
None dared approach him, save the king only.

17. VÖLUND: "There shines at Nidud's side the sword
            I tempered the best I knew, and honed
            With all my skill.

18.   "My flaming blade is borne far away,
        Nevermore to return to Völund's smithy;
        Now Bödvild bears my own bride's ring
        Of reddest gold, and I can do naught."

19.   So sat he, never sleeping, beating with his
            hammer,
        Soon forging treachery toward Nidud.
        Two lads came running, looked in at the door:
        Two sons of Nidud in Sävarstad.

20.   They went to the chest, they demanded the key,
        Apparent was evil as they looked inside:
        Jewels aplenty they saw within,
        Of purest gold and precious stones.

21. VÖLUND: "Come back alone, you two, come back
            tomorrow
            And you shall be given the glittering gold!
            But tell neither man nor maid in the hall,
            Tell no one at all that you have seen me."

22.   Early they called, brother to brother,
             Each to the other: "To the smithy, away!"
             They came to the chest, they demanded the key,
             Apparent was evil when they looked therein.

23.   He cut their heads off and laid their limbs
             Underneath the water;
             But the pale skulls beneath the hair
             He silvered and sold to Nidud.

24.   The precious stones from their eyes' sockets
             He sent to Nidud's cunning wife;
             And from the teeth of the two boys
             He fashioned a necklace for Bödvild.

25.   Bödvild came to praise the ring,
             Brought it to Völund
             When it was broken.
             She dared tell no one else.

26. VÖLUND: "I shall mend the break in the gold,
             So that it shall fairer seem to your father,
             Better than ever to your mother,
             The same to yourself."

27.   He brought her a beaker,
             The best of beer,
             And soon in her seat
             She sank into sleep.

28.   "Now am I avenged
             For the harm to me,
             For all but one,
             The worst of all.

29.   "It is well," quoth Völund,
             "I stand on my feet

Although Nidud's men
Deprived them of power."

30.
Smiling, Völund rose on high;
Weeping, Bödvild left the island;
Fearful for her lover
And her father's fury.

31.
Out went Nidud's ill-willing spouse,
And entered into the endlong hall,
Where in the court he sat at rest:
"Wake you, Nidud, champion of Njars."

32. NIDUD:
"I ever awaken bereft of joy;
Ill do I sleep since my sons are dead.
Cold is my head, cold is your counsel;
Now will I consult with Völund.

33.
"Tell me, Völund,
Wise elf,
What became
Of my sons?"

34. VÖLUND:
"First shall you swear me by every oath:
By the hull of the ship, by the rim of the shield,
By the heart of the horse, by the edge of the
    sword,
That you bring no pain to Völund's woman,
Nor be the bane of this bride of mine;
If I own a woman known to you
Or have a child here in this hall.

35.
"Go to the smithy that you yourself made,
You will find the bellows bespattered with blood;
The boys' heads I there severed
And laid their bodies beneath the water.

36.   "The white skulls hidden beneath the hair
         I surfaced with silver and sent to Nidud;
         The jeweled eyes from their sockets
         I sent to Nidud's cunning queen.

37.   "But from the two lads' teeth I fashioned
         Pendant gems and sent to Bödvild;
         Now goes Bödvild heavy with child,
         The only daughter of both of you."

38. NIDUD: "No words could grieve me more than yours,
         Nor could I wish you aught worse, Völund.
         So high is no man he could unhorse you,
         None is so skilled he could shoot you down,
         Where you fly in the heavens."

39.   Smiling Völund rose in the air,
         Sorrowful Nidud stayed where he sat.

40. NIDUD: "Rise up, Tackrád, best of thralls,
         Bid Bödvild, the bright-browed,
         Go to her father,
         To speak with him.

41.   "Is it true, Bödvild, what he has said,
         That you and Völund met on the island?"

42. BÖDVILD: "It is true what he told you, Nidud,
         That I was with Völund
         Together on the island,
         For one brief moment of guilt.
         I could not withstand him.
         I could not resist him."

22

Lokasenna

(Loki's Flyting[1])

The Aesir and Ásynjor (deities) were assembled in the inviolable, spacious hall, lighted by bright gold, to feast on the ale brewed in Hymer's caldron by Äger. Thor was absent "in easterly ways" and Loki had not been invited. At this point in evolution, when ale was already brewed, Loki, the human mind, had become proud and selfish, intractable to the promptings of the spiritual soul, and therefore he had no place in the banquet hall of the gods. Elves, however, were present: the finest properties of human souls, which had united their essence, their ásmegir (godmaker), with the divine Self, and who therefore could enter the sacred precincts.

Loki slew Fimafeng (the nimblefingered), forced his way into the hall and demanded to share in the revels. He reminded Odin of their kinship, calling himself Lopt (lofty — aspiring human intelligence). At Odin's command Vidar then ceded his place to Loki and served him ale but, before drinking, Loki toasted all the gods, pointedly omitting Brage (intuition, bardic inspiration). He accused that noble virtue (Brage) of cowardice and, when Brage offered him bangles of gold (such as were used for money) and even his horse and sword to keep the peace of the sacred place, Loki still refused to be silenced. Idun rose to defend Brage, whereupon she too became the butt of Loki's ready tongue, and soon each Áse and Ásynja, rising to the defense of another (never of himself), received the renegade's insults. At length Frigga intervened. She tried to soothe the angry company, enjoining the gods to forget the follies

---

1. "Dispute in verse form" (Webster's Dictionary).

of their youth and cease upbraiding each other with long forgotten peccadilloes, whereupon Loki turned on her too, accusing the mother of the gods of infidelity. This brought a sharp retort from Freya who reminded Loki that "Frigg knows every being's fate though she herself says naught." Arriving on the scene, Thor too indulged in an altercation with Loki who, when threatened with Mjölnir, the pulverizer, finally ceased and left.

At first reading, the feast of the deities seems a pointless succession of insults but, on closer scrutiny, it illustrates how a materialistic and uninspired intellect looks at nature, and particularly how such a pragmatic mind regards the powers represented as gods in mythic stories. Loki's vituperations read like the language of a Billingsgate fishwife. He sees in the actions of universal powers only the reflection of his own limited and distorted perceptions. Regarded in this way the metaphor becomes quite transparent. In fact, Loki's accusations of infidelity and immorality are exactly duplicated in numerous books of mythology today, where adultery and incest among the deities are taken literally and at face value. But when the gods and goddesses are, more logically, regarded as overlapping, enhancing, or mitigating force fields which interact with one another physically — gravitationally and in other ways throughout the electromagnetic spectrum — their combined effects may well accord with what the mythic tales relate. When, in addition, their various spheres of influence are taken to include spiritual and divine interactions, their meaning enters a realm of sacred science.

The mind is dual. Born of giant forebears, Loki is also one of the Aesir and their constant companion, aide, and interpreter when they travel in the giant worlds. His pranks are, on the surface, a rich source of amusement but, as we seek to understand his place in the evolution of beings, we soon see the pitfalls into which Loki alone, uninspired by Brage, can lead us. Allied with poetic inspiration (Brage), the lower practical mind (Loki) becomes lofty (Lopt), the salvation of humanity, and provides the mead for the inner god. When alone, it alienates itself from the heart of Being; unheeding of intuition, it rails against the gods, against universal law, against justice, love, and compassion. Our own civilization illustrates this for, although most human beings are well disposed and inclined to compassionate action, often cleverness is prized above virtue and physical skills above wisdom. If the gentler qualities were entirely lacking our world would truly be a hell, for technology untempered with ethics leads to disaster (which literally means it divorces us from the stars). Human progress is best promoted not by mind alone but by an alliance of mind and heart.

As the Aesir at their revels partake of the garnered spiritual gains of the life just past, the elves rest among them. These are souls that have earned their association with the divinities, leaving "outside" that part of mind — Loki — which seeks its own and separate goals. But the sleeping elves are not yet conscious in the sphere of the gods and can take no active part in the festivities; their awareness is not adequate to enjoy those realms. They are the souls' increment of good, dreaming their heavenly dreams in the higher halls of Hel, while awaiting the urge to enter once more into incarnation as men and women.

There is also another explanation for the sleeping elves. In the sacred traditions each of nature's kingdoms in turn has its heyday in any one world; the other streams of life belonging to that world are then relatively inactive. Our earth, as we observe, is presently concentrating its life forces in the human sphere. The mineral and vegetable representatives, though present, are for the most part quiescent. It is said that when the mineral kingdom is active, volcanism is tremendously prevalent and, when the vegetation is most flourishing, plants are not gently rooted but move freely over the earth. When the next succeeding wave of life following the human comes to our planet, ours will "sleep" among the lowest kingdom of the gods who will then be the predominant evolvers of the globe, "quaffing the ale" of life.

Lokasenna

Äger, also named Gymer, had prepared a drinking bout for the Aesir, after receiving the great caldron, as has been told.[2] To this banquet came Odin and Frigg, his wife. Thor did not, as he was in easterly ways but Sif, his wife, was there. Also Brage and his wife Idun. Tyr also; he was one-handed, for the Fenris wolf had torn off his hand while being bound. There was Njörd, and his wife Skade, Frey and Freya, and Vidar, Odin's son. Loki was there, as also Frey's servants, Byggver and Beyla. There was a host of Aesir and elves.

Äger had two servants, Fimafeng[3] and Elder. Bright gold supplied the light instead of fire, the ale served itself, and the place was inviolable and spacious. Those present praised the excellence of Äger's servants; Loki could not bear this, so he slew Fimafeng, whereupon the Aesir shook their shields, shouted at Loki, and drove him into the forest while they went to drink. Loki returned and met Elder outside. He said:

LOKI: Tell me, Elder, before you take another step: At the ale feast, whereof speak the sons of the triumphant gods?

ELDER: They judge of their weapons and their battle honor, the sons of the triumphant gods. Of Aesir and elves in there none has a good word for you.

LOKI: I shall go into Äger's hall and see this drinking feast.

2. The Lay of Hymer, pp. 147, 153.
3. The deft.

I shall bring scorn and anger to the Aesir's sons and so blend evil in the mead.

ELDER: Know that if you go into Äger's hall to see this drinking feast and heap scorn and abuse on the gentle gods, they may wipe it off on you.

LOKI: And you know, Elder, if we two have it out with words together that I am far better armed with speech than you.

Then entered Loki into the hall. At his entrance all fell silent.

LOKI: Thirsty came Lopt into this hall from far away to beg the Aesir, that one of them might give me a sip of fine mead. Why are you silent, gloomy gods? Have you nothing to say? Either show me a seat or forcibly drive me away.

BRAGE: A seat at the festive board shall you never have from the Aesir because they well know what kind of person they choose to carouse with.

LOKI: Remember, Odin, how in the foretime we two mingled blood together; you then said you never would drink ale were it not served us both.

ODIN: Rise, Vidar, and let the wolf's father have a seat in the assembly, that Loki may not charge us with scorn here in Äger's hall.

Vidar rose and poured for Loki. Before he drank, Loki addressed the Aesir:

LOKI: Hail ye, Aesir, hail Ásynjor, hail all holy gods, excepting him who sits inmost on the bench — Brage!

BRAGE: My horse and sword I give you freely, also a ring I forfeit to you, that you pay not the Aesir with envy and make the gods angry.

LOKI: May you ever be robbed of horse and bangle, Brage! Of all Aesir and elves here you are the most craven.

BRAGE: Were I outside instead of inside Äger's hall I should bear your head in my hand. It would serve your lie right.

LOKI: You are brave when seated, Brage, bench ornament! Go and fight if you want to. A brave man hesitates not.

IDUN: I beg of you, Brage, by your children and your wished-for sons, tease not Loki reproachfully here in Äger's hall.

LOKI: Shut up, Idun. You of all women I think are the most man-crazy since your dazzling arms clasped your brother's bane.

IDUN: I will not tease Loki with accusations here in Äger's hall. I would rather appease Brage who is wrought up; I do not want you two angered to fight.

GEFION:[4] Why should you, two Aesir, use sharp words between you? Lopt knows not how he is joking and tempting the gods.

LOKI: Shut up, Gefion, let us not forget how you were seduced by the white youth who gave you the gem and whom you linked in your limbs.

ODIN: You are mad, Loki, out of your mind, angering Gefion, for she knows all the fates of the ages as well as I do.

LOKI: Shut up, Odin; you never did know how to choose justly among warriors; often you gave victory to those you should not, the very worst.

---

4. Gefion is a lunar aspect of Freya.

ODIN:	And if I gave victory to the worst whom I should not, you spent eight winters in the underworld, a milker of cows, a woman, and there you bore children, offspring of evil. This I call cause to name you wretch.
LOKI:	You are said on earth to have used seery, to have cheated in sibyl's wisdom, and walked the world in a sorcerer's guise.
FRIGG:	You should not talk of your doings in adolescent years, what you two Aesir practiced in the foretime. Folks forget old grudges.
LOKI:	Quiet, Frigg, you are Fjörgyn's maid and have ever sought dalliance, as when you, Vidrer's woman, clasped both Vile and Vi to your bosom.
FRIGG:	Had I a son such as Balder here in Äger's hall you would not escape the sons of the Aesir without being badly beaten.
LOKI:	Well, Frigg, will you that I tell more of my harmful runes? I shall work it so that you shall not again see Balder riding to the halls.
FREYA:	You are mad, Loki, ranting your evil doings; Frigg, I know, knows every being's fate, though she herself says naught.
LOKI:	Shut up, Freya, I know you well. You lack not faults: of the Aesir and elves who are here within, you have whored with them all.
FREYA:	Your tongue is false and I believe it will babble you evil and ills in the future. You have angered the Aesir and Ásynjor. In shame shall you wend your way home.

LOKI: Shut up, Freya, you are a witch full of evil; when the mild gods found you conjuring with your brother, ugly you snorted then.

NJÖRD: It matters little if the woman embrace a husband or lover, but it is a miracle that the Aesir's hermaphrodite could enter here, as he bore offspring.[5]

LOKI: Shut up, Njörd. When eastward hence you were sent as hostage of the gods, Hymer's maids used you for a jar and poured in your mouth.

NJÖRD: I have the consolation that when I was eastward sent as hostage of the gods, I begot a son whom no one hates, a doughty defender of the Aesir.[6]

LOKI: Stay, Njörd, hold your tongue; no longer shall this be hid: with your sister you begot such a son. It was to be expected.

TYR: Frey is the best of all the bold Aesir: no man's wife or maid laments on his account. He loosens all links.

LOKI: Shut up, Tyr, you never made peace between any two; let us speak of your right hand. Fenrer tore it from you.

TYR: I lost my hand, and you your star witness. The harm is ill for us both. The wolf is no better off, biding in fetters till the end of the ages.

LOKI: Shut up, Tyr. With your wife it happened that she bore a son by me; you never received an ell nor a penny for the dishonor, poor fool.

---

5. In a past age Loki imbodied as a mare and with the stallion Svadilfare (*svadil* a slippery place + *fara* travel, hence disaster) gave birth to Sleipnir (slider), Odin's eight-legged steed.

6. Frey.

FREY: I see the wolf lying at the river's mouth till the rulers' reign shall be rent. Beside him shall you also be chained if you cease not now, schemer.

LOKI: With gold you bought Gymer's daughter, and so sold your sword; but when Muspell's sons ride over the Mirkwood, how shall you then fight?

BYGGVER: Had I the noble birth of Ingunar-Frey and such a blissful abode, I should grind you finer than marrow, you bird of ill omen, and lame all your limbs.

LOKI: What toddler is this I see sneaking his fare, a sniffer of crumbs? You tattle in Frey's ear and tread the mill.

BYGGVER: Byggver is my name, and I am called smart among gods and men; I am privileged to drink good ale here with all Ropt's sons.

LOKI: Shut up, Byggver, you never could share fairly the food among men; and you were hidden beneath the bench-hay when men came to blows.

HEIMDAL: You are drunk, Loki, and robbed of your wits; why don't you cease, Loki? Overindulgence causes both young and old to lose control of their tongues.

LOKI: Shut up, Heimdal. In the morning of days you were ill-fated to be ever splashed on the back, watcher for the gods.

SKADE: You are funny, Loki, but not for long may you play with a wagging tail; for, tied with your cold son's guts on a sharp rock shall the angry gods bind you.

LOKI: If on a sharp rock the angry gods bind me with my

frostcold son's guts, I was both first and last in the battle when Tjasse[7] lost his life.

SKADE: If first and last you were in the tumult when Tjasse gave his life, then from my sanctuaries, my sacred groves, shall you meager counsel gain.

LOKI: Gentler were your words to the son of Löfö when you bade me to your bed; such things must be told if we are to narrate all our faults.

Beyla/Sif came forth and poured the tankard with mead for Loki:

SIF: Hail thee, Loki, take this cup filled with mellow mead, and may I alone of Aesir's children be held free from faults.

Loki took the horn and drank.

LOKI: Alone indeed were you, if you were so faithful and attentive to your spouse, but I know one who has lain in Lorride's bed, and that is sly Loki.

BEYLA: The mountains quake; I believe Lorride is on his way here from home: he will silence the traducer whether god or man.

LOKI: Shut up, Beyla, you are Byggver's woman, full of evil, a more insolent nuisance came not among the Aesir's children, you dirty dairymaid.

Thor entered and spoke:

THOR: Quiet, miserable wretch, I shall rob you of speech with Mjölnir, my fire-hammer; I shall strike your head from your neck, thus shall you lose your life.

LOKI: Now is come the son of Earth. Why so noisy,

7. Skade's father.

Thor? You dare not brag of battling the wolf who swallows Victory-father whole.

THOR: Quiet, miserable wretch, my force-hammer Mjölnir shall rob you of speech. I shall hurl you aloft in the eastern space that none may see you again.

LOKI: Of your eastern journeys you never should speak before men since you crouched in the thumb of the giant's mitt, warrior.[8] You seemed unlike Thor then.

THOR: Quiet, miserable wretch, my force-hammer Mjölnir shall rob you of speech; with this my right hand I shall slay you with Rungner's bane, that all your bones break.

LOKI: I mean to live yet a long, long age, though you threaten me with the hammer; dreadfully tight did Skrymir's knots seem to you; though hale and strong you went hungry.

THOR: Quiet, miserable wretch, my force-hammer Mjölnir shall rob you of speech; Rungner's bane shall bring you to Hel, below the gates of death.

LOKI: I sang for the Aesir and for Aesir's sons whatsoever I chose, but only for you do I leave hence, for I know that Thor will strike at last. Ale you brewed, Äger, but never more shall you make feast again; may all that you here have with you be burned over and fire burn your back.

After this, Loki went in the shape of a salmon into the Frananger stream, where the Aesir caught him. He was

---

8. Cf. Thor and Loki in Jotunheim, p. 144.

bound with the guts of his son Nare. Narfi his [other] son became a wolf. Skade suspended a poisonous viper above Loki. The venom drips from it. Sigyn, Loki's wife, sits holding a bowl under the venom and when she goes to empty the bowl, the venom drips on Loki. He writhes in pain so that the earth shakes. These are called earthquakes.

23

Allvismál

(The Lay of Allwise)

TRANSLATOR'S NOTES

Allvis (allwise or allknowing) is a dwarf who desires to wed the daughter of Thor. Doubting that the dwarf is worthy of this union, Thor nevertheless gives him an opportunity to prove himself and subjects him to an intensive examination concerning the attitudes and vision that characterize different grades of beings which compose the world. Allvis gives satisfactory replies to all questions, but Thor keeps him talking till daybreak when the first rays of the rising sun strike him, and he turns to stone or, in some versions, blends with the mountain from which he had emerged.

Many fairy tales have this surprise ending, where a dwarf or troll turns to stone when faced with the dawn of day. Several possible interpretations present themselves. One is that the forces belonging to the night side of nature, having no business with the concerns of the day, cease from activity when light returns. Allvis, however, conveys something more than this. He is a knowledgeable dwarf, who presumes to demand union with the daughter of the god who is sustainer of life: as a human nature, he is well informed but unenlightened; he is seeking immortality on the strength of his considerable knowledge, but his "dwarf" nature is still immature and, unless inspired and receptive to the solar radiance, it cannot gain the desired union with divinity. When the neophyte faces the solar essence, the dwarf element, unfit to blend with it, "turns to stone."

Many mythologies, including the biblical, use stone or rock to symbolize dogmatic, dead-letter religion. This is exemplified by

Moses drawing living water from the rock — explaining the teachings within the ritual; and later, Christianity reverted to the "rock" (*petra* or Peter) as the foundation of the church.

This lay is probably susceptible also of other, equally valid interpretations; it is very revealing of different viewpoints that characterize consciousnesses at various stages of awareness and comprehension — from the simple matter-standpoint of the giants, through the differing perceptions of the dwarfs and of the elves, to the overview of nature commanded by the gods.

Allvismál

1. ALLWISE: The benches are being adorned.
   Now a bride shall go to her home
   With great haste it seems.
   No rest is awaiting at home.

2. THOR: What dastard is this? Why so pale in the face?
   Did you sleep with the dead last night?
   Meseems there is something thurselike
       about you.
   You are not born for a bride.

3. ALLWISE: Allwise is my name. I live below ground
   And my city lies beneath stone.
   The wagon-warrior[1] I come to seek.
   Let no one break his word!

4. THOR: I break it though, for I, as her father,
   Have the best right to decide.
   I was not home when she was promised.
   I alone among gods am marriage-maker.

5. ALLWISE: Who is this fellow who says he rules
   Over the fair and blessed woman?
   By your bowshots far there are few who know
       you.
   Who has borne you to golden rings?

6. THOR: Wingthor am I. I have traveled widely

---

1. Thor.

And I am the son of Broadbeard.[2]
Not against my will shall you have the maiden
Or receive her troth.

7. ALLWISE: Soon shall I have your promise, though,
And receive that troth.
I would rather have than forgo
The snowwhite maiden.

8. THOR: Nor shall her love be denied to you,
Wise guest, if from every world
You can give me tidings of all
That I wish to know.

9. ALLWISE: Try me, Wingthor, in all you would ask,
See what the dwarf is good for!
I have traveled in all the nine worlds
And have learned something of all.[3]

10. THOR: Tell me, Allwise, for you must know
The fates of all the kingdoms:
What is that earth disposed for the sons
Of ages in every world?

11. ALLWISE: Men call it Earth, but the Aesir[4] Humus;
The Vans call it Ways.
Giants say Evergreen, elves name it Growth;
The aspiring name it Origin.

12. THOR: Tell me, Allwise, as you must know
The fates of all kingdoms:
What is the heaven, the lofty-domed,
Named in each world?

---

2. Odin.
3. This verse is missing in Codex Regius.
4. Codex Regius has elves.

13. ALLWISE: Men call it heaven, the gods say defense,
Windmaker is he to Vaner;
The giants say upper home, elves say fair-roof,
The dripping hall is it to dwarfs.

14. THOR: Tell me then, Allwise, as you must know
The fates of all kingdoms:
What is the moon that people see
In every world?

15. ALLWISE: It is moon to men but to gods the diminisher,
Turning wheel in the house of Hel;
Giants say hastener, dwarfs call it shine;
Elves name it tally of time.

16. THOR: Tell me then, Allwise, as you must know
The fates of all kingdoms:
What is the sun that people see
In every world?

17. ALLWISE: Men call it sun but gods say the southernmost,
Dwarfs call it Dvalin's toy;
Giants say ever-glowing, elves call it fairwheel,
All transparent is it to Aesir's sons.

18. THOR: Tell me then, Allwise, as you must know
The fates of all kingdoms:
What are the clouds that drench with rain
Named in each world?

19. ALLWISE: Men call them clouds, the gods shower-wont,
The Vans say wind river;
Giants say weatherbode, elves tempest-boder,
Hel's folk say the hiding helmet.

20. THOR: Tell me then, Allwise, as you must know
The fates of all kingdoms:

What is the wind that fares so far
In every world?

21. ALLWISE: He is wind to men, but wafter to gods,
Neigher to the highest gods (Vaner),
Howler to giants, din-maker to elves,
Whirler in the house of Hel.

22. THOR: Tell me then, Allwise, as you must know
The fates of all kingdoms:
What is that calm that shall one day come
And settle on every world?

23. ALLWISE: To men it is calm, to gods the law,
Vaner say end-of-wind;
Giants say stifling, elves a day's sleep,
Dwarfs call it end-of-being.

24. THOR: Tell me then, Allwise, as you must know
The fates of all kingdoms:
What is that sea whereon one rows
In every world?

25. ALLWISE: It is sea to men, the funnel's eye to gods,
Waves to the wise Vaner:
Eelhome to giants, to elves staff-of-law,
To dwarfs the deep sea.

26. THOR: Tell me then, Allwise, as you must know
The fates of all kingdoms:
What is the name of fire that burns for all
In every world?

27. ALLWISE: To men it is fire, to Aesir the spark that lights,
Wagon to Vaner;
Giants say gluttonous, burning to dwarfs,
The swift in Hel's house.

28. THOR: Tell me then, Allwise, as you must know
              The fates of all kingdoms:
              What is that forest that, shading, grows
              In every world?

29. ALLWISE: He is forest to men but earth-man to gods,
              To Hel he is barrow-kelp,
              Fuel to giants, to elves flower-twigs,
              Vaner say willow-wand.

30. THOR: Tell me then, Allwise, as you must know
              The fates of all kingdoms:
              What is the night, daughter of dark,
              Named in each world?

31. ALLWISE: Men call her night, the gods say dark,
              The highest gods say the disguiser;
              Giants say unlight, elves joy-of-sleep,
              Dwarfs call her dream-binder.

32. THOR: Tell me then, Allwise, as you must know
              The fates of all kingdoms:
              What is the harvest sown by the sons of the ages
              In every world?

33. ALLWISE: Men call it grain, the gods yet-to-bear,
              Vaner say growth;
              Giants, food; elves the staff-of-law,
              In Hel's house a heavy head.

34. THOR: Tell me then, Allwise, as you must know
              The fates of all kingdoms:
              What is that ale the sons of the aeons
              Quaff in each world?

35. ALLWISE: To men it is ale, but with Aesir beer,
              To Vaner a draught of power;

Pure law to giants, mead in Hel's house,
But festive drink to Suttung's sons.

36. THOR: In one man's breast I never saw so many staves
                    of wisdom.
             With subterfuge have I misled you;
             Till daybreak, dwarf, you are still up.
             Now shines the sun in the hall.

24

Grogaldern and Fjölsvinns Ordskifte
(*The Spells of Groa* and *Verywise's Exchange*)

TRANSLATOR'S NOTES

GROGALDERN

The two lays that follow belong together and it would be misleading to separate them. The first enumerates the necessary qualities that must have been acquired by a candidate for initiation, while the second relates the culminating test itself. Together they tell the story of Svipdag, and his "Appearing as Day."

Od[1] (man) is sent forth by his stepmother Skade on the supposedly impossible errand of finding and gaining admission to the hall of Menglad ("she who enjoys a jewel," a name for Freya, owner of the Brisingamen, humanity). Skade is the sister, wife, and also a daughter of Njörd (time). It was she who suspended the venomous serpent over Loki's face when he was confined in the underworld.

To meet the all but insurmountable difficulties of his quest, Od invokes the aid of his dead mother, who is named Groa (growth). She rises from the dead to sing him nine protective charms. Represented as a sibyl, she symbolizes the hero's past, his former selves which have shaped his character and given him birth as he now is. If the lives of preparation have brought him the qualities he needs for success, he will be equipped for the great trial before him.

The "protective charms" are of course the strengths and virtues he has earned. First of these is freedom from all external pressures; the second is self-control; third, immunity from the powerful currents that flow towards the realms of death (of the soul); fourth is

---

1. Od is derived from *Odr*, spiritual mind, and stands for the evolved man. Similarly, the English word *man* is derived from the Sanskrit *manas*, which also means the higher intelligence, from *man*, to reflect upon, to think.

the power to turn enemies into friends, to transmute negative traits into positive, useful attributes; fifth is the magic sword which will loosen all bonds, all limiting weaknesses which by now the hero must have overcome. They are the personal ties that attract the soul away from its high purpose. Sixth, she endows him with the aid of the natural elements, even those of that "sea, more dread than men may know" (11) — the astral light with its baleful illusions; seventh, he gains immunity from the "frost of the high mountain" (12) — the chilling fear that grips the soul when faced with the unfamiliar heights of purer worlds. Eighth is the power to pass unharmed among the shades of the dead.

From all this a theosophic interpretation shows clearly that the adventure on which Od has embarked is an initiation into a high estate of spiritual awareness. Such initiation demands first a descent into the regions beneath our physical world. Each great Teacher of mankind has to "descend into hell" to render aid to lower grades of beings and to feel and understand their condition, while proving his integrity and remaining unaffected by the noxious miasmas of these worlds.

Ninth, the sibyl enjoins: "If you exchange words with the spear-renowned giant, of words and man-sense of tongue as of heart, may you have enough!" (14)

The nine charms also denote qualities that have been, or should have been, developed by each human being who has traversed the nine worlds we have experienced in this cycle. Certain it is that they are necessary equipment for any soul to become truly enlightened.

FJÖLSVINN'S EXCHANGE

We find Od in this lay seeking admittance to the hall of Menglad, whose name we know as a kenning for Freya. The guardian at the gate to Menglad's hall calls himself Fjölsvinn (Verywise) and is none other than Odin, here standing for the man's inner god and hierophant. He rebuffs the traveler, calling him "giant" and "wolf," but Od insists on gaining access to the gilded hall. Asked his name he responds:

"Windcold is my name, Springcold was my father. His sire was Verycold" (6).

Od then asks whose hall this is and learns that it is indeed that of Menglad, "born of her mother and the son of the Sleep-enchanter" (7).

Here is the origin of the tale of the Sleeping Beauty. In Sweden she is Törnrosa (thornrose), the rose pricked with the thorn of sleep: she is man's spiritual soul, the unawakened beauty who is the aim of life for man. The sleep-enchanter is in certain respects identified with Njörd, as Time, and also with Springcold, a far-past age of innocence. The seeker and the sought are thus descended from the same divine source, as are the human soul and its inner god. It is the aim of the individual to gain reunion with the universal after fulfilling its self-awareness through evolution in all the realms of matter: with Menglad-Freya — the higher self of man, his spiritual intelligence — to become one with the divinity that is awaiting its human champion.

In the guise of Windcold, Od poses questions of the keeper at the gate, and Odin-Verywise responds: he gives the name and function of the gate that binds like a fetter any pilgrim who lifts the latch; and of the court made from the limbs of the mud giant — the substance from which were made the first forms of men which were rejected as unfit vehicles by the gods and which were superseded by a later creation. Its task is to repel all comers. The two fierce watchdogs, according to Verywise, have eleven watches yet to keep before this life term ends.

When Windcold asks the name of the tree whose branches spread over all the land he is told it is Mimameid, the Tree of Knowledge, "which falls not for fire or iron" (20), and whose fruit helps what is hidden within to be revealed. Not to be confused with the Tree of Life its name links it with the "wise giant" Mimer, owner of the well of the wisdom to be gained through existence in matter. In the biblical Genesis, too, the trees of life and knowledge are quite distinct. It is clear that the "fall" from innocence was an inevitable part of the evolutionary process. Man *must* leave the childlike con-dition and enter what the Edda terms the "victory worlds" in order to earn, consciously and self-consciously, his ultimate access to the

Tree of Life. Here the human soul or elf, Od, must by its own self-determined efforts attain the godlike state that enables it to unite with its hamingja (immortal essence). We shall see how thorough a familiarity with the Tree of Knowledge is needed for the human initiant to gain this union.

Windcold asks about the golden bird in the topmost branches of Mimameid and is told it is Wideopener. The hero must conquer him, but in order to do this he must enter the underworld and there obtain the magic potion brewed by Lopt (lofty: aspiration), the inspired aspect of Loki, mind guided by its hamingja. The brew was made from remorse in the lower hells and is kept in a tub of tough iron, secured by nine strong locks. He must wrest it from its keeper, the dreaded hag Sinmara who, like Ceridwen of the Welsh, guards the caldron. The brew, like the mystic soma-drink supposedly given to initiants in the East, aids in opening the consciousness to the fearsome hells of the soul. These the candidate must successfully traverse — "endless woes" concentrated by the Wideopener "in one great sorrow" (23).

But there is a paradox here: in order to obtain from Sinmara the magic potion which will make accessible the Wideopener in the topmost branches of the Tree of Knowledge, the hero must bring her a shining feather from that golden bird!

The candidate who seeks the wisdom of the gods must thus gain access to the spiritual heights in order to descend to the nether-most regions and return unscathed; only after his successful rise from the descent into hell may he claim his bride — attain union with the immortal essence of himself, the universal heart of his being, and achieve the vistas of unlimited consciousness — for this world or branch of the Tree of Life.

There is here a story within a story, as so often happens in myths. Od, who stands at the gateway leading to the final revelation, in his exchange with the guardian of the gate who is his initiator, guide, and examiner, receives information which is clearly intended for the listener, or reader: a description of the types of experience and enlightenment of mind and soul which must be undergone by one who aspires to enter the hall named Calm, "long poised on the point of a spear, whereof only hearsay reached the people of old" (31) — (when there were as yet none who could receive it?)

At length Windcold stands revealed as Svipdag, the radiant — "Appearing as Day." Now he names himself son of Sunbright, "tossed forth on windcold ways" (46). The Egyptian Mysteries refer to the risen initiate as a "son of the sun," for a radiance is visible about him. This is the long forgotten origin of the *uṣṇīṣa* or halo above or about the heads of Bodhisattvas, Christs, and saints in ancient and mediaeval art. Svipdag, the successful initiate, represents one of such rare perfected humans in the history of mankind. "Tossed on windcold ways" are we all, every monad, each spark of divine fire which emerged from IT at the beginning of time and descended into spheres of life; destined at the end of the cycle to become reunited with its divine parent, every monad of consciousness brings with it the increment of experience earned throughout its existence.

The end of this lay reveals the Edda as a transmission of the one universal theosophy which is expressed through the Buddhist, Christian, and other sacred traditions throughout history. The story of Svipdag points to the true goal of life — hastened in initiation — something which has been consistently overlooked by modern mythologers. It is the very crux of the hero's venture, his selfless progress, success, and the crowning reunion with his hamingja. When Menglad welcomes him as her beloved, saying she has long awaited him on the sacred mountain, he responds, "Both have we yearned; I have longed for you, and you to meet me. Atonement is now as we two together share the tasks of the years and the ages" (48).

These few words are among the most important in all mythologies extant: the hero united with his spiritual self — not triumphant in his glory or content to rest eternally in heavenly peace — undertakes to aid his higher self in performing henceforth "the tasks of the years and the ages." This final verse places the Norse myths among the noblest scriptures of the world, those which enjoin the divine sacrifice whereby the aspirant aims to serve mankind and gains universal peace only in order to renounce it for the benefit of all beings. This is the ideal of the schools of genuine occultism down through the ages and the motivation of all the world's saviors.

Grogaldern

1. SON: [OD]	Waken, Groa, good woman. I call you at the doors of death. Mind you not that you enjoined your son to come to the barrow-tomb?
2. MOTHER: [GROA]	What fate has stricken my only son, to what ill is my child born, That you call your mother from the dead, where she is gone from the world of men?
3. SON:	An ill trick played me the sly woman who embraced my father; She has sent me where none may go — to seek Menglad.
4. MOTHER:	Long is the journey, far are the roads: far-reaching human passions; If you succeed in your desire, Skuld[2] will also be content.
5. SON:	Sing me spells that are good, help your son, Mother! On wide ways Shall I helpless stray. I feel too young for the marriage.
6. MOTHER:	First, I sing you the song of fortune that Rane sang to Rind: Shake all ills from your shoulders and steer your own steps.

---

2. Future.

7.

I sing you a second: As you wander on
  unwilling ways: Urd's[3] bolts
Hold you fast if you find abuse.

8.

I sing you a third: If towering torrents
  threaten to engulf you,
They shall hasten to Hel and for you they
  shall lower their level.

9.

I sing you a fourth: If enemies lurk, armed,
  on the roads of men,
That their minds may be turned toward you,
  their anger soothed to friendship.

10.

I sing you a fifth: If fetters be laid on your
  limbs, a sword I sound over you
That shall spring the locks from your limbs
  and the fetters shall fall from your feet.

11.

I sing you a sixth: If you be on a sea more
  dread than men may know,
The race of the wind and the roar of the
  waves shall aid you on your journey.

12.

I sing you a seventh: If you freeze from frost
  on the lofty mountain,
The chill of death shall spare your flesh and
  your limbs keep their life.

13.

I sing you an eighth: If on cloudy paths
  overtaken by night,
No harm may befall you from the shade of
  a Christian woman.

14.

I sing you a ninth: If you exchange words
  with the spear-renowned giant,

3. Past.

Of words and man-sense of tongue as of
heart, may you have enough!

15.   Travel no roads where evil you sense. No
obstacle hinders you then.
On the earth-fast rock I stood within the door
chanting these spells for you.

16.   Take your mother's words, son; take them
hence. Let them ever live in your heart.
All that is good shall you ever reap, as long
as you heed my words.

Fjölsvinns Ordskifte

1.   Outside the court he saw rising upward a
giant toward the fort:
"Who is that wretch standing before the court
and turning himself about at the purify-
ing flames?
"Whom do you seek, whose trail do you follow? What seek you to know, friendless
one?
"Wander away once more on wet ways. You
have no champion here, defenseless one."

2. WANDERER: Who is the wretch who stands at the gate and
bids not the wanderer welcome?
Discourteous discourse you dispense. Hie
you hence homeward!

3. THE WATCHMAN: Verywise is my name. I am knowing
enough but waste not much food.

> Into this house you shall never come. Wend
> your ways, wolf!

4. WANDERER: None turns away from his eyes' delight,
> when he sees some sweet sight.
> The courts seem to gleam round the gilded
> hall. Here may I happy dwell.

5. VERYWISE: Tell me of what past you are born, of what
> forebears you are the scion.

6. WANDERER: Windcold is my name, Springcold was my
> father. His sire was Verycold.
> Tell me, Verywise; I must ask and wish to
> know:
> Who rules here and wields the power over
> lands and sumptuous halls?

7. VERYWISE: Menglad is her name, born of her mother and
> the son of the Sleep-enchanter.
> She rules here and wields the power over
> lands and sumptuous halls.

8. WINDCOLD: Tell me, Verywise; I must ask and wish to
> know:
> What is that gate than which even the gods
> have not one more deceptive?

9. VERYWISE: Noisy her name and she was created by the
> three sons of Sunblind.
> Like a fetter she fastens each wayfarer fast
> who unlocks her and opens her up.

10. WINDCOLD: Tell me, Verywise; I must ask and wish to
> know:
> What is that court than which even the gods
> have not one more perilous?

11. VERYWISE: Repeller of strangers is his name. I made him of the mud giant's limbs;
So have I made him that he shall stand as long as men live.

12. WINDCOLD: Tell me, Verywise; I must ask and wish to know:
What are these hounds than which I never saw any more vicious?

13. VERYWISE: One is named Gifr, the other Gere, if you must know.
Eleven watches they have to stand ere the Rulers' reign be rent.

14. WINDCOLD: Tell me, Verywise; I must ask and wish to know:
May any man enter while such beasts slumber?

15. VERYWISE: They have been charged with alternately sleeping since they were trained to watch.
One sleeps by night, the other by day. No one enters here.

16. WINDCOLD: Tell me, Verywise; I must ask and wish to know:
Is there any food one could give them and enter while they eat?

17. VERYWISE: Two steaks there lie in Wideopener's members, if you must know.
That is the only food a man might give them and enter while they eat.

18: WINDCOLD: Tell me, Verywise; I must ask and wish to know:
What family tree spreads here its branches over the land?

19. VERYWISE: Mimameid is the tree and no man knows of
what roots it is grown;
What evil may fell it but few may guess. It
falls not for fire or iron.

20. WINDCOLD: Tell me, Verywise; I must ask and wish to
know:
What will cause to languish the glorious tree
that falls not for fire or iron?

21. VERYWISE: When its fruit shall be burned on the fire by
doting crones, then will go out
What should be within. Then is the tree
rotten among men.

22. WINDCOLD: Tell me, Verywise; I must ask and wish to
know:
What is that rooster high in the tree, all of
him shining of gold?

23. VERYWISE: Wideopener is his name who, shining, perches
high in Mimameid's crown.
He amasses in one great sorrow the endless
woe from Sinmara's fire.

24. WINDCOLD: Tell me, Verywise; I must ask and wish to
know:
Is there a weapon whereby Wideopener may
be brought to the house of Hel?

25. VERYWISE: Lävaten is its name. It was made with remorse by Lopt 'neath the chasm's gate.
In the iron vat in Sinmara's keeping, it is
guarded by nine firm locks.

26. WINDCOLD: Tell me, Verywise; I must ask and wish to
know:
Comes he again who seeks to take that magic
lever?

27. VERYWISE: He may come again who seeks to take that magic lever,
If he bear that which few may own to the fruitful earth's healing-woman.

28. WINDCOLD: Tell me, Verywise; I must ask and wish to know:
Is there anything costly a man might own to delight the hag?

29. VERYWISE: The shining pinion on its quill from Wide-opener's wings shall you bear
As a gift to Sinmara ere she deigns give you the weapon.

30. WINDCOLD: Tell me, Verywise; I must ask and wish to know:
What is that hall which is girt about, wisely, by purging fires?

31. VERYWISE: Calm is his name, and long may he poise on the point of a spear.
About that glorious house only hearsay has reached to the people of old.

32. WINDCOLD: Tell me, Verywise; I must ask and wish to know:
Who of the sons of the gods built the hall I saw through the gates?

33. VERYWISE: *Une* and *Ire*, *Bare* and *Ore*, *Varr* and *Vägdrasil*, *Dore*, *Ure*, and *Delling*; also the sly elf Loki.

34. WINDCOLD: Tell me, Verywise; I must ask and wish to know:
What is that mountain where the bride is to be found ensconced in dreams?

35. VERYWISE: Sacred Mountain its name, a haven since of
old for the sick and wounded;
Though sick unto death, each woman who
ascends here shall be healed.

36. WINDCOLD: Tell me, Verywise; I must ask and wish to
know:
Who are the maids who sit at Menglad's
knees, in harmony together?

37. VERYWISE: Haven is one, Survivor another, a third
Custodian; Bright and Gentle,
Tender and Peace, Compassion, and
Commander of Clemency.[4]

38. WINDCOLD: Tell me, Verywise; I must ask and wish to
know:
Do they save those who sacrifice to them, if
they deem it needful?

39. VERYWISE: They wisely save those who sacrifice in a
holy place.
So harsh an evil comes not to man that he be
not delivered therefrom.

40. WINDCOLD: Tell me, Verywise; I must ask and wish to
know:
Is there a man who may sleep on the lovable
Menglad's arm?

41. VERYWISE: No man is there who may sleep on the lovable
Menglad's arm,
Only Svipdag; to him the sunbright maid is
trothplight for spouse.

42. WINDCOLD: Open wide the gates! Here you see Svipdag!

---

4. Lif, Lifthrasir, Tjodvarta, Bjärt, Blid, Blöd, Frid, Eir, and Örboda.

> It is still unknown whether Menglad will deign to take me for her joy.

43. VERYWISE TO MENGLAD:

> Hear, Menglad. A man is come. Go see the guest yourself.
>
> The hounds are content; the house has opened of itself. Meseems it is Svipdag.

44. MENGLAD:

> If you are lying when you say the man has come from afar to my halls,
>
> Vicious ravens shall tear out your eyes on the high gallows.

45. MENGLAD TO SVIPDAG:

> Whence have you come? Why did you undertake the journey?
>
> By what name are you known in your own house?
>
> By your kin and your name I shall know by portent if I were meant for your wife.

46. SVIPDAG:

> Misty Morn is my name. Sunbright is my father. Thence I was tossed forth
>
> On windcold ways. None may lament Urd's decree though the cause be weak.

47. MENGLAD:

> Be you welcome! What I have wished for I now have; a kiss greet the dear arrival.
>
> Long have I awaited you on the mountain of sleep. Now my hope is fulfilled.
>
> You have once more returned, man, to my halls.

48: SVIPDAG:

> Both have we yearned; I have longed for you, and you to meet me.
>
> Atonement is now, as we two together share the tasks of the years and the ages.

25

Skirnismál

(The Lay of Skirner)

Translator's Notes

Frey, the deity whose imbodiment is in the many-mansioned earth, was seated on Lidskjälf whence he espied the giant maiden Gerd in her father's court. He was consumed with love for her and wished to woo her for his bride. The divine being cannot, however, enter the matter worlds directly and therefore Frey sent his henchman Skirner to woo the maiden on his behalf. Skirner introduces himself to Gerd as "not of the elves, nor of Ása-sons, nor yet am I one of the wise Vaner" (18). What, then, is he?

Skirner means Radiance, a ray of divinity, an avatāra which descends into a lower world in order to enlighten a race of humanity — a giant maid. Equipped with the steed and sword of the god, Skirner rides to the giant world and gains speech with Gerd, but she repels all his overtures. The apples of immortality do not tempt her, nor does "the ring that was burned with Odin's son" (Balder), which drops eight like itself every ninth night — her father, she says, has gold aplenty. Nor is she moved by threats of continuing evils in the giant world with worse to come. However, when her future is revealed to her — extinction in "powerlessness, witlessness, and lust" — she finally agrees to meet with the god in the inviolable sacred grove Barre "where one travels in peace" (39).

The lay of Skirner might easily be dismissed as fantastic nonsense were it not for a certain suggestive quality that parallels other tales relating to the incarnation of a divinity in our world: an avatāric descent. This, like the "hostages" sent by the Vaner to the Aesir, is the penetration of a divine ray from a superior sphere into a lower world and its imbodiment there, to bring an ennobling influence to bear on the thought atmosphere of that world. At certain junctures earth has experienced such events, when a divine teacher has taken human form to teach and inspire humanity. Krishna, Lao-tse, Śankarāchārya, the one whom tradition has named the Christ, and others, are examples of such avatāras. They come at certain cyclic periods; in the words of Krishna, "I produce myself among creatures, O son of Bhārata, whenever there is a decline of virtue and an insurrection of vice and injustice in the world; and thus I incarnate from age to age for the preservation of the just, the destruction of the wicked, and the establishment of righteousness." Each time such an avatāra imbodies among human beings, he strikes anew the keynote of truth which resounds for a longer or shorter epoch, depending on the age; eventually a new cycle begins, bringing a fresh dispensation of the eternal message.

In the light of this, Skirner's mission appears as such a periodic event, one which took place in some dimly remembered prehistoric time — a divine incarnation for the enlightenment of Gerd, daughter race of a grossly materialistic giant race, her father.

Before the descent, however, certain obstacles must be overcome. The radiant messenger must be equipped with the steed that can traverse the "purging fires" that surround the realm of the gods; he must be armed with Frey's sword which wields itself in battling giants "if the bearer is resourceful" (9). In the stories told of Frey, his sword is relatively short: a mere yard long. The one who wields it must be both courageous to approach close to the foe, and resourceful to be able to do so unharmed: the bearer of the weapon of spiritual will is fearless and also wise.

Gerd is evidently an age much like our own, one of material skills and pursuits: she is quite content with the riches of the giant world that are hers and cares not at all for those offered by the god's messenger. Only when the realization of the ceaseless sorrows attendant on a clinging to matter is gradually brought home to her does she choose at last to meet with her divine companion in the sacred grove of peace.

An interesting point raised by this poem revolves around the stepmother, Skade, whose name means "injury." She is the lovely young wife of Njörd, the ageless Saturnian god of time. We have seen that she was the one who hung the venomous serpent over Loki's face to aggravate his suffering in the nether worlds; she is also the instigator of Skirner's errand to inquire of Frey what is troubling him. This is not an easy problem to resolve but it is one that bears consideration. Is it possible that Skade could represent the Norse equivalent of the highly mysterious Nārada of eastern philosophies — the power which brings much immediate suffering but whose long-range effects are to clear the way for productive future growth? Whether she is intended to represent such an agent of natural calamity to further the evolution of beings must remain a moot question.

Skirnismál

Frey, son of Njörd, sat on the Shelf of Compassion one day and looked over all the worlds; he gazed into the realm of the giants and there saw a fair maiden walking from her father's hall to the women's quarters. Thence had he much heartache. Skirner was Frey's squire. Njörd's wife Skade sent him to engage Frey in conversation.

1. SKADE:	Stand forth, Skirner; Go try to engage our son in speech; Ask who it is Who makes the wise one unhappy.	
2. SKIRNER:	I may expect angry words If I ask your son Whom he wishes to espouse.	
3.	Tell me, Frey, prince among gods: Why sit you alone In your infinite hall, Day after day, my lord?	
4. FREY:	How can I reveal to you, Friend of my youth, My heart's great sorrow? Though the sun shines Blessingly each day, It shines not on my desire.	

5. SKIRNER: Surely your wish could not be so lofty
It might not be told to me;
We were young together in ancient days;
We two may trust each other!

6. FREY: In Gymer's courts I saw walking
A maid who pleases me;
Her arms glistened so they reflected
All the heavens and seas;

7.   The maid is more dear to me
Than my childhood friend;
But of Aesir and elves
None wish to see us united.

8. SKIRNER: Bring me the horse that can bear me at dusk
Over the protective purging fires;
That sword as well that wields itself
In battle with giants.

9. FREY: I bring you the steed that can bear you at
dusk
Over the protective purging fires;
The sword also that wields itself
If the bearer thereof is resourceful.

10. SKIRNER TO THE HORSE:
It is dark outside; our aim is to journey
Over moist mountains, close to the thurses;
We both shall be safe or both shall be taken
By the greedy giant.

Skirner rode into the giant world, to Gymer's courts; there angry hounds were bound by the gate of the yard surrounding Gerd's hall. He rode to a herdsman seated on a mound.

11. SKIRNER: Tell me, herdsman who sit on the mound
Watching all roads;

How shall I gain speech with the maiden
For Gymer's angry hounds?

12. HERDSMAN: Are you condemned to death or dead already,
You so high on your horse?
It will be hard for you to gain speech
With Gymer's maiden, the virtuous one.

13. SKIRNER: There are better things to do than haggle,
When wishing to advance.
One day only is my age waxed now,
And all my destiny laid forth.

14. GERD TO HER SLAVE GIRL:
What is the noise,
The roaring din I hear?
The earth trembles
And Gymer's courts quake.

15. SLAVEGIRL: Here is a man, dismounted,
Letting his horse crop grass.

16. GERD: Bid him enter our hall
And drink splendid mead!
Yet I sense a foreboding
That outside stands my brother's bane.

17.   Who among elves or of Ása-sons,
Or of wise Vaner are you?
Why came you alone over oak-lighted fires
To see our hall?

18. SKIRNER: I am not of the elves, nor of Ása-sons,
Nor yet am I one of wise Vaner;
Yet came I alone over oak-lighted fires
To see your hall.

19.   Eleven golden apples I have
To give, Gerd, to you,

To buy your peace and that you
Be not indifferent to Frey.

20. GERD: Eleven apples I will not take
To have a man;
Frey and I may not build
Our lives together.

21. SKIRNER: Then I offer you the ring
That was burned with Odin's young son;
Eight like itself drop therefrom
Every ninth night.

22. GERD: I care not for the ring
Though it was burned with Odin's young son;
For gold I lack not
In Gymer's courts.

23. SKIRNER: See you this sword,
Supple, adorned with runes,
Which I hold in my hand?
I shall sever your head from your neck
If you refuse.

24. GERD: Force shall never cause me
To take a man;
But I know that if you and Gymer meet in
battle,
It will be a lusty fight.

25. SKIRNER: See you the sword,
Supple, adorned with runes?
By it shall fall the ancient giant;
Your father were doomed to die.

26.   I smite you with a magic wand,
For I must tame you to my wish;

You shall go where the children of men
Nevermore shall see you.

27.   You shall sit on the eagle's mound
With your gaze turned from the world,
Staring toward Hel's house;
Food shall disgust you more
Than the shining serpent does men.

28.   You shall be a monster on the road;
Rimner shall stare at you;
Your aspect confusing all;
Better shall you be known
Than the watcher of the gods,
As you greedily gawk at the gate.

29.   Emptiness, lamentation, compulsion,
    impatience,
Your tears shall swell in anguish;
Sit while I conjure over you a flow of bitter
    curses,
Double lust and disgust.

30.   You shall be hagridden from morning till
    night
In the giants' courts;
To the frost giants' hall shall you daily walk
Defenseless and lame,
Weeping shall be as joy to you,
And sorrow suffered with tears.

31.   With a threeheaded thurse shall you walk,
Or be without man and mate;
Lust shall burn you, yearning tear you,
You shall be like the thistle that grows under
    the eaves.

32.
I went to the woods,
To the damp willow thicket,
The wand to take.
The wand I took.

33.
Wroth at you is Odin,
Wroth at you is Brage,
Frey shall heartily hate you;
Ill-willing maid,
You have provoked
The wrath of the gods in a matter of import.

34.
Hear ye, titans,
Hear ye, frostgiants,
Sons of Suttung,[1]
And even you, Aesir:
Hear how I curse, how I ban the maid
From pleasuring with man.

35.
Rimgrimner is the giant that shall hold you
Beneath the gates of death;
There shall slaves by the roots of trees
Give you sour liquid of goats;
No nobler drink shall you ever have, maid,
By your desire, by your own decree.

36.
"Giant" I carve you three rune-staves:
Powerlessness, witlessness, and lust.
Then I tear off that on which I scribed it,
If need be.

37. GERD:
Hail you, lad, rather now
Receive the festive beaker filled with aged
        mead!
Never dreamed I that I ever would wish
The Vana-son well.

---

1. Fire.

38. SKIRNER: I would know all
                Before I ride homeward:
                When shall you at Ting
                Plight your troth to the son of Njörd?

39. GERD: Barre is the grove where one travels in peace,
                As we both know.
                Nine nights from now shall Gerd there
                        plight her troth
                To the son of Njörd.

Skirner rode home.   Frey stood outside, greeted him and
asked for news.

40. FREY: Tell me, Skirner, before you unsaddle
                The steed and take one step:
                How went the matter in the giant world?
                According to your way or mine?

41. SKIRNER: Barre is the grove where one travels in peace,
                As we both know.
                Nine nights from now shall Gerd there
                        plight her troth
                To the son of Njörd.

42. FREY: Long is one night;
                Longer two;
                How shall I for three be yearning?
                Often a month seems less to me.

26

Vägtamskvädet
(*The Lay of Waywont*)

This much-told story is well known in many versions. Balder, the sun-god, was beset by ominous dreams, which alarmed the Aesir. When Odin learned that the House of Hel, goddess of death, was being prepared to welcome his son, Odin's consort Frigga, mother of the gods, set out to exact an oath of all creatures that they would not harm Balder. All gladly gave her the assurance she craved, and it seemed the danger was averted. One thing only had been overlooked: the mistletoe, too slight and frail to pose a threat.

Loki learned of this oversight. He plucked the little plant, fashioned a dart from it and went to where the gods were amusing themselves hurling weapons against Balder, who stood laughing and invulnerable as the missiles rebounded and fell harmless to the ground. Only Balder's twin, the blind god Höder, stood apart. Loki approached him and asked if he would not like to join the sport and he offered to guide Höder's aim so that he too might enjoy the pastime. But the dart he placed on Höder's bow was the fateful mistletoe. It pierced the sun-god's heart, and Balder forthwith journeyed to the House of Hel.

Disguised as Hermod (divine courage) Odin rode to entreat the queen of the dead to relinquish the sun-god, which she agreed to do if all beings without exception would weep for him. Frigga resumed her weary round and all creatures wept for the beloved Áse. When all appeared to be well she encountered an aged crone — Loki in disguise — who refused. It was decisive: Balder must remain in the House of Hel.

The sun-god was laid on his pyre ship; his loving wife Nanna (the moon) died of a broken heart and was laid beside him. Before the burning ship was set adrift, Odin is said to have bent and whispered something in his dead son's ear.[1]

There are many keys which fit this story: the sun-god dies each year at the winter solstice and is reborn, as his successor "but one night of age" strides to avenge his death, whereupon a new year dawns with the returning sun. The festival of the "unconquered sun" was celebrated throughout the lands north of the equator at the sacred season which later became Christmas. It is the time of the "virgin birth" when the divine self is born within the successful aspirant initiated into the Mysteries. Christ's birth was given that date to identify him as one of these initiates.

Another interpretation refers the tale to the end of the solar or golden age. In the days of humanity's youth, innocence prevailed in the newly aroused mind of man. It was an age of peace and serenity, of instinctual obedience to nature's laws, when the influence of the gods governed the lives of creatures. As the budding human intelligence began to test its power, freedom of choice and will led to inevitable wrongs and the law of moral responsibility came into play; together with the forces of ignorance and darkness, represented by the blind god Höder, they were instrumental in bringing to an end this gentle vegetating existence. Similarly, in the biblical tale, Adam and Eve were driven from Eden after tasting the fruit of the tree of knowledge of good and evil, because they had become as the gods (elohim), responsible for their evolution. The human mind must be free to choose its course; the automatic drifting of childlike innocence no longer became the human soul which must now begin to direct, purposefully and intelligently, its own progress toward perfection and manifest its divinity ever more fully.

The evolutionary urge of intelligence in action — Loki, disguised as the aged crone — refused to mourn the passing of that golden age, for the real work of man's inner growth must take its place. Bound in the underworld, Loki must suffer torment until the end of the cycle. Beautiful Skade, the adverse aspect of Njörd, the

---

1. Cf. Vaftrudnismál, 53.

Saturnian age, suspends a serpent over his face, and its venom drips unceasingly on the bound titan, compounding his agony, while his devoted wife Sigyn remains by his side, catching the poison in a goblet. It is when she must go to empty the cup that Loki writhes in agony and the earth quakes.

It is a sad reflection that in most, if not all, scriptures, the agent that forced man's ejection from the innocence of infancy into adulthood and responsibility, is regarded as evil. Perhaps it has been so regarded because, as a humanity, we have been reluctant to grow up. Even now, there are many who would prefer to lay their shortcomings at the door of some deity, real or fictitious, and who resent having any burden to bear, though a little observation and reflection must convince us that in order to fulfill a greater destiny evolving beings must leave childhood behind and undertake purposeful participation in the functions of the universe. Thus Loki is forced to abide in the depths of matter and to suffer until the cycle's culmination. His pain is enhanced by the venom produced by the serpent of knowledge, just as that of Prometheus is aggravated by the vulture gnawing at his liver. Both torments represent human misuse of the divine gift of mind. The enlightener's sacrifice will end only when the human travail shall have been successfully accomplished; when Fenris, Loki's offspring, shall be free and shall devour the sun at the end of its life, and Vale shall continue the sun-god's work on a grander level of existence. Then, maybe, we too shall know what Odin whispered in Balder's ear.

Vägtamskvädet[2]

1.   All the Aesir, gods and goddesses
     Sat in session together at Ting;
     The mighty powers took council of this:
     Why Balder was troubled by terrible dreams.

2.   Mighty slight was the sun-god's slumber,
     Rest and refreshment seemed gone from his sleep;
     The giants requested prophetic response
     As to how this might affect his creation.

3.   The lots cast thereon showed that doomed to die
     Was the dearest of Ull's kin;[3]
     Anguish assailed Frigga and Svafner[4]
     And the other rulers. They agreed on a plan:

4.   Word was dispatched to all of creation,
     Seeking assurance that Balder be spared;
     All gave an oath that he would be unharmed.
     Frigga received all agreements and promises.

5.   Yet Allfather feared an uncertain outcome.
     He felt that hamingjas were keeping away;
     He summoned the Aesir, demanded decision.
     Much was discussed at this congregation.

6.   Up rose Odin, father of eons,
     Saddled Sleipnir, his eightlegged steed;

---

2. Vägtam (way wont, accustomed to roads): pilgrim.
3. Balder, the sun-god.
4. Svafner: the Closer (he who puts to sleep); Odin.

Thence rode he downward, the road toward Niflhel,
Met here the hound that hails from the hollow.

7.   Bloody the beast was on brisket and breast,
Long did he bay at the father of runes.
Odin rode forth; loud thundered the fields
As he halted at Hel's high hall.

8.   Eastward rode Odin before the door,
Where he knew the sibyl's barrow to be.
Death-runes he sang to the magic maid
Until, forced to rise, she spoke from the dead.

9.   "Who among men, unknown to me,
Compels my heavy journey?
I was covered with snow, lashed by rain,
Drenched with the dew. Long was I dead."

10. ODIN: Waywont my name, I am son of Deathwont,
Speak you from Hel's home as I speak from Life's:
For whom are the benches adorned with rings
And the couch covered over with gold?

11. SIBYL: The mead is made, for Balder brewed,
The precious draught sheltered by a shield;
The kin of the Aesir anxiously wait.
Forced have I said it. Now may I cease.

12. ODIN: Cease not, sibyl. I will inquire
Until I know all. More will I know:
Who shall the bane be unto Balder
And rob Odin's son of his age?

13. SIBYL: Höder[5] brings hither the lovely scion.
He shall be unto Balder his bane
And rob Odin's son of his age.
Forced have I spoken. Now may I cease.

---

5. The blind god of darkness and ignorance.

14. ODIN: Cease not, sibyl. I will inquire
Until I know all. More will I know:
Who shall avenge him harshly on Höder
And bring Balder's bane to the pyre?

15. SIBYL: Rind[6] bears Vale[7] in western halls.
But one night old shall Odin's son battle;
He laves not his hands, nor combs he his hair
Ere he bears Balder's foe on the pyre.
Forced have I spoken. Now may I cease.

16. ODIN: Cease not, sibyl. I will inquire
Until I know all. More will I know:
Who are the maidens who then shall weep
And their kerchiefs fling to the skies?

17. SIBYL: No pilgrim you, as the sibyl thought.
You are Odin, father of eons.

18. ODIN: Nor sibyl you, nor wise seeress.
Rather are you three thurses' dam.

19. SIBYL: Ride home, Odin, with mind at rest!
So close comes no one again to me
Until Loki from fetters is free, and the forces,
Dissolvers of all, come to Ragnarök.[8]

---

6. Rind: the cold winter earth.
7. Vale: son of Odin.
8. End of a world.

27

Odens Korpgalder

(The Lay of Odin's Corpse
or The Lay of Odin's Ravens)

TRANSLATOR'S NOTES

This lay suggests the aftermath following the death of a planet. It has been omitted from many translations as scholars, led by the eminent Sophus Bugge, have tended to ignore it as being quite incomprehensible. It is a lay of great beauty, with a strong mystical appeal, as the reader senses the unsaid, dreamlike, all but unimaginable hiatus between periods of life when the planetary soul is immersed in the quiescence following death. Every kingdom of nature is held in breathless suspension, unmoving, unaware, unliving, awaiting the electrifying urges of a new dawn. Allfather alone is active. In all the *Edda* there is no more poignant piece of music than this stilling of the pulse of life, leaving each group of beings fixed in its own characteristic state of awareness for the long rest until the gods return.

Odin's two ravens, Hugin and Munin (mind and memory), "daily fly over the battlefield earth"[1] and report back to Allfather by night. Here we again find mention of the gods' anxiety for Hugin, lest he fail to return. There is cogent reason for this. Mind entails choice: beings who possess this faculty, who have attained the function of intelligence and free will, as has humanity on earth, are faced with the options these present. They can, if they so choose, ally themselves totally with the matter-side of nature, the giants, in extreme cases severing their connection with their inner god, so that their characteristic contribution to the cosmic purpose

---

1. Grimnismál, 20.

is lost and the soul forgoes its opportunity to become immortal. Or they can gradually blend with the divine source of their existence. The critical choice is not made all at once; it is the cumulative effect of numberless small choices made through progressive stages of life. In the natural course of growth the soul unites each increment of experience with its divine source and so little by little merges with it.

So it is that at the end of a "day" of life, Hugin returns to Odin, bringing tidings of the manifest world and rejoining the divinity whence it originally flew. Its companion, Munin, is the container of all the record of events since the beginning of time. It is on the report of Munin that is built all attainment, as memory remains eternally as the foundation of future awareness.

It should be noted that both birds refer not merely to human consciousness but to corresponding properties as they manifest differently and in varying degrees throughout nature. A planet, such as Idun personifies, possesses the characteristics contributed by all its components, from elemental consciousnesses through the rudimentary condition of minerals, the greater sensitivity of plants, the budding awareness of animal lives, and self-conscious human souls; it includes also the grander status of perfected men and women as well as kingdoms of life superior to the human. Each awakening consciousness at any stage proceeds through life to gain greater scope and cognition, ever modifying its malleable, growing awareness and comprehension, but it is in the human that we first are able to distinguish the process.

At the end of her life, the planetary soul, Idun, is besieged at the fount of Urd by the anxious gods who seek to learn from her of the past life's growth and to imbibe the mead she can provide. Applying the theosophic keys it seems probable that her father Ivalde represents the previous world, the chain of lunar globes of which our present earth is the successor. Idun, his daughter, is "oldest of Ivalde's younger brood," hence belongs to our earth, and is the offspring of the corresponding globe of the former moon chain. However, this is not the most physical part of it: that was Nanna, the body which is no longer visible to us. Nanna died before our earth was born, before it was made from the materials that had composed her discarded form. She is the planet's lower constituents and so sinks into unconsciousness at death, pricked with the thorn of sleep, the "son of the sleep enchanter." This is the very thorn that brought oblivion to Sleeping Beauty (in another interpretation of the same tale), whose long sleep was ended by the kiss of life. The paralyzing thorn is borne on the icicle waves from the frost giant (22) whose minions characteristically begin to die each midnight, slain by the approaching dawn. As the poem tells us, the sorrowing Idun had but little to contribute to the feast of the Aesir. However, the final verses of this poem bring us to the birth of a new life: as the hags and giants of the night slink away to their lairs "'neath the noble ash tree's farthest root" (25), the gods reappear and there bursts into triumphant life a new world with new hope, heralded by the "mighty clarion-blower on the mountains of heaven" (26).

Odens Korpgalder

1. Allfather acts, elves discern,
   Vaner know, norns point the way.
   Trolls nourish, aeons give birth,
   Thurses wait, Valkyries yearn.

2. The Aesir suffered grim forebodings,
   Seers mistook the fruit-maid's runes.[2]
   Urd's mead she guarded but could not defend it
   From the insistence of the great host.

3. Hugin soars high to seek her out.
   The Aesir are anxious if he delays;
   To Longing-for-life[3] dreams become suffering;
   Dim dreams surfeit the dead.

4. Dwarfs grow numb; their powers fail;
   Worlds into Ginnung's waning sink;[4]
   The Allwise fells beings often,
   And again reassembles the fallen.

5. No longer stand fast the earth or the sun;
   The stream of destruction stays no more aloft;
   Hidden deep in Mimer's well
   Lies all wisdom. Know you as yet or what?

---

2. The planetary equivalent of Bärgälmer, the "fruit giant."

3. What the Buddhists call *tanhā*, thirst for life. It characterizes the lower elements which are drawn to matter.

4. Ginnungagap: the Unfathomable Void.

6. Dwells in the dells the knowing maiden,[5]
   Fallen from Yggdrasil down, from the ash;
   The elves named her Idun; she is the oldest
   Of Ivalde's younger brood.

7. Unhappy she seemed over this misfortune,
   Lying captive under the lofty tree.
   She liked it not with the daughter of Night,
   Accustomed to having worlds for her dwelling.

8. The victory gods saw the sorrow of Nanna;[6]
   They sent her in Hel's house a wolf-disguise;
   She put it on and changed disposition;
   Confused with illusion, altered appearance.

9. Odin selected the watcher of Bäfrast[7]
   To ask of the dead sun's sorrowing widow
   All that she knew of the fate of the world.
   Brage and Lopt bore the testimony.[8]

10. Incantations they chanted, they rode on wolves,
    The ruler and powers, to the ends of the world.
    Odin, listening from Lidskjälf,[9]
    Lets them journey far and wide.

11. Wise Heimdal asked if the mead-provider
    Knew of the origin, age, and the end
    Of the races of gods and her journey's companions,
    Of heaven, the void, and the earth.

---

5. Idun: the soul of the dead planet is being questioned by the gods and
made to yield its increment of consciousness.

6. Nanna: the lowest elements of the dead planet which, when the soul has
left, become transformed into the illusory material to be reused in future forms.

7. Heimdal: the "white sword-Áse."

8. Intuition and aspiring mind.

9. The Shelf of Compassion.

12. Naught would she say, not a word would she utter
    In response to the askers, nor discourse with them;
    Her tears fell fast from her brain's shields;
    Her power was numbed, exhausted, and dead.

13. Filled with sorrow Jorun appeared[10]
    Before the gods, unable to speak;
    The more they asked, the less she said;
    All their words flowed in vain.

14. Foremost at the questing was Heimdal, the watcher
    Of the horn of the father of hosts;
    He brought with him Loki, the one born of Nál,
    While Brage, the bard, stood guard.

15. The warriors of Odin attained to the Winehall,
    Brought to the place by the sons of the past;
    There entered Ygg's heroes to salute the Aesir,
    And share in the feasting on mead.

16. They wished Hangatyr[11] health and contentment,
    With well-being ever to brew his ale;
    The drinkers were blissful to joy at the tankard,
    Eager to feast with the Ever-young.

17. Each benched by Odin, the rulers together
    Eat and are sated with Särimner;[12]
    With the ladle of Nikar[13] Skögul at the tables
    Serves mead in the horns of memory.

---

10. The earth-to-be, Idun reborn.

11. The hanged god: Odin, the Great Sacrifice. Cf. Hávamál, 137–42.

12. One of the boars that feed the One-harriers: Andrimner, air; Eldrimner, fire; Särimner, water; the elements of earth experience.

13. The Shaker: Odin as misfortune. Skögul is a Valkyrie who serves the gods and the One-harriers who have united with their inner god.

18. At the feast much was asked by the gods of Heimdal,
    By the goddesses of Loki.
    All day long until darkness fell
    They sought the seeress' wisdom and prophecy.

19. Ill they thought was resolved
    This matter, and little commendable.
    Cunning was needed to elicit
    An answer from the sly witch.

20. Darkening, Odin speaks. All listen:
    "Night shall be used for renewal of counsel;
    Each one who can shall by the morrow
    Find some solution for the Aesir's weal."

21. At the mountains' rim round the wintry earth
    The offspring of Fenris, exhausted, fell.
    The gods left the feast, saluting Ropt[14]
    And Frigg, at the departure of the steed of night.

22. Soon from the east, out of icicle-waves,
    Comes the thorn of sleep to the frozen giant,
    Whose minions are slain in beautiful Midgárd
    Every night at the midnight hour.

23. Then wanes the power. Hands grow numb.
    A swoon assails the white sword-Áse;[15]
    Unconsciousness reigns on the midnight breath;
    Thought fails in tired beings.

24. But the son of the Dawn spurs on his charger,
    Caparisoned gaily in precious gems.
    Over Manhome flows radiance from the steed's mane;
    He draws in the chariot Dvalin's toy.[16]

---

14. The maligned: Odin as the hierophant.
15. Heimdal, watcher of the gods on the rainbow bridge, who blows the horn at Ragnarök.
16. Dvalin's toy is the solar disk.

25. At the nourishing earth's northern horse-door,
    'Neath the noble ash-tree's farthest root,
    Went to their lairs hags and giants,
    Spooks, and dwarfs, and the black elves.

26. Up rose the gods. Forth shone the sun.
    Northward to Niflheim night drew away;
    Heimdal once more sprang up upon Bäfrast,
    Mighty clarion-blower on the mountains of heaven.

28

A Summing Up

THE READER WHO HAS persisted thus far will have noticed a lack of the illustrations of gods and giants which usually adorn books on mythology: Norse myths generally sport a one-eyed Odin in a slouch hat and a brawny Thor wielding a primitive stone hammer. All embellishments of that kind have been omitted because such images have done more to discredit the myths than almost anything else. Instead a deliberate effort has been made to de-personify the natural powers and substances of the universe, in an attempt to reverse the accustomed tendency to see mythic deities in human form and endow matter with qualities it does not possess. The first is an indignity to which no planetary or stellar power should be subjected; the second attaches to inert substance properties out of keeping with its nature.

Having roamed through a small part of the Saemundar *Edda*, with brief excursions into other sources, we should by now have a reasonable familiarity with the method used by the bards to record the science of the gods. Through the peculiar magic of myths we find ourselves learning of the origin, age, and the end of things, for we are, each one of us, the questing Odin. The problems that confront us, when reduced to their most basic form, are the very same demands made by the spirit of existence as it hangs, suspended from higher worlds, in the Tree of Life: Odin below consecrated to Odin above in the tree, while he searches the depths for runes of wisdom, raising them with *song* — sound, motion, activity.

In the Völuspá and Grimnismál we are given an overview of cosmogony, a panorama of living worlds returning to action after a cosmic rest; we see the gods draw to their judgment seats, assemble to take council and determine the disposition of heavenly beings in the shelves and mansions of the Tree of Life. We learn as well of our human origins and parentage: that we are descended from the creative cosmic powers, *composed* of the universal elements which endow us with the properties that belong to our species.

Others of the lays have reference more particularly to our own globe and to the humanities that have succeeded one another thereon. We find a succession of giants and giantesses, races of mankind which display different characteristics and encounter fresh experiences to nourish the enduring consciousness. The human spirit traverses the shelves and mansions of our universal Tree of Life in search of experience, just as we play host to myriads of atomic worlds on the various levels of our own nature, while our elf, our ego, either acts on the behest of its divine hamingja or permits itself to be swayed by the importunities of the dwarf nature in us. At the same time our bodily organisms, along with the minerals and other kingdoms, help constitute the globes of our universe, just as the atomic lives in us provide the bodies that belong to us in the world we are currently inhabiting.

The myths are eminently reasonable. There are no extra-ordinary demands on credulity: the systems interlock, the twigs on their branches of the Tree of Life are themselves trees of life which ramify within the greater system. All the while the gods, the beneficent powers, are in command of their own domains; not interfering in human concerns, nor subject to human cajolery and whims, they are intelligent worlds, austerely unapproach-able by us yet always there, a realistic prospect of our own future. For we, like toddlers in a world of grownups, stand knee-high to their majesty and see only the least, most basic of their attributes.

The worlds are shown to live and die, and again live, and once again depart. After each planetary life the gods seek to learn from the "fruitful spirit" what has been gained on its sphere of duty. Within the human realm, we too enter our globe of action, gain some mead to regale the inner god, and exit into other worlds: worlds having different composition, different substantiality, other ranges of experience for the evolving consciousness to partake of. The squirrel of awareness has free access to all the many levels of its Tree of Life, and what pertains to one world does not have identic application in some other, though we have affinities with all. We live and learn in them, while each part of our nature has its own home base.

Ever since the mind and will of early humanity were quickened to think and choose, and since their — our — first steps as human beings were guided by the "beneficent powers" anthropomorphized as Rig, our paths have ranged through many a swamp and quicksand where the inner light has been dimmed, and also over peaks of grand inspiration. The human mind being part and parcel of the mind of an intelligent universe cannot be divorced from, or contain something that is lacking in, the whole of which it forms a part but must constitute an integral portion of it. We have the assurance of the myths that when our weary journey through the self-discovering vales of matter will be completed, we shall regain our divinity and rightfully assume a conscious and responsible role in the governance of the world. For within us is a potent and undeniable link with the bright intelligences that govern planetary and solar systems; they are the hierarchs whose essence pervades their domain just as a human being permeates with consciousness all the teeming lives within its soul and body. And lest we lose touch with the source of our inspiration, the thought world we inhabit is impregnated with the signals whereby we may find truth.

Never in all our ventures has the light of inspiration been wholly lacking; always there have existed the mythic ideals, so that those who seek truth earnestly can find response in every age. For this the world's legends and allegories endure. When inward necessity and altruistic love impel, they can become more fully known; at other times they remain concealed within their disguises of epic and fairy tale. When studied, they reaffirm eternal values and virtues, and they teach us how to live: for, as they clearly show, our task as a human kingdom is to transmute the grosser substance of our giant world into the more enduring treasures of consciousness — the sustenance that feeds the gods — in us and in the systems of worlds.

Withal myths teach us to know truth and to value it: not data such as may be stored in a computer memory, but the growing sphere of truth that affords us ever freer vision and opens the inner worlds of a living kosmos to our comprehension. This assurance of our divine origins and universal destiny gives us a basis for discrimination that is always valid: no mere codified set of virtues (which, as everyone knows, can become vices when misapplied), but a solid foundation of character, an inner direction finder that points to the true in any situation.

The interpretations offered here are far from exhaustive, presenting merely an outline of a few of the main themes of theosophic philosophy recognized in some of the lays and stories of the Edda. Not every symbol has been noted, nor every kenning explained; many will strike the reader without having to be pointed out. Other passages are too obscure to be readily understood and, rather than confuse or, possibly, mislead the reader, they are left to the intuitive to discern for themselves. It is believed that with the general keys to symbolism that are proposed, a thoughtful and perceptive mind may find successive layers of understanding of not only the Norse but also other world myths. What has been scrutinized is also incomplete, being only a small proportion of the material available in the Edda. If this fragment of runic wisdom can encourage others to undertake a more complete study of the ancient records, it will have served a purpose. There is a real need in our present world to restore spiritual reverence and reason to human endeavor, before we immerse ourselves further in a universe without meaning. The ancient gods are not dead; far from it. They go about their tasks of keeping worlds in continuing, harmonious functioning, they ensure the balance of nature's elements and maintain on all levels the delicate efficiency that so astounds the naturalist in our physical environment. The maverick of nature is man. The kingdoms that trail behind us are largely dependent on us and suffer unduly from our mistakes, while those that precede us on the ladder of existence, though not bound by our foolishness, are nevertheless deprived of our cooperation when we act with less than the best of our humanness.

It is needful that we acquire awareness of the next step in our journey. Od, the human soul, must successfully gain his heavenly bride at the end of his travail through windcold vales of matter, aided by the talents and qualities bestowed on him by his mother, the past. Only when prepared and willing can we fulfill our human destiny and, as Svipdag united with Menglad, our hamingja, share in the tasks of the years and the ages.

PRONUNCIATION GUIDE

Each language really has an alphabet all its own; even though the same written symbols may be used, the sounds they represent are subtly different in each spoken tongue. Particularly is this true of the vowels, whereof English has five, Swedish nine, and Old Icelandic seventeen. Many of the names of the Edda's characters have several spellings, all equally valid, some Icelandic, others Old Norse, others Swedish, Danish, or Norwegian. We have used Swedish or Icelandic spelling, substituting for the extra Icelandic letters the closest English equivalents. Thus þ is commonly *th* as in Thor, while ð is given as *d*. The following pronunciation guide is a compromise giving merely an indication of the actual sounds. The vowels:

Long	*Short Equivalent*
a as in f*a*ther	s*a*t
e as in s*ay*	s*e*t
i as in fat*i*gue	s*i*t
o as in m*o*ve	s*oo*t
u as u minus the "ee" sound	h*u*t
y as in French t*u*	Gl*ü*ck
á as in c*o*rps	s*o*t
ä as in c*a*re	s*e*t
ö as in French d*eu*x	n*eu*f

Consonants are pronounced approximately as in English. The *g* is hard before hard vowels (a, o, u, á), but soft, like *y*, before the other (soft) vowels; *r* is trilled as in Scottish speech or like the French.

Glossary

Aesir (ay-seer) [gods] Active deities. See Áse

Äger (ay-gear) [a titan or giant] Space: brewer of mead for the gods

Agnar (ang-nar) Name of two early humanities; one was taught by Grimner (Odin)

Alf (alv) [channel] Elf, soul

Allvis (al-veece) [*all* all + *vis* wise] A dwarf: worldly wise wooer of Thor's daughter

Andrimner [*and* air + *rimner* computation, calendar] One of the boars that feed the One-harriers

Áse (aw-seh) [*ás* topmost roofbeam of a house] An active god. See also Aesir (pl.), Ásynja (f.), Ásynjor (f. pl.)

Ásgárd (aws-gawrd) [*ás* god + *gárd* court] Home of the Aesir

Askungen (ask-ung-en) [*ask* ash + *unge* child] Ash child, Cinderella

Ásmegir (aws-may-gir) [godmaker] Potential god: the human soul

Ásynja (aw-sin-ya) [goddess, f. of Áse] Active deity

Ásynjor (aw-sin-yore) [pl. of Ásynja, f. of Aesir] Goddesses

Audhumla (a-ood-hum-la) [mythic cow] Symbol of fertility

Balder (bahl-der) An Áse: the sun-god

Bärgälmer, Bergelmir (bare-yell-meer) [a titan] Fruitage of a universal lifetime

Barre (bar-reh) [*barr* pine needle] The sacred grove of peace. Snorri speaks of the ash as having *barr*, having never seen a tree. There were none in Iceland.

Bele's bane (bay-leh) The sword of Frey

Bifrost, Bäfrast, Bilrast (bee-frost, bayv-rast, beel-rast) The rainbow bridge between men and gods

Bilskirner (beel-sheer-ner) [flashing, shining] Valhalla's shelf

Bleknäbb (blayk-neb) [pale beak] Eagle, the giant Räsvälg

Bödvild (beud-vild) Daughter of King Nidud

Brage, Bragi (brah-geh) An Åse: poetic inspiration, wisdom

Brimer (bree-mer) [ocean surf] An aspect of Äger. See Ymer

Brisingamen (bree-sing-a-mayn) [*brising* fire + *men* jewel] Freya's gem, human intelligence

Brock A dwarf: the mineral kingdom

Budlung (bood-lung) A king (poetic)

Bur (boo-r) [birth?] Space, first emanation of Buri

Buri (boo-ree) Frozen, unmanifest, abstract Space. Traditionally King Buri or Bore personifies winter

Byleist (bee-layst) [wildfire] The destructive side of Loki, mind

Draupnir (drawp-neer) [dripper] Odin's magic ring: proliferating cycles

Dvalin (dvah-leen) [comatose] The human, unawakened soul; Dvalin's toy, the solar disk

Dwarfs Souls less than human in evolutionary status

Edda [great-grandmother] Matrix of human wisdom

Egil (ay-gil) An early humanity, the age of innocence

Eldrimner [*eld* fire + *rimner* computation, calendar] One of the boars that feed the One-harriers

Elf [channel] The human soul between spirit and dwarf in man

Eli-vágor (ay-lee-vaw-goor) [icicle-waves] Cold streams of matter

Elohim (ello-heem) [gods, Heb. pl.] Deity as an aggregate of many infinite forces

Fenja (fen-yah) [*fen* water] One of the giantesses who turn the magic mill Grotte

Fenris, Fenrer Loki's son, werewolf which will devour the sun

Fimbultyr (fim-bul-teer) [*fimbul* mighty, great + *tyr* god] The highest divinity, the god of secret wisdom

Fjölsvinn (fyeul-svinn) [*fjöl* very + *svinn* wise] Odin as instructor and initiator

Flyting [Eng. dial.] Dispute in verse, personal abuse

Fohat [Tib.] Electromagnetic radiation

Forsete (for-set-eh) An Áse: justice, karma

Freke (fray-keh) [gluttony] One of Odin's wolfhounds

Frey (fray) An Áse: planetary spirit of earth; valor

Freya (fray-a) An Ásynja: planetary spirit of Venus, protectress of humanity

Frigga [AS *frigu* love] An Ásynja: Odin's consort

Frode (froo-deh) [*frodr* wise] A legendary king

Frodefrid (froo-deh-freed) [*frodr* wise + *frid* peace] Age of peace and wisdom: the golden age

Frost Giant Age of non-life between active lives of a cosmos

Gagnrád (gang-n-rawd) [*gagn* gainful + *rád* counsel] Odin in Vaftrudnismál

Galder (gahl-der) Incantation

Gánglära (gong-lay-re) [*gáng* wandering + *läre* learner] King Gylfe seeking wisdom

Garm The hound that guards the gate of Hel, queen of death

Geirröd (gay-reud) [*geir* spear + *röd* red] An early humanity

Gerd (yayrd) A giantess: spouse of Frey

Gere (yay-reh) [greed] One of Odin's wolfhounds

Giant, Giantess Matter vivified by divinity

Gimle (gim-leh) [heavenly abode] A superior shelf of existence

Ginnungagap (yinn-ung-a-gahp) [*ginn* the void + *unge* offspring + *gap* chasm] The mystery of Nonbeing

Gladsheim (glahds-haym) [gladhome] Location of Valhalla

Grimner [disguised] Odin as teacher of the younger Agnar

Groa (groo-a) [growth] A sibyl: the evolutionary past leading up to the present

Grotte (grott-eh) [growth] Magic mill of change, creation, destruction: evolution

Gudasaga (goo-dah-sah-ga) [*gud* god + *saga* spell] A divine tale given orally, a god-spell or gospel

Gullveig (gull-vayg) [*guld* gold + *veig* drink or thirst] The soul's yearning for wisdom

Gunnlöd (gun-leud) Giantess who served mead to Odin in the mountain

Gylfe (yil-veh) A legendary king and seeker of wisdom

Gymer (yi-mayr) A giant: father of Gerd

Hamingja (ha-ming-ya) [fortune] Guardian spirit

Hávamál (haw-va-mawl) [*hár* high + *mál* speech] Lay of the High One

Heid (hayd) [*heid* bright sky] A vala or sibyl: nature's memory of the past

Heidrun (hayd-run) [*heidr* heath or honor] The goat that nibbles the bark of the Tree of Life

Heimdal (haym-dahl) [*heim* home + *dal* dell] "The whitest Áse." Celestial guardian of Bifrost

Hel (hayl) [death] The daughter of Loki, ruler of the kingdom of the dead. She is represented as half blue, half white

Hel's road The path from birth toward death

Hermod (hayr-mood) [*herr* a host + *modr* wrath, mood] An Áse: a son of Odin

Höder (heu-der) [*böd* war, slaughter] An Áse: blind god of darkness and ignorance; brother of Balder

Höner (heu-ner) One of the creative trinity; the watery principle

Hostage A Vana god among the Aesir: an avatāra from a higher to a lower world

Hugin (hoog-in) [*hug* mind] One of Odin's two ravens

Hvergälmer (vayr-yell-mer) [*hverr* caldron] Source of the rivers of lives. It rises in Niflheim and waters one root of the Tree of Life

Hymer (hee-mer) The first titan of a life cycle. See Rymer

Idun (ee-dun) An Ásynja: "the fruitful spirit" who feeds the gods the apples of immortality; soul of the earth. She is the wife of Brage, poetic inspiration

Ifing (ee-ving) [*ef* or *if* doubt] River that separates men from gods

Iörmungandr (yer-mung-andr) [*jörmun* immense + *andr* breath] An offspring of Loki: the Midgárd serpent. (May be the equator, the plane of the ecliptic, or the Milky Way)

Ivalde (ee-vahl-deh) A giant: the previous imbodiment of earth

Järnsaxa (yern-sax-ah) [*järn* iron + *sax* a short sword] An age: mother of Thor's son Magne. On earth the Iron Age, in space one of Heimdal's nine mothers

Kenning A descriptive epithet used in lieu of a name

Kvasir (kvah-seer) A hostage given to the Aesir by the Vaner, and whose blood is epic poetry

Lá and **Laeti** (law, lay-tee) Genetic bloodline and distinctive character or appearance

Lidskjälf (leed-shelv) [*hlid* aligning with, or *lid* suffering + *skjälf* shelf] The plane of aid or compassion

Lif and **Lifthrasir** (leev, leev-trah-seer) [life and survival] Immortal principles

Lin (leen) [*lin* flax] Frigga, Odin's consort

Loddfáfner (lodd-fawv-ner) A dwarf: a learning human soul

Lodur (loo-dur) One of the creative trinity; the fiery principle

Lofar (loo-vahr) [*lof* hand or praise] Highest member of animal kingdom

Logi (loo-gee) [*log* flame] Wildfire, the uninspired mind

Lokabrenna [*brenna* burning] A name for Sirius

Lokasenna [*senna* banter] Loki's Flyting

Loki [*lokka* entice, *logi* light] An Áse of giant stock: the enlightener, dual mind

Lopt [lofty] Aspiring mind

Lorride (lor-ree-deh) Thor as electric power on earth

Magne (mang-neh) [godly power: gravitation?] One of Thor's sons in cosmic space

Mead Drink of the gods: experience of life.

Menglad [*men* jewel + *glad* happy] Freya whose jewel is humanity

Menja (men-yah) [*men* jewel] One of the two giantesses who turn the mill Grotte

Midgård (mid-gawrd) [*mid* middle + *gård* court] Our physical planet

Mimameid (mee-mah-mayd) [*mima* of Mimer + *meid* tree] The tree of Mimer, owner of the spring of experience

Mimer (mee-mer) [the nine-layered sky] A giant: owner of the well of wisdom from which Odin drinks daily: matter

Mjölnir (myeul-neer) [miller] Thor's hammer of creation and destruction

Mjötudr (myeut-oodr) [*mjöt* measure + *udr* exhausting] The Tree of Life in its dying phase

Mjötvidr (myeut-veedr) [*mjöt* measure + *vid* increasing] The Tree of Life in its growing phase

Mode (moo-deh) [godly wrath: radiation?] One of Thor's sons in cosmic space

Mundilföre (mun-dill-feu-reh) [akin to *möndull* handle + *före* to fare, move] A giant, father of sun and moon: the "lever" or "axis" that turns the "wheels" in space

Munin (moo-nin) [mind, love, memory] One of Odin's two ravens

Muspellsheim (muss-pells-haym) [*muspell* fire + *heim* home] A cosmic principle. See Niflheim

Mysing (mee-sing) A sea-king who conquered Frode

Nagelfar (nahg-el-fahr) [*nagel* nail + *far* travel] The ship of death, built of dead men's nails

Nanna Soul of the moon, who died of sorrow when her husband Balder was killed. Predecessor of Idun

Nidhögg (need-heugg) [*nid* beneath + *högg* biter] Serpent undermining Yggdrasil, the Tree of Life

Nidud (nee-dud) [*nid* beneath, evil] A legendary king: the most material age of earth.

Niflheim (nee-vel-haym) [*nifl* cloud, nebula + *heim* home] A cosmic principle. See Muspellsheim

Niflhel (nee-vel-hayl) [*nifl* cloud, nebula + *hel* death] Extinction of matter

Niflungar (nee-vel-ung-ahr) [*nifl* mist + *ungar* children] An early human race that was still formless, nebulous

Nikar (nee-kahr) [ladler] Odin as bringer of misfortune

Njörd (nyeurd) A Vanagod: the regent of Saturn, father of Frey and Freya

Norns [*norn* weird, doom] Spinners of destiny for gods, worlds, and men

Od, Odr (ood, ood-r) [*odr* wit, intelligence] The higher human soul, spiritually inspired

Od's maid (Freya) The hamingja or higher self of man

Odin [*odr* intelligence, wisdom] Allfather: the divine principle in all levels of universal life. Consciousness

Odraerir (ood-reur-er) [*od* wisdom + *raerir* rearer] Inspirer of divine wisdom

Ofner (ohv-ner) [opener] Odin at the beginning of a cycle

Okolner (oo-kol-ner) [unfreezing] The "waters" of space

One-harrier Odin's warrior; one who has conquered himself

Örgälmer (eur-yell-mer) [*ör* original] First vibration: the big bang. See Ymer

Ragnarök (rang-na-reuk) [*ragna* rulers + *rök* ground] When the ruling deities withdraw to their ground; end of a world's lifetime

Ratatosk (rah-tah-tosk) [*rate* travel + *tosk* tusk] Squirrel in the Tree of Life: consciousness

Rate (rah-teh) [a drill] Bored through matter for Odin

Rig (reeg) [descent, involvement] Divine awakening of human mind

Rimgrimner [*rim* rime + *grimner* mask] A thurse, giant: cold, utter matter

Rind (rhymes with *sinned*) Earth in winter or in sleep

Rödung (reud-ung) [*röd* red + *ung* child] Father of the early races Agnar and Geirröd in Grimnismál

Ropt, Roptatyr (rop-tah-teer) [*ropt* maligned + *tyr* god] Odin as bringer of trials to the soul; the initiator, hierophant

Röskva (reuss-kvah) [vigor] Daughter of Egil and servant of Thor

Runes Wisdom gained by living

Rungner (rung-ner) [loud roar] A giant

Rymer (ree-mer) A giant: end of a life cycle. See Hymer

Saga Spoken or recited instruction in the guise of a story

Särimner (say-rim-ner) [*sär* sea + *rimner* computation, calendar] One of the boars that feed the One-harriers

Sejd (sayd) Prophecy

Sif (seev) [*sif* affinity, the sanctity of marriage] An Ásynja: Thor's wife. Her golden hair is the harvest

Sigyn (seeg-in) Loki's wife

Sindre (sin-dreh) [dross] A dwarf: the vegetable kingdom

Sinmara (sin-mah-ra) Hag who guards the caldron of matter, experience in the underworld

Skade (skah-deh) Sister-wife of Njörd, daughter of the giant Tjasse

Skald Bard

Skaldemjöd (skal-deh-myeud) [*skald* poet + *mjöd* mead] Inspiration

Skidbladnir (sheed-blahd-neer) [*skid* slat + *blad* leaf] Ship created by dwarfs for Frey. The planet earth

Skirner (sheer-ner) [radiance] Ray of the god Frey, an emissary to the giant world

Sleipnir (slayp-neer) [slider] Odin's eight-legged steed

Surt [fire] Destroyer of worlds; kenning also for Sinmara's drink

Suttung A giant, keeper of the divine mead of wisdom and poetry

Svadilfare (svah-dil-fahreh) [*svad* slippery + *fare* travel] A mythical steed, father of Odin's eightlegged Sleipnir

Svafner (svahv-ner) [closer] Odin at the end of a cycle

Svipdag (sveep-dahg) [*svip* flash + *dag* day] The successful initiant

Svitjod (sveet-yod) [the cold, the great] Sweden

Tables Stars and planets whereat the Aesir feast

Thor [*thorr, thonor, thur* thunder, consecrator, guileless power] An Áse: god of power, life force, electricity, and of the planet Jupiter. Also called Trudgälmer, Vior, Lorride in different applications

Thurse [dull, stupid] Uninspired matter giant

Ting, Thing [costly articles, inventory] Parliament

Tjalfe (chal-veh) [speed] Son of Egil and servant of Thor

Tjasse (chass-eh) A giant: an earlier life period

Tjodvitner (chod-veet-ner) [*tjod* tether + *vitner* witness] Fenris; wolf that fishes for the souls of men

Tomte (tom-teh) [*tom* empty] Nature sprite, helpful

Troll Nature sprite, mischievous

Trudgälmer (trood-yell-mer) Cosmic Thor

Trym (trim) [noise, battle] A giant: our physical planet Earth

Tund [tinder] A river: time

Tyr (teer) [Áse, god] A divine power, also the regent of Mars. Tyr sacrificed his hand to help bind Fenris

Ull An Áse: the god of a highly spiritual, unmanifest world

Vác or Vách (vahch) [Skt. voice, speech] Hindu first sound. See also Audhumla

Vaftrudnir (vahv-trood-ner) [*vaf* wrap, weave + *thrudr* doughty] The weaver of strong webs (of illusion)

Vägtam (vayg-tahm) [*väg* way + *tam* wont] Pilgrim

Vala, völva (vah-la, veul-va) [sibyl, prophetess] Indelible record of cosmic life

Vale (vah-leh) A son of Odin

Valhalla [*val* choice or slain + *hall* hall] Odin's hall where One-harriers celebrate

Valkyries [*val* choice or slain + *kyrja* chooser] Odin's agents

Van, Vanagod, Vanagiant (vahn-a-) Gods superior to the Aesir; unmanifest deities and corresponding giants

Ve, Vi (vay, vee) [awe] Cosmic prototype of Höner

Vidar (vee-dahr) A son of Odin, successor of Balder

Vidofner (veed-awv-ner) [wide opener] Cock in the crown of the Tree of Life

Vigridsslätten (vee-grids-slett-en) [*viga* consecrate + *slätt* plain] The battlefield of life

Vile (vee-leh) [will] Cosmic prototype of Lodur

Vingner, Vingthor [winged Thor] Epithets for Thor

Vior (vee-or) Thor as vital force in beings

Völsungar (veul-s-ungar) [*völsi* phallus + *ungr* children] Early bisexual humanity

Völund (veu-lund) Name of a mythic smith and skillful artisan. The soul of the fourth humanity

Völuspá (veu-luss-paw) [*vala* sibyl + *spá* to prophesy] Principal lay of the elder Edda

Yggdrasil (ig-dra-seel) [Odin's steed, Odin's gallows] The Tree of Life

Ymer (ee-mer) [frost giant] Örgälmer

'Bibliography

SOURCES OF THE LAYS:

Codex Regius af den ældre Edda: Håndskriftet No. 2365 4to gl. kgl. Samling printed by S. L. Møllers Bogtrykkeri, Copenhagen 1891.

Codex Wormianus.

Edda, Saemundar hinns Fróda: *Edda Rhythmica seu Antiqvior, vulgo Saemundina dicta,* Havniae 1787, from a fourteenth century parchment

Swedish versions of Gödecke and Sander are taken from the above and also from

Hauksbok

Sörla Tháttr, "little thread," which is part of the Younger Edda.

The Younger Edda by Snorri Sturlusson

GENERAL WORKS:

Anderson, R. B., *Norse Mythology,* Scott Foresman & Co., Chicago, 1907.

Asimov, Isaac, *The Universe, From Flat Earth to Quasar,* Walker and Company, New York, 1966.

Barker, A. T., ed., *The Mahatma Letters to A. P. Sinnett,* facsimile reprint of 2nd ed., Theosophical University Press, Pasadena, 1975.

Bhattacharjee, Siva Sadhan, *The Hindu Theory of Cosmology,* Bani Prakashani, Calcutta, 1978.

———, *Unified Theory of Philosophy,* Rama Art Press, Calcutta, 1981.

Blavatsky, H. P., *Isis Unveiled* (1877), Theosophical University Press, Pasadena, California 1976.

————, *The Secret Doctrine* (1888), facsimile reprint, Theosophical University Press, Pasadena, 1977.

————, *The Voice of the Silence* (1889), Theosophical University Press, Pasadena, 1976.

Cleasby, R., and G. Vigfusson, *Icelandic Dictionary*, Clarendon Press, Oxford, 1869.

Cruse, Amy, *The Book of Myths*, George G. Harrap & Co. Ltd., London, 1925.

Gödecke, P. Aug., *Edda*, P. A. Norstedt, Stockholm, 1881.

Gordon, E. V., and A. R. Taylor, *An Introduction to Old Norse*, Clarendon Press, Oxford, 1957.

Hapgood, Charles H., *The Path of the Pole*, Chilton Book Co., Philadelphia, 1970.

Harrison, Edward R., *Cosmology, The Science of the Universe*, Cambridge University Press, Cambridge, 1981.

Judge, W. Q., *Bhagavad-Gita*, Recension combined with *Essays on the Gita*, Theosophical University Press, Pasadena, 1969.

King, Ivan R., *The Universe Unfolding*, W. H. Freeman & Co., San Francisco, 1976.

Krupp, E. C., *Echoes of the Ancient Skies*, Harper & Row, New York, 1983.

————, ed., *In Search of Ancient Astronomies*, Doubleday & Co., New York, 1977.

Kurtén, Björn, *Not From the Apes*, Random House, New York, 1972.

Mutwa, Vusamazulu C., *Indaba, My Children*, Blue Crane Book Co., Johannesburg, 1965.

Nilson, Peter, *Himlavalvets sällsamheter*, Rabén & Sjögren, Stockholm, 1977.

————, *Främmande världar*, Rabén & Sjögren, Stockholm, 1980.

Purucker, G. de, *Fountain-Source of Occultism*, Theosophical University Press, Pasadena, California, 1974.

————, *Fundamentals of the Esoteric Philosophy*, 2nd & rev. ed., Theosophical University Press, Pasadena, 1979.

————, *Man in Evolution*, 2nd & rev. ed., Theosophical University Press, Pasadena, 1977.

————, *The Esoteric Tradition*, Theosophical University Press, Pasadena, 1935.

Rydberg, Viktor, *Undersökningar i Germansk Mitologi (Teutonic Mythology)*, Albert Bonnier, Gothenburg, 1886, 1889.

Sander, Fredrik, *Edda*, P. A. Norstedt, Stockholm, 1893.

Santillana, G. de, and H. von Dechend, *Hamlet's Mill*, Gambit, Inc. Boston, 1969.

Sullivan, Walter, *Continents in Motion*, McGraw-Hill Book Co., New York, 1974.

Turville-Petre, E. O. G., *Myth and Religion of the North*, Weidenfeld & Nicolson, London, 1964.

Vigfusson, Gudbrand, and F. York Powell, *Corpus Poeticum Boreale, The Poetry of the Old Northern Tongue*, Clarendon Press, Oxford, 1883.

Zeilik, Michael, *Astronomy: The Evolving Universe*, Harper & Row, New York, 1979.

Index